BEAUCHESNE'S

RULES AND FORMS

of the

HOUSE OF COMMONS
OF CANADA

with

ANNOTATIONS, COMMENTS AND
PRECEDENTS

Fifth Edition

by

ALISTAIR FRASER, B.A., LL.B.
CLERK OF THE HOUSE OF COMMONS

G. A. BIRCH, B.Sc., D.P.A., M.A.
CLERK OF COMMITTEES, HOUSE OF COMMONS

W. F. DAWSON, B.A., M.A., D.Phil.
PROFESSOR OF POLITICAL SCIENCE, UNIVERSITY OF WESTERN ONTARIO

1978
The Carswell Company Limited
Toronto, Ontario

First Edition, 1922.
Second Edition, 1927.
Third Edition, 1943.
Fourth Edition, 1958.

ISBN 0 459 32210 9

To
The Honourable
James Jerome, Q.C., M.P.
Speaker of the House of Commons
and to
The Honourable
Lucien Lamoureux, P.C., Q.C.
Speaker of the House of Commons, 1966-1974

Who were the Speakers of the House of Commons
during the preparation of the Fifth Edition
of this Book.

PREFACE

Twenty years have now lapsed since Arthur Beauchesne published his Fourth Edition. With the extensive amendments to the Standing Orders of the House of Commons in 1968, the procedural advice offered by his book soon became outdated. In this regard, we decided to update and revise Beauchesne's work.

Our decision was based upon the fact that it was a Canadian book dealing directly with the parliamentary procedure in our House of Commons. It had a system of numbered paragraphs for quick reference and, of course, some of its citations were still useful in interpreting the rules and practices of the House. Initially, our task involved deleting the obviously outdated citations and replacing them with Speakers' Rulings and with references from Sir Erskine May's Nineteenth Edition. In addition, we inserted headings to divide the various sections of the Chapters for easier, quicker reference.

Since 1958, there have been many changes in our procedure. During the 1960's, Special Committees on Procedure met regularly, reporting their recommendations for improving the Standing Orders. The revised Rules were adopted on December 20, 1968, with further amendments being adopted in subsequent years.

Two of the many important changes introduced abolished all appeals to a Speaker's Ruling and debate or amendment to the motion "That the Speaker do now leave the Chair".

In the area of legislation, there is now no debate on the Resolution preceding a bill. All bills are referred to one of the Standing Committees where they may be extensively amended. In addition a Report Stage has been instituted following the Committee Stage, at which time Members may amend specific clauses of the bill in the House with the Speaker in the Chair.

The financial procedures in the House have been altered quite significantly. The Committee of Supply has been abolished. The Estimates are referred directly to the Standing Committees, where they may be adopted, reduced or rejected. The Committee of Ways and Means has also been dropped. Ways and Means motions are adopted without debate or amendment with the bill based thereon being studied in the Committee of the Whole. In each of the three supply periods in the year, several days are allotted to the Opposition Parties to debate almost any subject they wish to set down. Two of these motions in each period are votes of non-confidence in the Government. On the last day in each period, Supply is passed in all its stages at the end of that sitting.

Finally the House has established a more useful committee system. The increased powers of the committees are set down in the Standing Orders allowing the committees to study and adopt both legislation and Estimates and, at times, to investigate important subject matters.

With these and many other changes to the Standing Orders, it became quite evident that a new edition of Beauchesne's book was not only necessary but vital if the House and its Members were to have a meaningful Canadian text on parliamentary procedure. Therefore, faced with this challenge and with some assistance from our colleagues and staff, we trust that we have produced an endeavour that is worthy of the tradition established by Arthur Beauchesne.

In particular we would like to extend our appreciation to the following persons who have offered us the benefit of their time and wisdom in the revision of the various drafts of this work: R-L. Boivin, Lois A. Cameron, J.D.W. Campbell, James Cooke, Fernand Despatie, Greg Fyffe, M. Guitard, Mary Ann Griffith, D. Gussow, Michael B. Kirby, C.B. Koester, Nora S. Lever, A.B. MacKenzie, J.M. Robert Normand, Gary O'Brien, M. Pelletier, R.E. Thomas and R.V. Virr.

Also the editors thank Suzanne Sauvé and Wendy Harris for painstakingly typing this book through its many revisions and the Index and Reference Branch for the preparation of the Index. Finally we are grateful to our very able artist, Julie Birch, for her drawing of the House of Commons.

Ottawa, June 1978.

A. Fraser
G.A. Birch
W.F. Dawson

TABLE OF ABBREVIATIONS

Bourinot ... Sir John Bourinot, Parliamentary Procedure and Practice in the Dominion of Canada, 4th Edition, Toronto, 1916.

B.N.A. Act ... British North America Act, 1867.

Debates ... *Debates of the House of Commons of Canada.*

Journals ... *Journals of the House of Commons of Canada.*

May ... Sir Erskine May, Treatise on The Law, Privileges, Proceedings and Usage of Parliament, 19th Edition, London, 1976.

R.S.C. ... Revised Statutes of Canada.

S.O. ... Standing Orders of the House of Commons.

§ ... paragraph symbol.

LIST OF DIAGRAMS

TABLE OF CONTENTS

CHAPTER 3

MACHINERY OF PARLIAMENT:
OFFICERS AND RECORDS

CHAPTER 4

A NEW PARLIAMENT; OPENING AND CLOSING
OF A SESSION

CHAPTER 7

RULES OF DEBATE

CHAPTER 8

ADDRESS IN REPLY TO HIS EXCELLENCY'S SPEECH

CHAPTER 9

QUESTIONS, REPORTS AND RETURNS

CHAPTER 10

NOTICES

CHAPTER 11

MOTIONS; AMENDMENTS; NOTICES OF MOTIONS; THE PREVIOUS QUESTION

CHAPTER 12

COMMITTEE OF THE WHOLE HOUSE

CHAPTER 13

BUSINESS OF SUPPLY AND WAYS AND MEANS

CHAPTER 14

FINANCIAL RELATIONS BETWEEN THE CROWN AND PARLIAMENT

CHAPTER 15

STANDING, SPECIAL AND JOINT COMMITTEES

CHAPTER 16

PETITIONS

CHAPTER 17

PROCEEDINGS ON PUBLIC BILLS

APPENDIX I

FORMS AND FORMULAE

Motions

1

Content and Sources of Parliamentary Procedure

1

Content and Sources of Parliamentary Procedure

Principles of Parliamentary Law — The British North America Act — Statute — Written Rules — Precedent and Tradition — Speaker's Rulings — The Authorities — Unanimous Consent.

PRINCIPLES OF PARLIAMENTARY LAW

§1. The principles that lie at the basis of English parliamentary law, have always been kept steadily in view by the Canadian Parliament; these are: To protect a minority and restrain the improvidence or tyranny of a majority; to secure the transaction of public business in an orderly manner; to enable every Member to express his opinions within limits necessary to preserve decorum and prevent an unnecessary waste of time; to give abundant opportunity for the consideration of every measure, and to prevent any legislative action being taken upon sudden impulse. Sir John Bourinot, Parliamentary Procedure and Practice in the Dominion of Canada (4th ed., 1916), pp. 200-1.

§2. Procedure in the Canadian House of Commons is derived from many sources — the British North America Act, statute, written rules and tradition.

THE BRITISH NORTH AMERICA ACT

§3. It may be claimed that the most significant portion of the Act is the preamble which established that Canada should have a Government similar in principle to that of the United Kingdom. Although this is no great development from colonial times, it represents a clear statement of the general form that the Government will take, and adopts for Canada many procedurally important features of the parliamentary system. Without further elaboration, Canada thus was ensured a responsible Cabinet system with the assumption that there will always be a recognizable Government with a legislative programme. If the electorate so wishes, the system also presupposes an Opposition ready and willing to attack the Government in an attempt to have its legislation altered or rejected. It is well known moreover that a grant of money must be introduced on the recommendation of the Governor General, and that the Cabinet Ministers are the only Members capable of obtaining this recommendation. Similarly, the whole concept of the parliamentary Question Period depends on the tradition that the Cabinet is willing to submit its conduct of public affairs to the scrutiny of the Opposition on a regular basis. More tentative are such traditional features as respect for the rights of the minority, which precludes a Government from using to excess the extensive powers that it has to limit debate or to proceed in what the public and the Opposition might interpret as unorthodox ways.

§4. Beyond the vast legacy of tradition implanted in Canada by the preamble to the British North America Act, one section above all affects procedure. Section 18 permits the adoption in Canada of all of the privileges of Parliament available to the British House of Commons. Few of these are of greater importance than the right to regulate the internal proceedings of the House, or more specifically, to establish binding rules of procedure. Other sections deal with an apparent random selection of procedural questions. No fewer than five apply to the Speaker: his election, vacancies in the office, the temporary absence of the Speaker, his obligation to preside over the House and his casting vote. The Act provides also for the quorum of the House and the settlement of questions by majority vote in normal circumstances. Bills to raise or spend money must originate in the House of Commons and all spending bills must be recommended to the House by the Governor General. Finally, s. 133 guarantees the rights of both the French and English languages in debate and in the records of the House.

STATUTE

§5. Three Canadian statutes are basic to procedure and the administrative operation of the House. The Senate and House of Commons Act, R.S.C. 1970, c.S-8, makes the formal claim to privilege authorized by the British North America Act. It gives complete protection to those responsible for the publication of parliamentary papers and a qualified protection for those publishing extracts from them. The Act further provides for the administering of an Oath to those giving evidence at the Bar of the House or before any committee. Other sections deal with such matters as the independence of Parliament and the salaries of Members. The House of Commons Act, R.S.C. 1970, c.H-9, covers some of the disqualifications of Members, their resignation, procedure in case of vacancies and the Commissioners of Internal Economy. The Speaker of the House of Commons Act, R.S.C. 1970, c.S-13, provides for the succession to the Chair during the temporary or unavoidable absence of the Speaker and guarantees the validity of all procedural acts done by temporary occupants of the Chair.

§6. In recent years, other statutes have increasingly impinged on the procedure of the House. The Statutory Instruments Act, 1970-71-72 (Can.), c.38, for instance, specifies that all Statutory Instruments stand referred automatically to any committee of the House or Senate established to examine them. Although the Act does not specifically set up a Committee of Parliament, its terms are sufficiently specific to have caused the establishment of a joint committee and given it a permanent order of reference. Other statutes are more direct, such as the Electoral Boundaries Readjustment Act, R.S.C. 1970, c.E-2, which provides for objections to be filed with the Speaker and compels a debate on them within a specific time.

WRITTEN RULES

§7. Standing, Sessional and Special Orders are the rules and regulations which the House has agreed on for the governance of its own proceedings.

§8. A Standing Order has a continuing effect until changed or repealed. On one occasion a Standing Order has been declared obsolete by a decision of the Speaker. *Debates,* October 4, 1967, p. 2786. A Sessional Order has effect for only the remainder of the session in which it is passed. A Special Order may have effect for only a single occasion or such longer term as may be specified. It has become the custom in modern times to apply the term Special Order to all rules which have only temporary effect.

§9. All rules are passed by the House by a simple majority and are altered, added to, or removed in the same way. By custom, changes in the Standing Orders are generally made after study and a recommendation by the Standing Committee on Procedure and Organization. There is no procedural reason why any private Member or Minister of the Crown could not introduce a motion to alter the rules and, on occasion, such as the introduction of the closure, this has been done. *Journals,* April 24, 1913, p. 508. Sessional and Special Orders are normally moved by the Government after consultation with the Opposition parties.

PRECEDENT AND TRADITION

§10. Behind the written rules and filling in the gaps, lies the vast quantity of precedent. Although the House normally assumes that a ruling is binding for the future, Speakers have used the flexibility available to them to develop procedure regardless of conflicting precedents in the past. Changes in the Standing Orders from time to time also give ample opportunity for the House to adjust the interpretation of its precedents and tradition in the light of changing circumstances. It is impossible to estimate the extent of this body of traditional parliamentary law. In Canada, not only is there more than a century of native practice, but also Standing Order 1 adopts for Canada all the centuries of tradition (where applicable) of the United Kingdom House of

Commons. Custom and precedent are basic to the parliamentary system. Parliament, and the manner in which it works, has developed over centuries and the written rules are relative newcomers to the procedural field. Indeed, increasingly, the written rules are being used, not to codify existing practice, but rather to trim and adjust historic traditions to modern needs.

SPEAKER'S RULINGS

§11.   The interpretation of both the written rules and tradition is in the hands of the Speaker and his deputies, with their rulings forming a fundamental part of procedure. Some problems attach to these rulings. When the Standing Orders change, for example, rulings based on the old rules must obviously become obsolete. More important, many rulings must be made with little opportunity for reflection or consultation. When possible the Speaker may defer a decision to give time for research and full consideration. Time, however, is not always available and unsatisfactory rulings may result. Finally, it must be noted that rarely are two points of order precisely the same. While previous rulings may be useful guidelines, they may well lack the precision and certainty which might be desired.

THE AUTHORITIES

§12.   Members also have recourse to various publications known collectively as "the authorities". The term is used to describe the small number of books that attempt to collect and organize the traditions, precedents and procedure of parliamentary bodies. The extent of this group is uncertain. Traditionally, in Canada, the House has recognized the usefulness of Beauchesne's Parliamentary Rules and Forms and Bourinot's Parliamentary Procedure. Erskine May's Parliamentary Practice is a guide to relevant current British procedure. For wider ranging discussions of procedure, Members have also consistently referred back to Redlich's Procedure of the House of Commons and Hatsell's Precedents, as well as a variety of lesser known works.

UNANIMOUS CONSENT

§13.   (1) Within the ambit of its own rules, the House itself may proceed as it chooses; it is a common practice for the House to ignore its own rules by unanimous consent. Thus, bills may be passed through all their stages in one day, or the House may decide to alter its normal order of business or its adjournment hour as it sees fit.

(2) The House is perfectly able to give consent to set aside its Standing

Orders and to give its unanimous consent to waive procedural requirements and precedents concerning notice and things of that sort. *Debates,* June 28, 1977, p. 7154.

§14. Whenever the House proceeds by way of unanimous consent, that procedure does not constitute a precedent. *Journals,* May 3, 1974, p. 161.

§15. It is not in order for one Member to ask for unanimous consent to compel another Member to do something. *Debates,* November 18, 1977, p. 1030.

2

Privilege

2

Privilege

DEFINITION

§16. Parliamentary privilege is the sum of the peculiar rights enjoyed by each House collectively as a constituent part of the High Court of Parliament, and by Members of each House individually, without which they could not discharge their functions and which exceed those possessed by other bodies or individuals. Thus, privilege, though part of the law of the land, is to a certain extent an exemption from the ordinary law.

The distinctive mark of a privilege is its ancillary character. The privileges of Parliament are rights which are "absolutely necessary for the due execution of its powers". They are enjoyed by individual Members, because the House cannot perform its functions without unimpeded use of the services of its Members; and by each House for the protection of its members and the vindication of its own authority and dignity. Sir Erskine May, Treatise on the Law, Privileges, Proceedings and Usage of Parliament (19th ed., 1976), p. 67.

§17. A question of privilege ought rarely to come up in Parliament. It should be dealt with by a motion giving the House power to impose a reparation or apply a remedy. A genuine question of privilege is a most serious matter and should be taken seriously by the House.

§18. ". . . it is clear that many acts which might offend against the law or the moral sense of the community do not involve a Member's capacity to serve the people who have chosen him as their representative nor are they contrary to the usage nor derogatory to the dignity of the House of Commons. Members of the House of Commons, like all other citizens, have the right to be regarded as innocent until they are found guilty, and like other citizens they must be charged before they are obliged to stand trial in the courts. Parliament is a court with respect to its own privileges and dignity and the privileges of its Members. The question arises whether the House, in the exercise of its judicial functions with respect to the conduct of any of its Members, should deprive such Member of any of the safeguards and privileges which every man enjoys in any court of the land." *Journals,* June 19, 1959, p. 583.

§19.   (1) A dispute arising between two Members, as to allegations of facts, does not fulfill the conditions of parliamentary privilege.

(2) The failure of a Minister of the Crown to answer a question may not be raised as a question of privilege.

(3) Statements made outside the House by a Member may not be used as the base for a question of privilege.

(4) Many matters, such as the absence of a Minister of the Crown from a committee studying his Estimates, may constitute a grievance but not a question of privilege.

CLAIMS TO PRIVILEGE OF THE UNITED KINGDOM HOUSE OF COMMONS

§20.   (1) While privilege in the United Kingdom has always been based on the common law, it has never been transferable to the colonies except by statute. The right of the Canadian Parliament to establish its privileges is guaranteed by the British North America Act and the privileges thus claimed may, at present, not exceed those of the United Kingdom House of Commons.

(2) Parliament, in 1868, laid claim to all of the privileges of the United Kingdom House of Commons without specifying their exact extent. Three times since then (in 1868, 1873 and 1894) Parliament has clarified minor aspects of its privileges by statute.

(3) The privileges of the House of Commons are also claimed on the opening day of each new Parliament when the Speaker, after introducing himself to the Governor General, claims on behalf of the House "all their undoubted rights and privileges, especially that they may have freedom of speech in their debates, access to Your Excellency's person at all seasonable times, and that their proceedings may receive from Your Excellency the most favourable construction." Although this request is granted, it has no legal validity as privilege in Canada rests on statute and not on common law.

(4) As Parliament has never delimited the extent of privilege, considerable confusion surrounds the area. Recourse must therefore be taken, not only to the practice of the Canadian House, but also to the vast tradition of the United Kingdom House of Commons.

PRIVILEGES OF THE HOUSE

§21. The most fundamental privilege of the House as a whole is to establish rules of procedure for itself and to enforce them. A few rules are laid down in the British North America Act, but the vast majority are resolutions of the House which may be added to, amended, or repealed at the discretion of the House. It follows, therefore, that the House may dispense with the application of any of these rules by unanimous consent on any occasion, or, by motion, may suspend their operation for a specified length of time.

Enforcement of the Privileges of the House

§22. The power of the House to enforce its rules extends not only to Members and others admitted within the precincts of Parliament, but also to members of the general public who may interfere with the orderly conduct of parliamentary business.

§23. Within the walls of the Commons chamber, the authority of the House is clear. The Speaker is given the authority to "maintain order and decorum" and he is given the authority to clear the galleries at his own discretion. S.O. 12 and S.O. 13. On all occasions the House itself holds the ultimate power. When a Member is named, for instance, his suspension from the service of the House is not ordered by the Speaker, but rather by vote of the House.

§24. Tradition and British precedent have provided the occupants of the Chair with ample powers to enforce order in the House. There is little doubt that the Speaker may suspend a sitting because of disorder on the floor and may resume the Chair, without motion or report, to quell disorder in Committee of the Whole.

Naming of a Member

§25. (1) The most serious penalty in the hands of the Speaker is naming. It is rarely used and on many occasions the threat of using the power has been sufficient to gain compliance with the Speaker's decisions.

(2) When a Member is named (by the Speaker stating: "Mr. X, it is my duty to name you for disregarding the authority of the Chair" or some such similar formula), he has the right to make a statement to the House and should then withdraw while the House makes its judgment.

(3) If the Member satisfies the House by an apology, no further action is necessary. If the Member's statement is insufficient, it is the duty of the Government House Leader to present a motion proposing a suitable penalty.

(4) A Government House Leader in a statement in the House explained his role:

> "Mr. Speaker, because of the importance of the situation that has

arisen I feel I should explain the proceeding in which I am now engaged.

"It has been the tradition of the House of Commons that when the Speaker names any particular member, the leader of the government in the House supports the Speaker in that decision. That, I believe, has been the unvarying tradition of the House of Commons with one exception, and when that occurred the Speaker of the day was left in a very exposed, unprotected and unsupported position. It is therefore my desire in discharging my responsibility to support the Speaker.

"I would add that while the Speaker did make the suggestion that I put this motion, it is a decision which the leader of the government in the House makes on his own account, and he can either agree or disagree to move the motion."

Debates, May 16, 1978, p. 5457

(5) The penalty common in Canada is suspension for the remainder of the sitting day. On one occasion the House decided upon a seven day suspension for a second offence by the same Member. *Journals,* July 4, 1944, p. 526.

(6) The Chairman of Committee of the Whole has no power to name a Member. If a Member fails to obey the rulings of the Chairman, the Committee will rise and report the incident to the Speaker. The Chairman's report takes the place of the actual naming by the Speaker with the remainder of the procedure following the course as mentioned above.

§26. It is desirable, on the rare occasions that it may be necessary, that proceedings to discipline a Member for his behaviour should be disposed of as expeditiously as possible. Before events have reached this stage, great care will have been taken by the Speaker to avoid a confrontation, and the Member will have persisted in his action in the sight of all Members present. It is the duty of all Members to uphold at all times the authority of the Chair, reflecting as it does the House itself. Thus, no other proceedings may intervene once the process has started and such motions as are necessary are not debatable. However, speeches as may be made should be limited to brief attempts to achieve a withdrawal by the member concerned and should not be directed to the merits, or otherwise, of the decision that the Speaker has made.

§27. The House is cautious in the use of its authority. On two occasions in recent years, the House has avoided making awkward decisions. One of those occasions was after the election of 1963, when the Social Credit Party, which had returned to the House as the third largest party, split into two separate groups, each smaller than the New Democratic Party. The Speaker refused to settle the question of seating in the House posed by this development and the Standing Committee on Privileges and Elections was given the task of examining the problems raised. *Journals,* October 9, 1963, p. 423.

The Press Gallery

§28. The authority of the Speaker and the House over the Press Gallery is uncertain. While technically the Gallery is under the jurisdiction of the House, in practice it enjoys a considerable degree of independence. In 1963 the Standing Committee on Privileges and Elections recommended that an appeal by a reporter who had been denied accreditation by the Gallery should be decided by the Speaker alone. *Journals,* December 20, 1963, p. 763. Since then the Speaker has granted special privileges to a reporter suspended by the Gallery and has refused to intervene in a labour dispute affecting the Gallery.

Exclusion of Strangers

§29. The House has always exercised the right to exclude the public from its deliberations. The House has discussed such questions as the abolition of its bar without the public being present and also has used such meetings to discuss the progress of the war in both World Wars. A fixed day may be set in advance for such meetings, or a general motion allowing any day to be set aside for a secret session may be passed. On the day chosen the sitting may begin in public and then the public may be excluded, or, with consent, the Speaker may simply not order the doors to be opened after Prayers. When secret sessions were held during the two World Wars, Senators were permitted to attend by courtesy of the House.

§30. (1) Any Member may move under S.O. 13 that strangers be ordered to withdraw from the galleries. The question is put forthwith without debate or amendment. In Committee of the Whole, the Chairman puts the question. If this motion is passed, all galleries, including the Senate Gallery, are cleared.

(2) A motion to clear the Galleries designed to prevent the entrance of the Gentleman Usher of the Black Rod will not be accepted. *Debates,* February 16, 1972, pp. 10959-60.

§31. Under S.O. 13 both the Speaker and the Chairman have the right to order the galleries cleared without a motion or decision of the House. It is customary to use this power when significant disorder occurs in the galleries.

§32. Individual members of the public who misconduct themselves in the galleries are normally dealt with by the Protective Staff without resort to corporate action by the House.

The Right of a Member to Sit

§33. One privilege of the House is the right to try controverted elections. The procedure proved cumbersome and time-consuming; therefore in 1873 Parliament gave its jurisdiction in this area to the courts. Other facets of electoral propriety have been examined by the House from time to time.

Sir John Bourinot, Parliamentary Procedure and Practice in the Dominion of Canada (4th ed., 1916), pp. 135-140.

§34. The Standing Committee on Privileges and Elections has also examined such questions as the right of Sir Charles Tupper to retain his seat while holding an appointment as High Commissioner in London and the circumstances under which a Member might retrieve a letter of resignation which had been mailed to the Speaker but had not yet been opened. *Debates,* March 4, 1898, p. 1772.

§35. The House has also been willing to examine possible offences against the provisions of the Senate and House of Commons Act. In 1969, the Standing Committee on Privileges and Elections examined the case of a Member who was entitled to a vacation credit from government employment at the time of his election, and in 1970 another case where a Member held leases on Crown land. *Journals,* April 24, 1969, p. 937. *Journals,* June 3, 1970, p. 917.

§36. The House has, on occasion, examined the activities of Members to establish if they were fit to hold their seats. It has examined an old conviction for forgery and the accusation that a Member's conduct was "discreditable, corrupt and scandalous" with respect to the granting of timber limits. *Journals,* March 11, 1890, pp. 172-5.

§37. There is no question that the House has the right to expel a Member for such reasons as it deems fit. Such expulsion does not affect the right of a Member to run again and be re-elected. On two occasions Louis Riel was expelled. On the first occasion he had fled from justice and had failed to obey an order of the House to appear in his place. *Journals,* April 16, 1874, p. 70. When re-elected, the House, after examination, decided that he had been judged an outlaw for felony and ordered the Speaker to issue his warrant for a new writ. *Journals,* February 24, 1875, p. 124.

§38. The case of Fred Rose in 1946 was rather different. The Speaker laid before the House court documents regarding the conviction and sentence to six years' imprisonment of Fred Rose for conspiring to commit various offences under the Official Secrets Act, 1939 (Can.), c. 49 and ordered the Speaker to issue his warrant for a writ. *Journals,* January 30, 1947, pp. 4-8. *R. v. Rose* (1946), 88 C.C.C. 14 (Que. C.A.).

§39. It is not necessary for the courts to come to a decision before the House acts. In 1891 charges were laid in the House against Thomas McGreevy relating to scandals in the Public Works Department. The Committee on Privileges and Elections examined the evidence and concluded that the charges were amply proven. Mr. McGreevy meanwhile had submitted his resignation, which was void since the matter had not yet been settled in the courts. The House judged Mr. McGreevy to be guilty of a contempt of the House as well as certain of the charges and ordered his expulsion. *Journals,* September 29, 1891, p. 561.

§40. In any case where the propriety of a Member's actions is brought into question, a specific charge must be made. The Speaker will not allow the Standing Committee on Privileges and Elections to examine the actions and statements of a Member relating to the question to report generally on the matter. *Journals,* June 19, 1959, pp. 582-6.

Control over Publications

§41. (1) The control of the House over its publications is absolute. For a number of years after Confederation the House made a formal claim each session "that the *Votes and Proceedings* of this House be printed, being first perused by Mr. Speaker and that no person but such as he shall appoint do presume to print the same". This motion is no longer passed each session, but the claim made is still enforced.

(2) In 1960, the Sperry and Hutchinson Company was judged guilty of a breach of privilege for having published and circulated, for advertising purposes, a copy of a portion of a day's Hansard report. *Journals,* March 16, 1960, p. 280.

§42. Alterations in the records of the House should rarely be made. Changes in the *Votes and Proceedings* are properly made by motion in the House and are entered in the *Votes and Proceedings* the next day. The alteration is incorporated in the *Journals* at the end of the session.

§43. Alterations in the *Debates* are traditionally limited to minor corrections of syntax and will often be made by the Member involved before printing. More substantial changes should be made the following day by a statement in the House. Such changes are accepted with consent and are printed in the daily report. On rare occasions the House will order the deletion of words from Hansard by formal motion.

§44. (1) Unauthorized recording or broadcasting of debates is not allowed. The House in the past has disapproved of an extension of the sound amplification system into a Member's office. Tape recorders in the galleries are forbidden. With the advent of radio and television coverage of House debates, this whole question is in a changing situation. The Special Committee on Television and Radio Broadcasting of the House, under the chairmanship of the Speaker, is attempting to reach a more reasonable solution in view of the present day operations.

(2) In 1973, the House considered briefly the unauthorized electronic transmission of caucus proceedings. Although it did not decide that a breach

of privilege had occurred, the reporter was ordered to surrender his tape to either the Speaker or the party concerned. *Journals,* October 17, 1973, p. 577.

REFLECTIONS ON THE HOUSE AS A WHOLE

§45. Traditionally, articles in the press reflecting badly on the character of the House have been treated as contempts. Two members of the staff of the House have been dismissed for writing such articles, and in 1873 the House judged an article written by a Member to be a "scandalous, false and malicious libel upon the honour, integrity and character of this House, and of certain Members thereof, and a high contempt of the privileges and constitutional authority of this House". *Journals,* April 17, 1873, p. 169.

§46. In 1906, Mr. J.E.E. Cinq Mars was examined at the Bar for an article in the press that the House eventually judged to "pass the bounds of reasonable criticism and constitute a breach of the privileges of the House". *Journals,* June 14, 1906, pp. 372-7.

§47. More recently, notice has occasionally been taken of such articles, but the House has failed to take any action. In 1920, a press report of a speech suggested that the expenditure of money would achieve certain results in Parliament. The Speaker requested an explanation and the clear denial of any such implication was accepted. *Debates,* June 15, 1920, p. 3557. In 1962, a derogatory article which appeared to reflect badly on a parliamentary delegation was referred to the Standing Committee on Privileges and Elections which failed to make a report. *Journals,* November 29, 1962, p. 334.

Reflections on Members

§48. The House has occasionally taken notice of attacks on individual Members. Most notably, in 1880 John Macdonell, while seated at his desk in the House, referred to a Member, L.S. Huntingdon, as "a cheat and a swindler". Removed from the House, he returned twice more to repeat the charge and finally concluded with a written note to the same effect. For the offence, Macdonell was judged guilty of a breach of privilege and was summoned to the Bar to apologize. *Debates,* May 10, 1879, p. 1940. *Debates,* February 24, 1880, pp. 182-195.

§49. Following reports in various newspapers in 1976, the remarks of Mr. Auguste Choquette, which appeared to accuse unnamed Members of accepting bribes, were referred by the House to the Standing Committee on Privileges and Elections. After examining Mr. Choquette, the Committee accepted a portion of his explanation and recommended that no further action be taken by the House because no evidence had been produced to support his remarks. *Journals,* May 21, 1976, p. 1305.

§50. A suggestion in a newspaper in 1941 that a Member nominated to a committee could not act impartially was noted by the Prime Minister to be a breach of privilege but the House took no action. *Debates,* March 4, 1941, p. 1234.

§51. It is always the responsibility of the House to decide if reflections on Members are sufficiently serious to justify action. In 1974 and again in 1976 Members complained about newspaper reports and the Speaker allowed that a prima facie case of privilege existed. After debate, the House declined to refer the matters to the Standing Committee on Privileges and Elections.

Reflections on the Speaker

§52. (1) The Speaker should be protected against reflections on his actions.

(2) In 1956, Mr. Colin Cameron submitted to the House two letters in a local newspaper reflecting on the actions of the Speaker. After a brief debate, the Speaker on the following day ruled that "because of the unprecedented circumstances surrounding this pipeline debate and because of the remarks that were made in this House by Members themselves, it was and it is impossible, if we are to consider freedom of the press, as we should, to take these two articles as being breaches of our privileges". He continued to describe them as "comments which do not go beyond the bounds of unfairness". *Debates,* June 1, 1956, p. 4537.

(3) Other press references have been considered. On one occasion, the apology of the Member who had written the letter to the Editor was accepted *Debates,* May 18, 1960, p. 3993. On another, the article complained of was referred to the Standing Committee on Privileges and Elections but the Committee failed to report. *Journals,* November 1, 1962, pp. 201-2.

(4) In 1976, the House took notice of an editorial in a newspaper and dealt with the question by passing a motion without debate, under S.O. 43, which condemned the editorial as a "gross breach of the privileges of this House". *Journals,* December 22, 1976, p. 270.

POLICE WITHIN
THE PRECINCTS OF PARLIAMENT

§53. It is still not clear whether the House of Commons regards as contempt the presence of members of federal, provincial or local police forces within the precincts of Parliament without the consent of the Speaker. The Standing Committee on Privileges and Elections found in 1973 that it was "well established that outside police forces should not enter the precincts without permission", but failed to establish such an entry as a contempt. *Journals,* September 21, 1973, p. 567.

§54. Parliament maintains two police forces of its own (called the Protective

Service) to maintain order and regulate the conduct of those admitted to the precincts. Outside police forces must inform the authorities of the House whenever one of their members wishes to approach a Member of Parliament or to be on duty within the buildings. The closest co-operation is maintained between the parliamentary authorities and the outside police forces and in cases such as official visits or disturbances on Parliament Hill, these forces co-operate with the Parliamentary Protective Service. When military troops were used to guard the Parliament Buildings in October 1970 they were quickly removed in favour of more conventional security forces.

FREEDOM OF SPEECH

§55.   The privilege of freedom of speech is both the least questioned and the most fundamental right of the Member of Parliament on the floor of the House and in committee. It is primarily guaranteed in the British Bill of Rights which declared "that the freedom of speech and debates or proceedings in Parliament ought not to be impeached or questioned in any court or place outside of Parliament". 1 William and Mary, Sess. 2, c.2, s.9.

§56.   (1) The privilege of freedom of speech has been reaffirmed by the courts. The decision of the Court of Appeal of Ontario was clear in the case of *Roman Corpn. v. Hudson's Bay Oil and Gas Ltd.,* [1972] 1 O.R. 444 at 448, 23 D.L.R. (3d) 292 at 296; affirmed [1973] S.C.R. 820, 36 D.L.R. (3d) 413, where it stated: ". . . the respondents [Mr. Trudeau and Mr. Greene] cannot be called upon to plead to or to defend against, in any ordinary Court of law, the allegations concerning statements they made in the House of Commons. For more than one hundred years no such Court has entertained an action based upon such statements, declaring it to be within the absolute privilege of the House itself to deal with them as the House may see fit." The Court of Appeal and the Supreme Court of Canada went further and extended this absolute privilege to a telegram sent to Mr. Roman and also to a press release relating to the same matter.

(2) In *Re Ouellet; R. v. Atlantic Sugar Refineries Co.* (1976), 34 C.R.N.S. 234 at 249, 28 C.C.C. (2d) 338 at 352, 67 D.L.R. (3d) 73 at 87; affirmed by the Quebec Court of Appeal at 36 C.R.N.S. 296, 32 C.C.C. (2d) 149 (*sub nom. Re Ouellet Nos. (1) and (2)*), 72 D.L.R. (3d) 95, the court made clear that freedom of speech was limited to the floor of the House. On this occasion, remarks made by the Minister to a journalist in the lobby were judged not to be covered by privilege. In the words of the judgment: "It is not the precinct of Parliament that is sacred, but the function and that function has never required that press conferences given by Members should be regarded as absolutely protected from legal liability."

Protection of Publications

§57.   Under the provisions of the Senate and House of Commons Act any "report, paper, votes or proceedings" of the House enjoys an absolute privilege and should any person be prosecuted for publishing them, a certificate from the Speaker or the Clerk stating that the document was published under the authority of the House is sufficient to stay proceedings. An extract from such documents, providing that it is published "bona fide and without malice", is similarly protected. Senate and House of Commons Act, R.S.C. 1970, c. S-8, ss. 7-9.

§58. The exact extent of the protection afforded the Press in reporting Parliament is still not clear. In *Re Clark and A.G. Can.* (1977), 17 O.R. (2d) 593, 81 D.L.R. (3d) 33, 34 C.P.R. (2d) 91 the decision of the Chief Justice of the High Court of Ontario indicated only that the absolute privilege of the Member of Parliament does not extend to the Press. The Speaker ruled that the court decision does not alter in any way the privileges, the powers and the rights possessed by Members and in the relationship with the Press in respect of proceedings in the House. *Journals,* December 5, 1977, pp. 166-171.

FREEDOM FROM ARREST

§59. The freedom from arrest of Members is more apparent than real. The wide freedom from arrest which historically existed at one time in England, and extended even to a Member's servants, has never existed in Canada. Freedom from arrest today extends only to civil actions and cannot be claimed for treason, felony, breach of the peace or any indictable offence. The House has always claimed its prior right to the attendance of its Members, but has never placed its claims above those of the community as a whole.

§60. Such freedom from arrest, as still exists, may be claimed traditionally not only while the House is sitting but also for a period of forty days before and after the session.

§61. Beyond the few exceptions made, a Member is fully responsible in the ordinary courts for any offence not "within the scope of his duties in the course of parliamentary business". *R. v. Bunting* (1885), 7 O.R. 524 at 563 (C.A.).

§62. The most notable modern example of the legal responsibility of a Member is that of Fred Rose. The Royal Commission investigating the Gouzenko spy accusations, faced with the necessity of arresting a Member of Parliament, took legal advice on the question. The answer of counsel was clear: "... a Member who had committed an indictable offence is liable to arrest at any time and any place except on the floor of the House when it is sitting." Documents relating to the *Proceedings of the Royal Commission* established by Order-in-Council P.C. 411 of February 5, 1946. The advice was accepted and Fred Rose was arrested at his home on the opening day of the 1946 session. Successful prosecution followed.

§63. From British practice it would seem that if a Member is arrested the House should be informed, through the Speaker, by the judge or magistrate concerned. There is no example of this ever happening in Canada, although in 1946 the Prime Minister made an extensive statement explaining the circumstances surrounding the arrest of Fred Rose. *Debates,* March 15, 1946, pp. 4-7.

FREEDOM FROM ATTENDANCE AT COURT

§64. No Member may be compelled to appear in court as a witness. Examples may be found of Members benefiting from this privilege, although in practice, except in unusual circumstances, a Member will not avail himself of the protection offered by privilege.

§65. A Member may similarly exercise his privilege to avoid jury duty. This privilege is further strengthened by the provisions of various provincial acts, which specifically exempt Members of Parliament.

§66. Neither the House nor its Members have ever made any specific claims to freedom from service of process within the precincts. Sir Richard Cartwright noted in 1877 that an attempt had been made to serve a subpoena on him in the corridors of the House, but he did not pursue the question. *Debates,* April 16, 1877, p. 1540. In 1965, Mr. G. Grégoire also mentioned in passing that he had been served with one summons in his office and that he had been called out of the House for the service of a second. The Standing Committee on Privileges and Elections looking into his allegations in that year did not even consider the question. *Debates,* February 16, 1965, p. 11358.

INFLUENCING MEMBERS

§67. It is generally accepted that any threat to a Member, attempting to influence his vote or his actions as a Member, is a breach of privilege. It seems probable that the extreme delegate theories of representation, favoured by minor parties in the west and manifesting themselves through undated resignations, was a breach of privilege. Although these were well known at the time, Parliament amended the Dominion Elections Act (Canada Elections Act, R.S.C. 1970, c.14 (1st Supp.), s.104) to make illegal any signed pledges which would force a Member's resignation at the request of any individual or group.

§68. During the second World War the Prime Minister admitted that letters and telephone calls to Members had been intercepted by the censors, but he defended the action on the grounds of national security. *Debates,* February 20, 1942, p. 743.

§69. A question of alleged wiretapping of telephones was referred to the

Standing Committee on Privileges and Elections in 1972, but the Member making the allegation refused to appear before the Committee and therefore no evidence of wrongdoing was discovered. *Journals,* May 24, 1972, pp. 321-6.

§70. Members have raised, as a matter of privilege, the question of police files being maintained on Members. The Speaker has refused to recognize a question of privilege, based on such allegations, unless the charge is specific and unless the dossier refers to the individual in his role as a Member of Parliament rather than as an ordinary citizen.

§71. Direct threats which attempt to influence Members' actions in the House are undoubtedly breaches of privilege. They do, however, provide serious problems for the House. They are often made anonymously and it is rarely possible for the House to examine them satisfactorily. The common practice today is to turn the responsibility for investigating them over to the ordinary forces of the law.

Bribery

§72. Since 1867, the House has had a rule specifically forbidding the offer of money, or any other advantage, to a Member. The present rule is S.O. 76. Section 108 of the Criminal Code, R.S.C. 1970, c. C-34, similarly forbids such action.

§73. In 1873, a Member stated in the House that an Ottawa Alderman had attempted to buy his vote for the government. The House ordered the immediate arrest of the Alderman and his appearance at the Bar. The Alderman was arrested, but proceedings were interrupted by prorogation and later dissolution. The matter was never concluded. *Journals,* November 3-7, 1873, pp. 134-142.

§74. A charge of attempted bribery was made in 1964 when a Social Credit Member alleged that the Liberal Party had attempted to persuade him, through promises of campaign funds, to change his Party affiliation. After investigation, the Standing Committee on Privileges and Elections reported that there was no evidence of bribery or attempted bribery, and therefore, no question of privilege was involved. *Journals,* June 15, 1964, pp. 425-6.

EXTENSIONS OF PRIVILEGE

Committees

§75. Many of the privileges of the House extend also to its committees. They may exclude the public from their meetings and commonly do so, particularly while considering their reports to the House. Members not on the committee may be requested to leave but cannot be forced to do so. Committee reports and the verbatim transcripts of committee hearings are documents published under the authority of the House and are entitled to the same absolute privilege as House documents. Extracts from committee documents enjoy the same qualified privilege as extracts from House documents.

§76.   Breaches of privilege in committee may be dealt with only by the House itself on report from the committee. Thus should a witness refuse to attend, or refuse to give evidence, the committee must report the fact to the House for remedial action.

Witnesses

§77.   Witnesses before committees share the same privilege of freedom of speech as Members. *Journals,* April 12, 1892, pp. 234-5. Nothing said before a committee (or at the Bar of the House) may be used in a court of law. Thus a witness may not refuse to answer on the grounds that he will incriminate himself. *Journals,* February 18, 1913, p. 266.

Employees of the House

§78.   The employees of the House are, of necessity, also covered by some of the privileges of Parliament. For the proper functioning of Parliament, not only the Members must be free to attend, but also the servants of the House. The House will often waive its privileges here, even to the point of allowing its employees to give evidence on the proceedings of the House. One right which is routinely maintained is the immunity of essential staff from jury duty.

Documents in Possession of the House

§79.   The House maintains sole control over documents in its possession. The public may see papers which have been tabled in the House. Even the Senate, however, has no right to such papers. In 1919, the Senate passed an Address for papers, including those "in the possession ... of His Honour the Speaker of the House of Commons". The Speaker drew the Address to the attention of the House and a Minister of the Crown moved that the Senate's action was a breach of the privileges of the House. The motion further suggested that the traditional way of obtaining such documents was a formal message from one House to the other. *Journals,* March 20, 1919, p. 80.

PROCEDURE ON A BREACH OF PRIVILEGE

Distinction Between Questions of Privilege and Questions of Order

§80.   (1) A question of order concerns the interpretation to be put upon the rules of procedure and is a matter for the Speaker or, in a committee, for the Chairman to determine.

(2) A question of privilege, on the other hand, is a question partly of fact and partly of law — the law of contempt of Parliament — and is a matter for the House to determine. The decision of the House on a question of privilege, like every other matter which the House has to decide, can be elicited only by a question put from the Chair by the Speaker and resolved either in the affirmative or in the negative, and this question is necessarily founded on a motion made by a Member.

(3) It follows that though the Speaker can *rule* on a question of order, he cannot *rule* on a question of privilege. His function, when a question of privilege is raised, is limited to deciding whether the matter is of such a character as to entitle the motion, which the Member who has raised the question desires, to move to priority over the Orders of the Day. *Report from the Select Committee of the House of Commons of the United Kingdom on Parliamentary Privilege,* February 20, 1967, p. 108.

Raising a Question of Privilege

§81. (1) By its nature, a question of privilege is of such importance that it may be raised at any time, and S.O. 17 makes provision for the precedence of a question of privilege over all other business of the House. A question of privilege arising out of proceedings in the Chamber, during the course of a sitting, may be raised without notice. For other questions of privilege a Member must give notice to the Speaker at least one hour prior to the opening of a sitting. It is customary for questions of privilege arising during the oral Question Period and those for which notice has been given to be considered at the conclusion of the oral Question Period.

(2) A complaint of a breach of privilege must conclude with a motion providing the House with an opportunity to take some action.

§82. A question of privilege must be brought to the attention of the House at the first possible opportunity. Even a gap of a few days may invalidate the claim for precedence in the House. *Journals,* June 9, 1969, p. 1136.

§83. Should a question of privilege be based on published material, the article in question must be submitted and read at the Table. *Journals,* November 1, 1962, p. 201.

Role of the Speaker

§84. (1) Once the claim of a breach of privilege has been made, it is the duty of the Speaker to decide if a prima facie case can be established. The Speaker requires to be satisfied, both that privilege appears to be sufficiently involved to justify him in giving such precedence (or as it is sometimes put, that there is a prima facie case that a breach of privilege has been committed); and also that the matter is being raised at the earliest opportunity.

(2) It has often been laid down that the speaker's function in ruling on a

claim of breach of privilege is limited to deciding the formal question, whether the case conforms with the conditions which alone entitle it to take precedence over the notices of motions and Orders of the Day standing on the *Order Paper;* and does not extend to deciding the question of substance, whether a breach of privilege has in fact been committed — a question which can only be decided by the House itself. May, pp. 346-347.

Reference to the Standing Committee on Privileges and Elections

§85.   A complaint of a breach of privilege must conclude with a motion providing the House an opportunity to take some action. That action is normally the reference of the matter to the Standing Committee on Privileges and Elections for examination. It may, however, be a statement of condemnation for a breach of privilege or an order for an individual to appear at the Bar.

§86.   The Standing Committee on Privileges and Elections has a free hand within its terms of reference to hear witnesses and call for papers. It is customary for the Law Clerk and Parliamentary Counsel to present a brief and to assist the Committee in reaching its conclusion.

Examination of Witnesses at the Bar of the House

§87.   Should the House wish to proceed without reference to the committee it may do so. Evidence may be taken from witnesses at the Bar of the House. When a charge has been laid, it is customary for the accused to request and be granted the right to be heard through counsel. However, this is a procedure which has rarely occurred in Canadian parliamentary history.

§88.   Witnesses to be heard at the Bar are normally summoned by the Speaker to appear on a specific date, although the terms "without delay" and "forthwith" have been used. It is not necessary to specify the reason for the summons. At the time stated, the Sergeant-at-Arms reports on the attendance of the individual. Should he not be present, the absence is noted and the House orders the Speaker to issue a warrant for him to be taken into custody.

§89.   With the individual at the Bar, the examination begins with the Clerk reading the original resolution. The examination proceeds by question and answer. Each question is a separate motion, properly moved and seconded and put to the House by the Speaker. The motions are debatable and amendable and may be ruled out of order by the Speaker. If passed, the Speaker puts each question to the individual at the Bar. The witness withdraws during procedural discussions and while the House considers its verdict. If necessary he will return to the Bar to hear the message of the House delivered by the Speaker.

Punitive Powers of the House

§90. Privilege grants considerable punitive powers to the House of Commons. The mildest form of punishment is a simple declaration that an act or an article is a breach of privilege. When an individual has been present at the Bar it has been customary to deliver this conclusion to the culprit in the presence of the House. On such occasions, censure of the individual is usually added to the conclusion that privilege has been offended.

§91. Occasionally the individual at the Bar will be given an opportunity to purge his contempt and promise better conduct in the future. Mr. J.B. Provost and Mr. O.E. Larose, for example, having failed to attend a committee investigation, were summoned to the Bar and there agreed to attend the committee and give evidence at any time the committee might appoint. *Debates*, June 7, 1894, p. 3866. *Debates*, June 11, 1894, p. 4040. *Debates*, June 13, 1894, p. 4189.

§92. For more serious contempts the House may proceed further. Louis Riel and Thomas McGreevy were both expelled from the House, partly at least, for their refusal to attend in their places and answer charges. Imprisonment has been used on only one occasion. Mr. R.C. Miller refused to answer questions before the Public Accounts Committee and had been reported to the House. Summoned to the Bar he persisted in his refusal. The House committed him to the Carleton County jail until prorogation or until the House otherwise decided. *Journals*, February 20, 1913, p. 278.

3

Machinery of Parliament:
Officers and Records

3

Machinery of Parliament:
Officers and Records

The Parliament Buildings — The Chamber — The Chair — The Table — The Mace — Place of Members — Attendance of Members — Access to the House of Commons — Members of Parliament — Members of the Public — The Galleries — Exclusion of Strangers — Officers of the House — The Speaker of the House of Commons — The Speaker as Representative of the House of Commons — The Speaker as Presiding Officer of the House of Commons — Procedural Duties of the Speaker — Administrative Duties of the Speaker — Functions of the Office of the Speaker after Dissolution — Unavoidable Absence of the Speaker — Resignation of the Speaker — The Deputy Speaker of the House of Commons — Other Presiding Officers — Officers in the Service of the House — The Clerk of the House — Procedural Duties — Administrative Duties — The Clerks Assistant — The Sergeant-at-Arms — The Law Clerk and Parliamentary Counsel — Directorates of the House — Journals Branches — Debates Branches — Committees and Private Legislation Branch — Parliamentary Publications — The Votes and Proceedings — The Journals — The Order Paper and Notices — The Official Report of Debates — Party Machinery in the House — The Official Opposition — The House Leaders — The Party Whips.

THE PARLIAMENT BUILDINGS

§93. (1) The Parliament Buildings comprise accommodation in which the proceedings of the two Houses and their Committees are conducted. In addition, office space is provided for all Members and officials of both Houses.

(2) Control of the accommodation and services in that part of the Parliament Buildings (the Centre and West Blocks, the Confederation Building and other buildings occupied on behalf of the House) and its precincts occupied by the House of Commons is vested in the Speaker on behalf of the House.

THE CHAMBER

§94. The Chamber is rectangular in shape, surrounded by galleries, with the seat of the Presiding Officer at one end and a barrier known as the Bar at the other; between these is the Table of the House. The House is divided lengthwise by a broad aisle with desks on each side, an arrangement which is said to facilitate the division of Members into two main groups — the Government supporters to the right of the Speaker, and supporters of the various Opposition groups to his left. Traditionally, the House does not recognize parties but merely the division of Government versus Opposition groups. However, increasing reference has been made in statutes and Standing Orders of parties. Around the upper level of the House, the galleries provide accommodation for the public. Refer to the Plan of the House at Figure No. 1.

§95.   (1) In the centre of the aisle are four small desks at which the Hansard reporters record the debates in both official languages.

(2) On each side of the Chamber opposite the Speaker there are booths in which simultaneous interpreters perform their tasks.

(3) Since October 1977, equipment has been installed on the floor of the House in order to provide radio and television coverage of parliamentary debates.

(4) The Sergeant-at-Arms sits at a desk on the floor of the House within the Bar.

(5) The Lobbies are directly behind the curtains on each side of the Chamber. The Speaker has been of the view that access to the Lobbies is controlled by the political parties.

(6) A sound reinforcement system has been installed which enables the individual microphones to be activated whenever a Member is recognized to speak. However, whenever the Speaker's microphone is activated, no others can be used.

The Chair

§96.   (1) The Speaker's Chair is a gift to the House of Commons by members of the Empire Parliamentary Association to replace the Chair destroyed by the fire of 1916. *Journals,* May 20, 1921, p. 305.

(2) On the right hand side of the Chair, the following phrases are incised in gothic type:

> "Nec prece nac pretio. (Neither by entreaty nor bribery.)
> Libertas in legibus. (Liberty under the laws.)
> Hostis honori invidia. (Envy is the foe of honour.)

On the left hand side:

> Manus justa nardus. (A just hand is a precious ointment.)
> Memor et fidelis. (Mindful and faithful.)
> Mens conscia recti. (A mind conscious of the right.)"

The Table

§97.   In front of the Speaker's Chair is the Table where the Clerk of the House and the two Clerks Assistant sit during sittings of the House. Arranged on each side of the Table are various parliamentary books for the use of the Members. The Mace is placed at the end of the Table.

FIGURE NO. 1 — THE PLAN OF THE HOUSE OF COMMONS

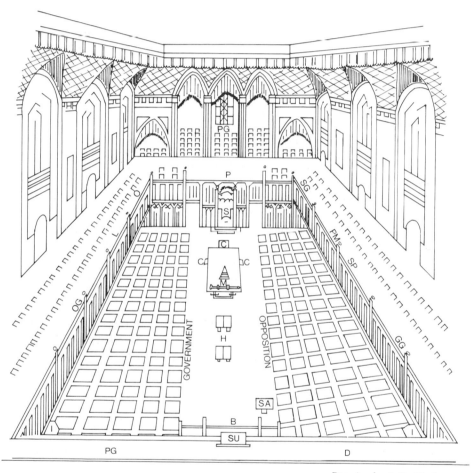

Drawing by Julie Birch

KEYS: S—Speaker. P—Press Gallery. H—Hansard Reporters. O—Official Gallery. C—Clerks of the House (When the House goes into Committee, the Speaker leaves the Chair, and the Chairman sits in the Chair of the Clerk of the House, which is the one at centre). T—Table of the House. M—Mace (when the House goes into Committee, the Mace, is put below the table on brackets). B—Bar of the House. SA—Sergeant-at-Arms. SG—Senate Gallery. PM—Prime Minister's Gallery. SP—Speaker's Gallery. GG—Gallery of the Government Party. D—Diplomatic Gallery. OG—Gallery of the Opposition Parties. L—Leader of the Opposition Gallery. I—Interpreters' Booth. PG—Public Gallery. SU—Sound Reinforcement Unit. Television Cameras (Under Galleries).

The Mace

§98. The symbol of the House's authority is the Mace. The original Mace was destroyed in the February fire of 1916 but was replaced in June, 1916, by Colonel the Rt. Hon. Sir Charles Cheers Wakefield, Lord Mayor of London, the Sheriffs of London, George Alexander Touche, Esq., M.P. and Samuel George Shead, Esq. Its general design is on similar lines to the Mace used in the United Kingdom House of Commons.

§99. During the election of a Speaker, the Mace is placed on a cushion on the floor under the Table. Later, when the Speaker is in the Chair, the Mace is placed on the Table. However, when he leaves the Chair for the House to go into a Committee of the Whole, the Sergeant-at-Arms places the Mace on a rack below the Table.

PLACES OF MEMBERS

§100. (1) Members are allocated desks in the Chamber by the Speaker on the advice of the party Whips who, in turn, have the concurrence of their Leader. By custom, the centre of the first two rows of desks on the Speaker's right are reserved for the Ministers of the Crown. The front row on the Speaker's left is reserved for the leading members of the Opposition Parties. Each Opposition Party is allocated a proportionate number of front desks as they have elected Members to the House.
  (2) By custom, the Speaker and Deputy Speaker are allocated desks on the right and near the Chair.

§101. If the majority party has more Members than there are desks on the Speaker's right, then the remaining government Members occupy desks across the aisle. This section may, at the discretion of the Speaker, be near his Chair or at the far end of the Chamber and is commonly referred to as the Rump.

§102. Members must be in their designated place in order to be recognized by the Speaker for purposes of debate or voting. The only exception occurs during proceedings in a Committee of the Whole, when Members may occupy any desk.

ATTENDANCE OF MEMBERS

§103. (1) Standing Order 5 states that every Member is bound to attend the service of the House unless leave of absence has been given him by the House.
  (2) Mr. Speaker Lamoureux ruled: "that the Chair should not be expected to take judicial and official notice every day of the absence of a Member of the House of Commons. Standing Order 5 does not apply only to Cabinet Ministers; it refers to the attendance of all Members. This point has

been raised from time to time. I recognize that the Standing Order is there. I have felt also that perhaps the Standing Committee on Procedure and Organization should look at Standing Order 5. I have suggested that before but for some reason the members of the Committee have thought that the Standing Order should not be interfered with and that it should be allowed to stay. According to my information, the last time that Standing Order was applied was back in 1877. I would not think, after all these years, that this Standing Order should be referred to signal the absence of any individual Member of the House." *Debates,* June 16, 1970, p. 8153.

(3) In modern times the ensuring of attendance in the Commons has become a principal function of the party machinery. The Whips of the various parties make it their duty to secure adequate representation for all important divisions. The publication of the official Division Lists in the *Journals* and *Debates* of the House, showing the names of Members and the total number of Members for each side of the question, provides an opportunity for a Member to place on record not only his vote but the fact of his attendance on that particular day.

(4) In addition, in accordance with s. 44 of the Senate and House of Commons Act, R.S.C. 1970, c.S-8, each Member is required to deliver a signed statement to the Clerk of the House, setting forth his attendance for the required period, in order that he may receive his sessional allowance.

ACCESS TO THE HOUSE OF COMMONS

Members of Parliament

§104. The time-honoured privilege of Members to have free and unimpeded access to the Parliament Buildings should be recognized even if there is some question as to the extension of the term "parliamentary precincts", and in particular whether the jurisdiction of the Speaker, exercised on behalf of Members, extends beyond the limits of the Parliament Buildings themselves. *Debates,* May 25, 1970, p. 7255.

§105. (1) Although the words "parliamentary precincts", by tradition and practice, are recognized as covering the buildings themselves and principally the Centre Block, West Block and Confederation Building, the definition has never been officially deemed to include the grounds surrounding the buildings. So far as the Centre Block is concerned, there is no question whatever that the protective staffs of both the Senate and the House of Commons, who are parliamentary employees, have sole and exclusive jurisdiction. Once outside this building, however, security and control of access are more directly under the control of the executive branch of the Government. *Debates,* May 15, 1970, p. 7007.

(2) There have been exceptions to this principle in times of emergency; other security forces have been invited to assist in the maintenance of order.

Members of the Public

§106.   Strangers, or to use its more common term, the public, are permitted to visit and use those areas of the Parliament Buildings not normally appropriated for the use of the Members.

THE GALLERIES

§107.   (1) The Galleries of the Chamber comprise a Press Gallery, two large visitors galleries at the ends of the Chamber called the Public Gallery, and galleries for the Diplomatic Corps and departmental officials. There are, also private galleries allotted to the Speaker, the Senate, the Prime Minister, the Leader of the Opposition and to each of the Government and Opposition Parties.

(2) All arrangements and matters concerning proper decorum with reference to the admission of strangers are the responsibility of the Sergeant-at-Arms.

Exclusion of Strangers

§108.   Under S.O. 13, the Speaker will not normally, on his own accord, order that the galleries be cleared, but puts the question: "Shall strangers be ordered to withdraw?" This is not debatable, but a division may take place. However, in view of the authority accorded to him by the Standing Orders, the Speaker has directed in cases of grave disorder, that the galleries be cleared. *Debates,* May 11, 1970, p. 6796.

§109.   The Sergeant-at-Arms or members of his staff, with or without an express direction from the Speaker, have removed from the galleries of the House strangers who were behaving in a disorderly manner. When the disorder has continued, the galleries have been cleared by the Speaker's direction.

§110.   Whenever the House decides to sit in secret sessions, strangers are cleared from the galleries, or if the House has agreed to sit in secret on a certain day, the gallery doors are not opened to the public after the Prayers.

Officers of the House

THE SPEAKER OF THE HOUSE OF COMMONS

§111.   The Speaker of the House of Commons is the representative of the House itself in its powers, proceedings and dignity. His functions fall into two main categories. On the one hand, he is the spokesman or representative of the House in its relations with the Crown, the Senate and other authorities and persons outside Parliament. On the other hand, he presides over the debates

of the House of Commons and enforces the observance of all rules for preserving order in its proceedings.

The Speaker as Representative of the House of Commons

(a) *In relation to the Queen and the Governor General*

§112. (1) The Speaker is elected by the House itself. Directly upon his election he petitions the Governor General for the continuance of the Commons' privileges.

(2) He personally delivers an engrossed Address in Reply to the Speech from the Throne to the Governor General.

(3) He leads the Commons when it is summoned to attend the Queen, the Governor General or his representative in the Senate. Upon returning to the House at the opening of a new Parliament or Session he makes available the Speech from the Throne. In addition, he reads messages from the Queen and the Governor General.

(b) *In relation to outside authorities*

§113. The Speaker communicates the resolutions of the House to those to whom they are directed, conveys its thanks and expresses its censure, its reprimands, and its admonitions. He issues warrants to execute the orders of the House for the commitment of offenders, for the attendance of witnesses in custody, and for giving effect to other orders requiring the sanction of a legal form. Whenever it seems to him a suitable occasion, he communicates to the House letters and documents addressed to him as Speaker, such as expressions of congratulation and condolence and other messages from foreign countries and legislatures, letters acknowledging a vote of thanks of the House or relating to the rights and privileges of the House or of its Members.

§114. Upon receipt of a resignation of a Member, he addresses his warrant to the Chief Electoral Officer for the issue of a Writ of Election for the election of a new Member. The Speaker is required by some statutes to ensure debates occur in the House, as in the Electoral Boundaries Readjustment Act, R.S.C. 1970, c.E-2, s.20.

(c) *In relation to the Senate*

§115. It is the function of the Speaker to direct the attention of the House, when the occasion arises, to a breach of its privileges in bills or amendments brought from the Senate, and to direct the special entries to be made in the *Journals* by which the House, in respect of particular amendments, signifies its willingness to waive its privileges without thereby establishing a general precedent.

(d) *The Rank of the Speaker*

§116. The Speaker's rank is defined by Order in Council of December 19, 1968, in which it is provided that upon all occasions and in all meetings, except where otherwise provided by Act of Parliament, the Speaker shall have precedence immediately after the Governor General, the Prime Minister of Canada, the Chief Justice of Canada, former Governors General, former Prime Ministers and the Speaker of the Senate and immediately before Ambassadors and Members of the Cabinet.

The Speaker as Presiding Officer of the House of Commons

§117. (1) The chief characteristics attached to the office of Speaker in the House of Commons are authority and impartiality. As a symbol of the authority of the House, he is accompanied by the Mace which is carried before him by the Sergeant-at-Arms and is placed upon the Table when he is in the Chair. He calls upon Members to speak and in debate all speeches are addressed to him. When he rises to preserve order or to give a ruling he must always be heard in silence. No Member may rise when the Speaker is standing. Reflections upon the character or actions of the Speaker may be punished as breaches of privilege. His actions cannot be criticized incidentally in debate or upon any form of proceeding except by way of a substantive motion. *Journals,* June 4, 1956, p. 692. Confidence in the impartiality of the Speaker is an indispensable condition of the successful working of procedure, and many conventions exist which have as their object, not only to ensure the impartiality of the Speaker but also, to ensure that his impartiality is generally recognized. He takes no part in debate in the House. He votes only when the voices are equal, and then only in accordance with rules which preclude an expression of opinion upon the merits of a question.

(2) The Presiding Officer, though entitled on all occasions to be treated with the greatest attention and respect by the individual Members, because the power, dignity, and honour of the House are officially embodied in his person, is yet but the servant of the House. He is selected and appointed to the trust of Presiding Officer in the confidence and upon the supposition of the conformity of his will to that of the House.

(3) In order to ensure his complete impartiality the Speaker has usually relinquished all formal affiliation with his political party. He does not attend the party caucus nor any outside partisan political activity. Mr. Speaker Lamoureux on two occasions (in 1968, 1972) was re-elected as an Independent Member of the House.

(4) The Speaker cannot be consulted, from the floor of the House, as to the consequences of the passage of a resolution. *Debates,* January 31, 1935, p. 355.

(5) Hypothetical queries on procedure cannot be addressed to the Speaker from the floor of the House.

(6) The Speaker will not give a decision upon a constitutional question nor decide a question of law, though the same may be raised on a point of

order or privilege. *Journals,* September 25, 1903, pp. 577-8. *Journals,* October 25, 1963, p. 488. Sir John Bourinot, Parliamentary Procedure and Practice in the Dominion of Canada (4th ed., 1916), p. 180.

(7) The opinion of the Speaker cannot be sought in the House about any matter arising or likely to arise in a committee. *Journals,* April 6, 1976, pp. 1183-4.

§118. The Speaker should be addressed as "Mr. Speaker" or "Sir". However, he has been addressed in the House as "Your Honour", although there is no written authority for such a title.

§119. (1) Speakers' rulings, once given, belong to the House which, under S.O. 12, must accept them without appeal or debate. They become precedents and form part of the rules of procedure. The Speaker is not vested with the power to alter them of his own accord. If they have been given under misrepresentation, the House itself, and not the Speaker, should take the initial steps to avoid the consequences or implications. Such actions would not be considered as an appeal against a decision of the Speaker. *Journals,* March 28, 1916, p. 201.

(2) The Speaker's rulings, whether given in public or in private, constitute precedents by which subsequent Speakers, Members, and officers are guided. Such precedents are collected and in course of time may be formulated as principles or rules of practice. It is largely by this method that the modern practice of the House of Commons has been developed.

Procedural Duties of the Speaker

§120. Foremost among his many responsibilities, the Speaker has the duty to maintain an orderly conduct of debate by repressing disorder when it arises, by refusing to propose the question upon motions and amendments which are irregular, and by calling the attention of the House to bills which are out of order. He rules on points of order submitted to him by Members on questions as they arise. Many powers have been vested in the Speaker by virtue of the Standing Orders.

§121. Under S.O. 26, he decides upon proposals to adjourn the House in order to discuss a specific and important matter that should have urgent consideration by ensuring that they conform to the provisions of the Standing Order.

§122. (1) When a complaint of breach of privilege is raised he decides whether a prima facie case has been made which would justify such proceedings taking precedence over the other business of the House. If the Speaker states that a prima facie case exists, he then puts the proposed motion so that the House may decide what action is required in the matter.

(2) It has often been laid down that the Speaker's function in ruling on a

claim of breach of privilege does not extend to deciding the question of substance whether a breach of privilege has in fact been committed — a question which can only be decided by the House itself.

§123.   (1) The Speaker may rule out any question which violates the procedures of the House in the same way as he deals with irregularities in motions and amendments. He may make alterations to proposed motions or he may refer them back to the Member for correction.

(2) In accordance with S.O. 40(5), the Speaker decides the order in which subjects are raised on the adjournment motion.

(3) Under S.O. 75(10), the Speaker has the power to select or combine proposed motions in amendment offered at the report stage of bills.

(4) The Speaker is normally given the discretionary power, after consultation with the Government, of recalling the House from an adjournment.

(5) He calls to order any Member who is being irrelevant or repetitious in debate.

Administrative Duties of the Speaker

§124.   (1) The Speaker has the control of the accommodation and services in that part of the Parliamentary Buildings and precincts occupied by, or on behalf of, the House of Commons.

(2) The Speaker is responsible, through the Clerk of the House, for the accuracy of the *Votes and Proceedings* and for the correctness of the *Official Report of Debates*.

§125.   The Speaker, as Chairman and with the other Commissioners of Internal Economy, approves all Budgetary Estimates for the coming fiscal year as prepared by the Clerk of the House and the Sergeant-at-Arms. The Speaker transmits these Estimates to the Minister of Finance for inclusion with the total Budgetary Estimates of the Government of Canada. The House of Commons Act, R.S.C. 1970, c.H-9, s.17.

Functions of the Office of the Speaker After Dissolution

§126.   (1) By s.15 of the House of Commons Act, the person who fills the office of Speaker at the time of any dissolution of Parliament shall, for the purpose of the provisions of the Act, be deemed to be the Speaker until a Speaker is chosen by the new Parliament.

(2) During this period the Speaker may perform only duties of an administrative nature.

Unavoidable Absence of the Speaker

§127.   Whenever the Speaker of the House of Commons, from illness or other cause, finds it necessary to leave the Chair during any part of the sittings of the House, he may call upon the Deputy Speaker or any other Presiding Officer of the House or, in their absence, upon any Member of the House to take the Chair and to act as Speaker during the remainder of such day, unless he himself resumes the Chair before the closing of the sitting for that day.

§128.   (1) At the opening of a sitting when the Speaker is absent, the Sergeant-at-Arms enters the House with the Mace, which he places upon the Table. The Clerk informs the House of the Speaker's unavoidable absence, and if necessary, of that of the Deputy Speaker.

(2) In accordance with the Speaker of the House of Commons Act, R.S.C. 1970, c.S-13, whenever the House is informed by the Clerk at the Table of the unavoidable absence of the Speaker, the Deputy Speaker, if present, shall take the Chair and shall perform the duties and exercise the authority of the Speaker in relation to all the proceedings of the House, until the meeting of the House on the next sitting day, and so on from day to day on the like information being given to the House until the House otherwise orders. If the House adjourns for more than twenty-four hours, the Deputy Speaker shall continue to perform the duties and exercise the authority of the Speaker for twenty-four hours only after such adjournment.

Resignation of the Speaker

§129.   The Speaker continues in office during the whole Parliament, unless in the meantime he resigns, dies or is dismissed by resolution of the House.

§130.   (1) The Speaker may offer his resignation in two ways. He may read from the Chair a statement tendering his resignation to be effective either immediately or at some future day, or he may write a letter to the Clerk of the House who will read it at the next sitting the same way as he notifies the House when the Speaker is unavoidably absent.

(2) The Speaker's resignation is addressed to the Clerk for the purpose of having it officially communicated to the House, which has to elect his successor. There is no precedent to show that the House's acceptance is necessary. Once the letter of resignation is signed it is effective and after the House has been officially apprised of it, it cannot be withdrawn. If it were desirable that he should remain in office, he would have to be re-elected in the same way as when he was first appointed to the Speakership.

THE DEPUTY SPEAKER OF THE HOUSE OF COMMONS

§131.   (1) Under the terms of S.O. 53, the House elects one of its Members to be a Chairman of Committees with the additional title of Deputy Speaker of the House. As with the Speaker, this Member is elected at the beginning of each new Parliament and holds office for the duration. In the event of a vacancy occurring in the office, the House proceeds to elect a successor.

(2) Every act done and warrant, order or other document issued or

published by the Deputy Speaker in relation to any proceedings of the House of Commons, or which under any statute would be done, shall have the same effect and validity as if the same had been done, issued, signed or published by the Speaker for the time being. Speaker of the House of Commons Act, s.5.

§132.   A Member from an Opposition Party has been elected to the position of Deputy Speaker. *Journals,* March 21, 1918, p. 32. *Journals,* January 4, 1973, p. 13.

§133.   Deputy Speakers have not taken a consistent position with respect to attendance at their political party's functions. During divisions they have voted but have not attempted to participate otherwise in the debates of the House.

OTHER PRESIDING OFFICERS

§134.   In addition to the Deputy Speaker and Chairman of Committees, the House has the power under S.O. 53 to appoint a Deputy Chairman and an Assistant Deputy Chairman of Committees, who, whenever the Chairman is absent from the Chair, are entitled to exercise all the powers vested in the Chairman of Committees, including his powers of Deputy Speaker during the Speaker's unavoidable absence.

§135.   Unlike the Speaker and Deputy Speaker, these other Presiding Officers are elected at the commencement of each session of Parliament.

§136.   During the unavoidable absence of the Speaker, and the Deputy Speaker, the Deputy or Assistant Deputy Chairman of the Committee of the Whole takes the Chair. If the House subsequently goes into Committee, he also presides. When the question for reporting from the Committee has been agreed to, he returns to the Speaker's Chair and a Member makes the report of the Committee.

OFFICERS IN THE SERVICE OF THE HOUSE

§137.   The Officers in the Service of the House of Commons are the Clerk of the House, the Clerks Assistant, the Sergeant-at-Arms, and the Law Clerk and Parliamentary Counsel.

THE CLERK OF THE HOUSE

§138.   The Clerk of the House of Commons is appointed by Letters Patent under the Great Seal and not by the Speaker or Parliament.

Procedural Duties

§139. (1) The Clerk is the chief procedural advisor to the Speaker and to the House.

(2) He signs the Addresses, votes of thanks and orders of the House, endorses the bills sent or returned to the Senate and reads whatever is required to be read in the House. The Clerk has the custody of all records or other documents and is responsible for the conduct of the business of the House in the offices within his department. He assists the Speaker and advises Members in regard to questions of order and proceedings of the House.

(3) The Clerk presides over the election of the Speaker.

(4) The Clerk is responsible for carrying out all divisions in the House and announcing the vote tally.

(5) It is the duty of the Clerk to deliver to the Minister of Justice two copies of every bill introduced in the House in order that they be examined with respect to the Canadian Bill of Rights. He also sends copies of the *Votes and Proceedings* daily to both the Governor General and the Speaker.

(6) He prepares and issues a daily *Order Paper* for each sitting of the House and, as required, a *Special Order Paper*.

(7) At each sitting of the House, the Clerk prepares the Scroll which is the official record of the actual proceedings that took place in the House. It is the record from which the Journals Branches prepare the *Votes and Proceedings*.

(8) The Clerk conveys and receives messages between the two Houses.

(9) Throughout all its stages and proceedings, legislation continues in the custody of the Clerk of the House. No alteration whatever is permitted to be made to it without the express authority of the House or committee as recorded by either the Clerks at the Table or the Clerk of the Committee.

Administrative Duties

§140. (1) The Clerk administers the Oath of Allegiance to all duly elected Members.

(2) The Clerk has the direction and control of all the officers and clerks employed by the House of Commons.

(3) The Clerk prepares the Budgetary Estimates for the House and submits them to the Speaker.

THE CLERKS ASSISTANT

§141. (1) There are two Clerks Assistant in the House of Commons — a Clerk Assistant (Administrative and Procedural) and a Clerk Assistant (Legal).

(2) The Clerks Assistant are appointed by Letters Patent under the Great Seal and take the Oaths of Allegiance and of Office before the Clerk. They are commissioners appointed under the Great Seal to administer the Oath of

Allegiance to Members of the House. They are authorized by the provisions of the Senate and House of Commons Act to certify the statements of the Members for the payment of their travelling expenses and indemnity. They sit at the Table on each side of the Clerk and all three are described as "the Clerks-at-the-Table". They receive the notices of questions, motions and amendments which have to be entered on the *Notice Paper*. They also receive amendments from Members proposing to amend the motion before the House at that time. It is their duty to see that these are drawn according to the rules of the House and to refer to the Speaker, the Clerk or the interested Member any that appear to be out of order.

(3) Although there are two Clerks Assistant, their responsibilities are interchangeable.

(4) During the unavoidable absence of the Clerk of the House, one of the Clerks Assistant performs his duties.

(5) In addition, the Speaker appoints, from time to time, persons as Second Clerk Assistant and Third Clerk Assistant. These Clerks, designated as "Clerks-at-the-Table", discharge such duties as are assigned to them by the Clerk of the House.

§142. (1) A Clerk Assistant calls out in both official languages the first, second or third reading of bills as they are passed by the House. A Clerk Assistant reads the reports from the Standing and Special Committees as required. When a bill or resolution is adopted, he certifies the dates of the different stages of procedure through which it has progressed, then endorses them. He acts as Reading Clerk for any document which forms part of a question which needs to be read. He reads the Orders of the Day as they are called by the Speaker. He is in constant communication, during the sittings, with the different branches of the staff supplying the needs of the House. When the House is in Committee of the Whole, a Clerk Assistant is the Clerk of the Committee, taking the Minutes of its proceedings.

(2) During a division in the House, one Clerk Assistant calls out the names of the Members rising; however, during a division in a Committee of the Whole, he only counts the number of Members rising.

THE SERGEANT-AT-ARMS

§143. (1) The Sergeant-at-Arms is appointed by Letters Patent under the Great Seal. He brings to the Bar persons to be examined as witnesses. He takes into custody strangers who are irregularly in the House or its galleries, or who misconduct themselves there; and causes the removal of persons directed to withdraw. For the better execution of his duties he has a chair close to the Bar of the House. He is a commissioner appointed under the Great Seal to administer the Oath of Allegiance to Members of the House. His ceremonial duties are to attend the Speaker, with the Mace, on entering and leaving the House or going to the Senate; he introduces, with the Mace, messengers from the Senate. Out of the House, he is entrusted with the execution of all warrants for the commitment of persons ordered into custody by the House and for removing them to a prison or retaining them in his own custody. He serves, by his messengers, all orders of the House upon those whom they concern. The Sergeant-at-Arms also maintains order in the lobby and passages of the House and may be directed by the Speaker to ascertain and report on the facts when a disturbance has occurred. He appoints and supervises the several officers in his department. He has control over the arrangements for the admission of strangers to the galleries.

(2) The Sergeant-at-Arms is the Housekeeper of the House of Commons. In this capacity, acting under the direction of the Speaker, he has the responsibility for the House's buildings, committee rooms, restaurants and all moveable property.

THE LAW CLERK AND PARLIAMENTARY COUNSEL

§144. (1) The Law Clerk and Parliamentary Counsel is appointed by Letters Patent under the Great Seal. He has the principal duty of advising the Speaker and officers of the House on all legal matters which do not fall within the sphere of procedure.

(2) It is also his duty under S.O. 84 to assist the Members of the House in drafting legislation.

(3) In particular his duties include the examination of all government legislative proposals prior to their introduction, to determine whether they entail an expenditure of public moneys; if they are found to do so, then he drafts the Royal Recommendation for inclusion with the proposal; preparing and sending bills for printing and reprinting following the various legislative stages; incorporating Estimates into legislation; incorporating amendments into bills; and the final responsibility for the annual statutes compilation.

DIRECTORATES OF THE HOUSE

§145. (1) There are three Directorates within the House. The Directors, who are responsible for their respective branches, report directly to the Clerk of the House. They are Administration and Personnel, Building Services and Legislative Services. Under the Director of Legislative Services are the three principal branches of the House of Commons — Journals, Debates and Committees, and Private Legislation Branches. Refer to the Chart of the Organization of the House of Commons at Fig. No. 2.

(2) These Directors and Chiefs of Branches are designated as officials of the House and not as officers of the House. *Debates,* October 28, 1963, p. 4071.

Journals Branches

§146. These Branches, one for each official language, are responsible for preparing the *Votes and Proceedings* and the *Order Paper and Notices* for each sitting day. The former forms the basis for the *Journals* at the end of the session and the latter has two parts; the *Order Paper* and the *Notice Paper*. The Branches are also responsible for the editing of all notices of questions, motions that are received from Members for publication in the *Notice Paper*. They operate as a secretariat for the Table Officers of the House of Commons. There is also a section called the Sessional Papers Office which receives and retains all documents tabled in the House.

Debates Branches

§147. The function of a Debates Branch is to transcribe the verbatim record of what is said in the House. These Branches, one for each official language, are responsible for preparing the *Official Report of Debates* for each sitting day.

Committees and Private Legislation Branch

§148. This Branch provides the Clerks of Committee for each of the committees established by the House. These Clerks of Committees are the procedural and administrative advisors to their committees. In addition, the Branch is responsible to the Clerk of the House for providing procedural advice concerning the presentation of petitions and private legislation.

PARLIAMENTARY PUBLICATIONS

The Votes and Proceedings

§149. (1) This is a record of the proceedings of the House. The entries are compiled under the responsibility of the Clerk of the House by the Journals Branches, mainly from the entries in the Scroll of the Clerks-at-the-Table. The *Votes and Proceedings* record all that is, or is deemed to be, done by the House, but they ignore everything that is said unless it is especially ordered to be entered.

(2) The usual entries, apart from those on the Scroll, include, from time to time, important rulings made by the Speaker, committee membership changes and reports, and lists of documents deposited with the Clerk of the House in accordance with any Act of Parliament or in pursuance of any resolution or Standing Order. In addition, Notices of Committee Meetings are included in an appendix plus such other matters as Ways and Means Motions, and Objections filed with the Speaker pursuant to the Electoral Boundaries Readjustment Act, R.S.C. 1970, c.E-2.

The Journals

§150. The *Journals* are the permanent official record of the proceedings of the House. They are an edited and corrected version of the *Votes and Proceedings,* but do not include any appendices. At the end of a session they are bound and published with an index as the *Journals of the House of Commons of Canada.*

FIGURE NO. 2 — ORGANIZATION CHART OF THE HOUSE OF COMMONS

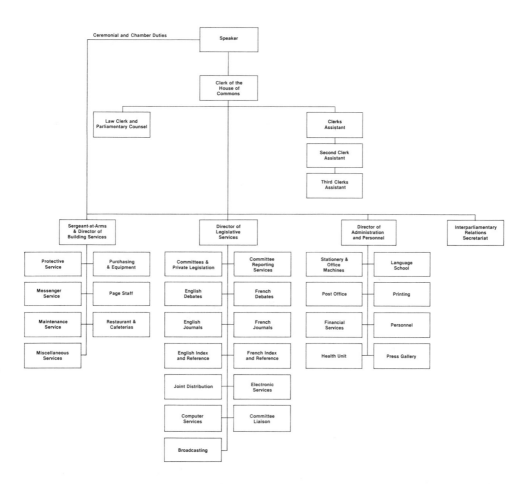

§151. (1) The *Journals* contain all the proceedings which have actually taken place, the res gestae, such as petitions presented, bills read a first, second or third time, references or questions to committees, resolutions amended or carried, votes taken, debates adjourned. The official record of what is "done and past," in a legislative assembly, is called the *Journal.* It is so called because the proceedings are entered therein, in chronological order, as they occur from day to day; the business of each day forming the matter of a complete record by itself; hence the record is frequently spoken of in the plural as the *Journals.*

(2) The *Journals* are prepared under the direction of the Clerk, by the Chiefs of the Journals Branches. They are prepared from the Clerk's Scroll; therefore, whenever any question arises as to any proceedings which have taken place the *Journals* alone are held to be correct. An entry therein may be amended or expunged, but only on a motion made in the House after due notice.

§152.   (1) Upon any enquiry touching the privileges, immunities and powers of the Senate and House of Commons, or of any Member thereof respectively, any copy of the *Journals of the House of Commons,* printed or purported to be printed by order of the House of Commons, shall be admitted as evidence of such *Journals* by all courts, justices, and others without any proof being given that such copies were so printed. Senate and House of Commons Act, R.S.C. 1970, c.S-8, s.6.

(2) When a person requires the *Journals* as evidence in a court of law, or for any legal purpose, he may either obtain from the Journals Branches a copy of the entries required without the signature of any officer and swear himself that it is a true copy or, with the permission of the House or, during prorogation, of the Speaker, he may secure the attendance of an officer to produce the printed *Journals* or extracts which he certifies to be true copies. Bourinot, pp. 186-7.

The Order Paper and Notices

§153.   The *Order Paper* includes Routine Proceedings, Orders of the Day and the Disposition of Business, it is the official agenda which lists the items that may be called during the sitting for that day. The *Order Paper* for the first sitting day of the week lists all items in detail; however, because of its immense size, it is considerably abridged for each of the other days of the week.

§154.   The *Notice Paper* is prepared in the Journals Branches and is appended to the *Order Paper* but numbered with roman numerals. It contains entries by which Members give notice of their intention to do something such as seek answers to written questions, introduce bills, or to move motions under Private Members' business.

The Official Report of Debates

§155.   (1) The *Official Report of Debates,* commonly referred to as Hansard, is the record of speeches made in the House; it also contains answers to written questions on the Order Paper. The debates of the House of Commons are reported verbatim, recording correctly what was said by each Member in the House. Slight verbal alterations are allowed to be made by a Member in order to make his meaning more precise and accurate; however, he may not, by the insertion of words or phrases, effect material changes in the meaning of what he actually said in the House. *Debates,* April 7, 1933, p. 3855.

(2) Corrections may be made to Hansard. If the correction is of a very important nature the Member shall rise in the House when Motions are called to explain his correction. At this time the House gives its approval to the change. However, if the change is minor the Member should inform the Editor of *Debates*, directly, in order to have the correction made. *Debates,* October 26, 1971, p. 7083.

§156.   The *Debates* are printed in bound volumes from time to time during a session.

PARTY MACHINERY IN THE HOUSE

The Official Opposition

§157.   (1) The importance of the Opposition in the system of parliamentary government has long received practical recognition in the procedure of Parliament. Statutory recognition has been accorded through the grant of a salary to the Leader of the Opposition. The political party which has the right to be called the "Official Opposition" is the largest minority group which is prepared, in the event of the resignation of the Government, to assume office. The Leader of the Opposition and some of his principal colleagues form a group, each member of which is given a particular range of activities on which it is his task to direct criticism of the Government's policy and administration and to outline alternative policies from the point of view of his party. The Opposition, both by usage and under the Standing Orders, has the right to exercise the initiative in selecting the subject of debate, on such occasions as the debate on the Address in Reply to the Throne Speech and on allotted days. The Leader of the Opposition is, by custom, accorded certain particular rights in asking questions of Ministers. Official Opposition spokesmen are also given some precedence in asking questions and in debate. Each party is usually organized, with chief spokesmen, for various areas of activities under the Government's control.

(2) An additional allowance is paid to each Member who is the Leader of a party that has a recognized membership of twelve or more persons in the House. Senate and House of Commons Act, s.41 [re-en. 1974-75, c.44, s.3].

(3) In addition, recognized parties within the meaning of the Senate and House of Commons Act are allocated, on a proportionate basis, funds for establishing and maintaining research groups to aid them in their parliamentary work. *Debates,* November 15, 1968, p. 2791.

The House Leaders

§158.   (1) The Member of the Government who is primarily responsible to the Prime Minister for the arrangement of government business in the House of Commons is known as the Government House Leader and has, in recent years, held the portfolio of President of the Queen's Privy Council for

Canada. This Minister has the authority to call any items of government business as he may decide. *Journals,* May 2, 1961, pp. 493-5.

(2) The Leader of the Official Opposition designates a Member of his Party to occupy the recognized position of Opposition House Leader. The Opposition House Leader is responsible for discussing his Party's priorities for the arrangement of the business of the House.

(3) The Government House Leader discusses with the House Leaders of other Parties, the business arrangements for the House and attempts to reach some compromise on the length of debate on each of the various items of business.

(4) As a matter of practice, since 1968, each Thursday following the Question Period, the Government House Leader states, in reply to a question put by the House Leader of the Official Opposition, the projected business of the House for the forthcoming week.

(5) The Government House Leader also moves housekeeping motions, allots supply days and generally ensures that the House is kept busy in as efficient a manner as possible.

The Party Whips

§159. (1) Each party has as one of its supporters a Member known as the Chief Whip. The names of these Members are communicated to the Speaker in order that extra allowances may be paid to those Members holding the officially recognized positions of Chief Government Whip and Chief Opposition Whip.

(2) The duties of the Whips are to keep their Members supplied with information concerning the business of the House, to ensure the attendance of their Members, to determine pairing arrangements for their Members who are unable to attend divisions, so that their votes may be neutralized and not lost, and to supply lists of Members to serve on the various committees of the House.

4

A New Parliament; Opening and Closing of a Session

4

A New Parliament; Opening and Closing of a Session

§160. This chapter describes the procedures involved in summoning, proroguing and dissolving Parliament.

PARLIAMENTARY AND SESSIONAL PERIODS

§161. "A Parliament" in the sense of a parliamentary period is a period between a general election and dissolution, not exceeding five years, which may be regarded as a cycle beginning and ending with a proclamation. Such a proclamation, on the one hand, dissolves an existing Parliament and, on the other, orders the issue of writs for the election of a new Parliament and appoints the day and place for its meeting. British North America Act, s.50.

§162. A session is a period of time between the meeting of a Parliament and its prorogation. There are a number of sessions within a Parliament, each lasting approximately one year. Parliament is usually prorogued by the Deputy of His Excellency the Governor General, with the House in attendance upon the Senate, to later that day or to the following day. The date so appointed may be deferred by a subsequent proclamation. During the course of a session either House may adjourn itself to such a date as it pleases. However, the practice evolving since 1968 is that the House adjourns for a duration and then is prorogued on the day after its first day's sitting of its return, with the next session commencing the following day.

§163. The period between the prorogation of Parliament and its reassembly in a new session is termed a "recess", while the period between the adjournment of the House and the resumption of its sitting in the same session is properly called an "adjournment". A prorogation terminates a session; however, an adjournment is only an interruption in the course of one and the same session.

Summons of Parliament

§164. A new Parliament is summoned in pursuance of a proclamation issued by the Governor General with the advice of the Privy Council. Proclamations, issued separately, dissolve the old Parliament, order the issue of writs by the Chief Electoral Officer and appoint a day for the meeting of the new Parliament.

Dissolution of Parliament

§165. Parliament is dissolved either by proclamation or by the expiration of its time of five years as mentioned in the British North America Act. The Parliament which assembled in 1911 was prolonged beyond this limit (to 1917) because of the exceptional circumstance of world war. *Journals,* February 8, 1916, p. 62.

Prorogation and Adjournment

§166. The prorogation of Parliament is a prerogative act of the Crown. Just as Parliament may only commence its deliberations at the time appointed by the Governor General, so it may not continue them any longer than he pleases. But each House exercises its right to adjourn itself independently of the Crown and of the other House. There shall be, however, a session once at least in every year as indicated in B.N.A. Act, s.20.

Effect of Prorogation and Adjournment

§167. (1) The effect of a prorogation is at once to suspend all business until Parliament shall be summoned again. Not only are the sittings of Parliament at an end, but all proceedings pending at the time are quashed. Every bill must therefore be renewed after a prorogation, as if it were introduced for the first time.

(2) An adjournment has no such effect on parliamentary proceedings. Upon reassembling, each House proceeds to transact the business previously appointed and all proceedings are resumed at the stage at which they were left before the adjournment.

§168. However, in accordance with S.O. 79, prorogation shall not have the effect of nullifying an Order or Address of the House for returns or papers. If they are not complied with in one session they shall be brought down during the following session without renewal of the Order.

Prorogation and Further Prorogation by Proclamation

§169. When Parliament stands summoned (after a dissolution) or prorogued to a specific day for the dispatch of business, it may be prorogued or further prorogued to a later day by a proclamation made by the Governor General on the advice of the Privy Council.

Procedure for the Prorogation of a Session

§170. (1) After the House receives the Message that the Deputy of His Excellency the Governor General desires their immediate attendance, the Speaker with the House, goes to the Senate Chamber where the Deputy of His Excellency the Governor General closes the session with a Speech. The Speaker of the Senate then reads out a message such as the following:

> "Honourable Members of the Senate
> "Members of the House of Commons:
> "It is the will and pleasure of the Honourable the Deputy of His Excellency the Governor General that this Parliament be prorogued until the .... day of ...., 19...., to be here holden; and this Parliament is accordingly prorogued until the .... day of ...., 19.... ."

(2) Accordingly, the Members of the House disperse.

Recall of the House from Adjournment

§171. (1) When the House is dispersed following its adoption of an adjournment motion, its reassembly can be effected either by proclamation or by the Speaker, by virtue of the powers specifically conferred upon him.

(2) The adjournment motion normally contains a paragraph such as the following:

> "That, when the House adjourns on ...., it shall stand adjourned until ...., provided that at any time prior to that day if it appears to the satisfaction of Mr. Speaker, after consultation with the Government, that the public interest requires that the House should meet at an earlier time during the adjournment, Mr. Speaker may give notice that he is so satisfied, and thereupon the House shall meet at the time stated in such notice, and shall transact its business as it it had been duly adjourned to that time;
> "And that, in the event of Mr. Speaker's being unable to act owing to illness or other cause, the Deputy Speaker or the Deputy Chairman of Committees shall act in his stead for the purpose of reconvening the House."

(3) The House has occasionally been recalled, usually to pass back-to-work legislation, at which time the Speaker causes to be published in the

Canada Gazette a notice such as the following:

> "In accordance with the provisions of the Resolution adopted by the House on ...., having been satisfied after consultation with the Government, that the public interest requires that the House should meet at an earlier time during the adjournment, I hereby give notice that the House of Commons shall meet on .... at .... o'clock, for the purpose of considering .... and to transact the business of the House as if it had been duly adjourned to that time."

A NEW PARLIAMENT

§172. The principal proceedings which distinguish the meeting of a new Parliament from the opening of any subsequent session are the taking and subscription of the Oath by Members of the House and the election of a Speaker.

THE OATH OF ALLEGIANCE

§173. Following receipt from the Chief Electoral Officer of a certificate listing Members returned to serve in the next Parliament, the Clerk of the House, or any other designated Commissioner, administers the Oath of Allegiance to all such duly elected Members of the House of Commons.

§174. (1) Only such Members as those who have taken and subscribed to the Oath, as required by law, may take their seats in the House of Commons. B.N.A. Act, s. 128.

(2) It is not the Oath that makes a person a Member of the House. He must be a Member before being sworn in. Unless he has first been duly elected under the terms of the Canada Election Act, R.S.C. 1970, c.14 (1st Supp.), he cannot take the Oath. The object of the Oath is to allow the Member to take his seat in the House. In accordance with this interpretation of the law, Members-elect, as soon as their election is reported to the Clerk by the Chief Electoral Officer, may receive such requisites as are necessary for the performance of their public duties. But if, for some reason or other, a Member were precluded from taking the Oath and sitting in the House, he would be deprived of his sessional indemnity. The form of the Oath is as follows:

> "I, ..., do swear, that I will be faithful and bear true Allegiance to Her Majesty Queen Elizabeth the Second." B.N.A. Act, The Fifth Schedule.

After taking the Oath of Allegiance, the Member signs the Roll.

Affirmation in Lieu of the Oath

§175. (1) In accordance with the Oaths of Allegiance Act, R.S.C. 1970, c.

O-1, s.5, members who object to being sworn may make a solemn Affirmation if the taking of an Oath is contrary to their religious belief or if they have no religious belief.

(2) The form of the Affirmation is as follows:

"I, ..., do solemnly, sincerely and truly affirm and declare the taking of an oath is according to my religious belief unlawful, and I do also solemnly, sincerely and truly affirm and declare that I will be faithful and bear true allegiance to Her Majesty Queen Elizabeth the Second."

OPENING OF A NEW PARLIAMENT

§176.   On the day appointed by Proclamation for the meeting of a new Parliament for the dispatch of business, the Members assemble in their Chamber.

§177.   When the Speaker has not yet been chosen and when the Members and the Clerk with the Clerks Assistant are in their places, the Gentleman Usher of the Black Rod presents himself at the door of the Commons and strikes it three times with his rod. The door is opened and he announces his message to the Sergeant-at-Arms who walks to the Table, makes an obeisance and, addressing the Clerk, says: "A message from the Deputy of His Excellency the Governor General." The Clerk says: "Admit the Messenger." The Gentleman Usher of the Black Rod then advances to the middle of the House, where he says in English and French:

"Members of the House of Commons:
    "His Honour the Deputy of His Excellency the Governor General desires the immediate attendance of Honourable Members in the Chamber of the Honourable the Senate."

§178.   The Members, preceded by the Clerk of the House and the Clerks Assistant, go immediately to the Upper House. The Gentleman Usher of the Black Rod, the Sergeant-at-Arms (without the Mace), the Chief of the Protective Staff, two constables and the Chief Messenger march in front in order to make the way clear for the Members in the execution of their duty. On their arrival in the Senate, they stand silently at the Bar facing the Deputy of His Excellency the Governor General, who is seated at the foot of the Throne. They receive a Message delivered by the Speaker of the Senate such as the following:

"Honourable Members of the Senate,
    "Members of the House of Commons:
    "I have it in command to let you know that His Honour the Deputy of His Excellency the Governor General does not see fit to declare the causes of his summoning the present Parliament of Canada until the

Speaker of the House of Commons shall have been chosen according to Law, but this afternoon at the hour of .... o'clock His Excellency will declare the causes of calling this Parliament."

ELECTION OF A SPEAKER

§179.   The Members return to their Chamber and proceed at once to the choice of a Speaker. The Mace is placed upon cushions on the floor under the Table. The Clerk presides at these preliminary proceedings and will stand up and point to a Member who rises to speak.

§180.   After a General Election, the Lower House is empowered to elect its Speaker by s.44 of the British North America Act, which says: "The House of Commons, on its first assembling after a general election, shall proceed with all practical speed to elect one of its Members to be Speaker." The Governor General does not give any orders to the Members of the Commons, neither does he tell them to present their Speaker to him for approbation.

§181.   (1) A Member, usually the Prime Minister, will propose the name of some other Member then present, in these words:

> That ...., Member for the Electoral District of ...., do take the Chair of this House as Speaker."

This motion is duly seconded and put by the Clerk, and in cases where there is no opposition it will be resolved, nemine contradicente.

(2) In practice, the proposer of the motion to elect the Speaker is normally the Prime Minister, with the honour of seconding the motion being given to the Leader of the Opposition or, at times, to another Minister of the Crown.

(3) The Clerk declares the Member in question duly elected. The proposer and seconder will accompany him from his seat to the Chair, where standing on the upper step he will return his humble acknowledgments to the House for the great honour they had been pleased to confer on him by choosing him to be their Speaker. The Mace, which up to this time has been under the Table, will then be laid on the Table.

(4) The person proposed should always be present, and should be properly a Member upon whose seat there is no probability of a question.

§182.   (1) In case there is opposition and two or more candidates are proposed for Speaker, not as amendments but as separate propositions, the Clerk will continue to point to each Member as he rises, and then sit down; when the debate is closed he will put the question first proposed, and if the majority decides in favour of that motion, the Speaker-elect will be immediately conducted to the Chair, but if it be otherwise, the second motion will be submitted to the House, and if it be resolved in the affirmative the Member so chosen will be conducted to the Chair.

(2) If a division is taken and there is equality of voices, the House not being then constituted, there is no casting vote and the question remains undecided. A decision to reject as well as to accept a motion must be given by the majority. A tie vote, when the Clerk is in the Chair, is not a decision.

§183. Prior to the Speaker being elected, it is not regular for the Clerk of the House to announce vacancies in the membership nor the election of new Members, as the Clerk does not preside over the House but occupies his chair at the meeting of the Members called for the purpose of completing the House by the election of a Speaker. *Debates,* February 7, 1878, p. 1.

Proceeding to the Senate for the Speech From the Throne

§184. (1) At the hour fixed for the purpose of appearing before the Governor General, for the formal opening of Parliament, the Speaker will communicate to the House a letter from the Governor General's Secretary, stating that His Excellency shall, at a certain hour, proceed to the Senate Chamber to open the session of the Parliament.

(2) The Gentleman Usher of the Black Rod makes his appearance a few minutes later, the door is rapped three times, and the Sergeant-at-Arms opens it. The Gentleman Usher of the Black Rod announces that he carries a Message from His Excellency the Governor General. The Sergeant-at-Arms walks to the Table, bows and says: "Mr. Speaker, a Message from His Excellency the Governor General." The Speaker says: "Admit the Messenger." The Sergeant-at-Arms takes the Mace from the Table, and carrying in on his shoulder, walks as far as the door, where he informs His Excellency's Messenger that he may appear before the House. Both enter. The Sergeant-at-Arms stops inside the Bar, holding the Mace, with the small end resting on the floor. The Gentleman Usher of the Black Rod advances past the Bar, bows, walks to the middle of the Chamber, stops and bows a second time, then he comes as far as the Table where he bows again and says in English and in French:

> "Mr. Speaker, His Excellency the Governor General desires the immediate attendance of this Honourable House in the Chamber of the Honourable the Senate."

The Speaker, with the House, then goes up to the Senate Chamber.

§185. (1) The Speaker, on arriving in the Senate, walks to a small platform at the Bar and raises his hat to His Excellency, who acknowledges the salutation. The Governor General is seated on the Throne; on his left Her Excellency occupies a chair close to the Throne. The Prime Minister sits to the right with the Leader of the Senate to the left of their Excellencies. Members of the House of Commons cluster around their Speaker and remain standing. When they are all in attendance, the Gentleman Usher of the Black Rod calls "Order".

(2) Then the Speaker, having been earlier elected, will address the Governor General, usually in the following words:

"May it please Your Excellency:

"The House of Commons have elected me as their Speaker, though I am but little able to fulfill the important duties thus assigned to me.

"If in the performance of those duties, I should at any time fall into error, I pray that the fault may be imputed to me, and not to the Commons, whose servant I am, and who through me, the better to enable them to discharge their duty to their Queen and Country, humbly claim all their undoubted rights and privileges, especially that they may have freedom of speech in their debates, access to Your Excellency's person at all seasonable times, and that their proceedings may receive from Your Excellency the most favourable construction."

(3) On behalf of His Excellency, the Speaker of the Senate will usually reply with the following words:

"Mr. Speaker,

"I am commanded by His Excellency the Governor General to declare to you that he freely confides in the duty and attachment of the House of Commons to Her Majesty's Person and Government, and not doubting that their proceedings will be conducted with wisdom, temper and prudence, he grants, and upon all occasions will recognize and allow their constitutional privileges.

"I am commanded also to assure you that the Commons shall have ready access to His Excellency upon all seasonable occasions, and that their proceedings, as well as your words and actions, will constantly receive from him the most favourable construction."

(4) This assertion of the Commons' privileges holds good for the full term of a Parliament and need not be repeated by a Speaker who is elected during the course of a Parliament.

§186.   The Speaker-elect does not submit himself to the Governor General's gracious approbation. The obligation to appoint a Speaker after a General Election is imposed by law, and it is therefore not necessary that his election should meet with the approval of the Governor General.

§187.   The Governor General then reads the Speech from the Throne; following its conclusion the Speaker and Members return to the House.

Election of Speaker in the Course of a Parliament

Announcement of vacancy

§188.   The Speaker continues in office during the whole Parliament, unless in the meantime he resigns, is dismissed by resolution of the House, dies, or accepts public office.

§189. (1) On February 8, 1878, there was no Speaker when the Members assembled for the Fifth Session of the Third Parliament, Mr. Anglin having resigned during the recess. The Gentleman Usher of the Black Rod delivered to the Commons the usual message demanding the Members' attendance in the Senate Chamber. They obeyed and were told in the Senate that the causes of summoning Parliament would not be declared until they chose a Speaker. This they did at once.

(2) On August 1, 1899, after the Speaker's death during the session, the Members did not go up to the Senate, but when they met at three o'clock, Sir Wilfrid Laurier immediately took the floor and said: "... the Governor General, having been informed of the death of Sir James Edgar, is pleased to give leave to the House to proceed to the choice of a Speaker." Strictly speaking, the information regarding the Speaker's death should be given to the Members by the Clerk of the House, but no objection was raised. The Prime Minister addressing the Clerk, then moved: "That Mr. Bain do take the chair of the House as Speaker." The motion was carried unanimously.

(3) On March 10, 1904, when the Members assembled for the Fourth Session of the Ninth Parliament and were without a Speaker, the same procedure was followed as on February 7, 1878, the procession to the Senate took place prior to the Speaker's election. The same practice was observed on January 12, 1916, when Parliament opened for the Sixth Session of the Twelfth Parliament and Mr. Sevigny was elected Speaker in the place of Dr. Sproule who had resigned through ill health.

(4) On January 15, 1935, Mr. George Black handed his resignation to the Clerk but it was addressed to the Prime Minister, Mr. Bennett, to whom it was immediately delivered. When the House met two days later, for the Sixth Session of the Seventeenth Parliament, Mr. Bennett read the letter, which was as follows: "Sir, I find it necessary to ask the House of Commons to allow me to retire from the Chair. In laying down the great office to which the House of Commons has called me, I trust that I can hand down its traditions unimpaired. If I have been able to discharge my official duties with any degree of success, it is because I have received the help and support of all my colleagues, for which I desire to express my sincere thanks." The Gentleman Usher of the Black Rod then delivered the Governor General's message and Members of the House proceeded to the Senate where they were informed that His Excellency did not see fit to declare the causes of summons until they elected their Speaker. They returned to the House, and, the Prime Minister, addressing the Clerk, moved that Mr. Bowman do take the Chair of this House as Speaker.

(5) During the 1956 session, the Speaker of the House of Commons, against whom a motion of want of confidence had previously been made and lost, said from the Chair: "I am anxious to regain my full freedom of speech. Were I to resign today the House would have to adjourn immediately. The Senate being adjourned for three weeks, it would have to be called back in session and the presence of His Excellency the Governor General or his

deputy would be required for the approval of a new Speaker. I place my resignation before the House to take effect at the pleasure of the House. I would wish that it be accepted as soon as possible. This is my farewell speech. I shall always remember with pleasure my term of office as Speaker. . . . Now I thank you very much for the privilege and the honour that you have given me of serving you as Speaker of the House." This statement was not followed by any resolution and no objection was taken to the Speaker continuing to perform his official duties. The Prime Minister stated that the Speaker had only declared his intention to resign. The Speaker then remained silent; his announcement was neither confirmed nor withdrawn and the House took no action. *Debates,* July 2, 1956, p. 5555.

Procedure for election to fill vacancy

§190.   (1) In the event of a vacancy in the Speakership during the session, the Governor General's desire that the House proceed to the appointment of a Speaker is not normally signified by the Speaker of the Senate in the Senate Chamber. Instead a Minister of the Crown, in the Commons, acquaints the House that His Excellency gives leave to the House to proceed forthwith to the choice of a new Speaker. *Journals,* August 1, 1899, p. 488.

(2) If the vacancy occurs during a recess, the same procedure is followed as in the first session of a new Parliament. *Journals,* February 7, 1878, p. 9. *Journals,* March 10, 1904, p. 10. *Journals,* January 12, 1916, p. 6. *Journals,* January 17, 1935, p. 2.

§191.   This procedure, which is one of the remnants of ancient practice followed when the Governor General's Instructions gave him a more direct role in the administration of public affairs, has no other value than that of a gesture of respect for His Excellency. It seems clear from s. 45 of the British North America Act that the House, being compelled by law to fill a vacancy in the Speakership, does not require the Governor General's permission to perform that duty.

THE OPENING OF A NEW SESSION

The Speech From the Throne

§192.   In every session but the first of a Parliament, as there is not election of a Speaker, the session is opened at once by the Governor General's speech, without any preliminary proceedings in either House. Until the causes of summons are declared, neither House can proceed with any public business; but the causes of summons, as declared from the Throne, do not bind Parliament to consider them alone, or to proceed at once to the consideration of any of them.

§193.   It will be noted that, under the B.N.A. Act, s. 38, the Governor General is bound to summon and call together, for the session, the House of Commons only and not the Senate.

§194. The Senate and Commons cannot open a session by their own authority. It is by the act of the Crown alone that they can be assembled, but the Governor General's power is restrained within certain limits. The B.N.A. Act, s. 20, declares that there cannot be an interval of twelve months between two sessions, which is emphasized by the practice of providing money for the Public Service by annual enactments. The Governor General's authority is only theoretical, as Parliament is always summoned on the advice of the Prime Minister. The opening of the session may, however, be deferred by Proclamation from the day to which it stands summoned to any further day, but it cannot be called for an earlier date. It is now customary for the House, prior to adjourning the session to a fixed day, to pass a resolution to the effect that the Speaker may, after consultation with the Government, recall the House to resume its sittings at any time.

§195. A session of Parliament is opened only by the reading of the Speech from the Throne. When the Members of the House of Commons, in compliance with a Proclamation, meet in the Chamber on an appointed day, prior to going to the Senate where the causes of summons will be imparted by the Governor General, they are not in Parliament Assembled. The point was raised in 1873, and the Speaker, in giving his decision, made the following statement:

"The first day of a session of Parliament is that day on which the Sovereign opens Parliament with a Speech giving the causes of summoning Parliament. Parliament is composed of three distinct branches, the Queen, the Senate and the House of Commons. It is true that on the 5th of March this year, the Members of the House of Commons went individually to the Senate Chamber, and were there informed by His Excellency, or by the Speaker of the Senate for His Excellency, that it was their duty to elect a Speaker. That was not an assembling of Parliament; the three branches of Parliament were not there; the House of Commons as a House of Commons was not there; the Mace, the symbol of its authority, was not there; the Speaker was not there. It is said that the House of Commons has no eye, no ear, nor mouth without a Speaker. It had no car to hear the Speech of His Excellency, no voice to ask that its ancient privileges be maintained; consequently, it was only there as a collection of individuals. The Commons then returned to this Chamber by command of His Excellency to elect their Speaker. They could do nothing more. It is clear from the authorities that they had no power to do anything else, because their powers were derived from the mandate of the Governor General and that was confined to the one subject to elect a Speaker, and then incidentally to this, to adjourn immediately afterwards. English precedents show that it is not open to

the House of Commons to transact any other business whatever, after the
election of the Speaker, except to immediately adjourn. The first day, the
5th of March, was not therefore the day of the assembling of Parliament.
It was not until the 6th of March, that Parliament was formally opened
by the Speech from the Throne.

"All the authorities go to show that the Parliament is only opened
when the three States of the Realm are met together, and is not supposed
to be seized of any public business until the Speech from the Throne is
delivered." *Journals,* March 24, 1873, p. 58.

Introduction of New Members

§196. (1) The introduction of Members elected at by-elections is not
required under the British North America Act or any statute. Members were
introduced in the Dominion Parliament until 1875. The practice was departed
from at the opening of the session of 1875 when twenty-one Members elected
during the recess took their seats without having been introduced while
several Members elected during that session went through the ceremony of an
introduction.

(2) Whether Members are elected in recess or during sessions is
immaterial. The introduction is a custom and does not affect a Member's right
to take his seat. When the Chief Electoral Officer's report of an election has
been tabled and a Member has taken the Oath and signed the Roll, he is, to all
intents and purposes, a Member of the House of Commons and may take his
seat without any ceremony. If he insisted on his right, the Speaker would have
to decide that introduction is a tradition which cannot override provisions of
the law.

(3) In 1878, the Speaker, Hon. T.W. Anglin, resigned his seat and was re-
elected during recess. When the session opened, he and other Members took
the Oath, signed the Roll and were in their seats at the sitting called for the
election of the Speaker. Mr. A. Mackenzie moved that Mr. Anglin take the
Chair as Speaker. Sir John A. Macdonald objected on the ground that Mr.
Anglin had not been and could not be introduced until there was a Speaker
and therefore he was not yet a Member and could not be elected as a Speaker.
Mr. Mackenzie retorted that introduction was not essential and the House
agreed with him. *Debates,* February 7, 1878, pp. 2-11.

(4) In the session of 1938, Hon. Earl Rowe, Member for Dufferin-
Simcoe, who had resigned and had been re-elected during the recess, took his
seat without being introduced to the Speaker. He had attended the whole
session of 1937, including prorogation, his place had not been taken by a new
Member nor had his constituency been vacant during a session after his
resignation. He was again in attendance as the same Member for the same
Electoral District, the House was fully acquainted with him, and there was no
need in going through the formality of an introduction.

§197. New Members are usually introduced immediately upon the opening of the sitting of the House. The new Member, flanked by his political Party Leader and his party's senior representative from his province, awaits at the Bar. Together the group advances to the Table, where the Party Leader states that the newly-elected Member has taken the Oath, signed the Roll and wishes to take his seat. The new Member is taken to the Speaker's Chair where he is introduced to the Speaker. Following this, the party whip escorts the new Member to his allotted seat.

Business Taken Before the Consideration of the Throne Speech

§198. When the House returns from the Senate, the Speaker first announces the vacancies in the membership and the election of new Members at by-elections. Then the Prime Minister, before His Excellency's speech is reported by the Speaker, introduces a Bill pro forma, intituled An Act respecting the Administration of Oaths of Office, which receives its first reading but is not ordered for second reading. It will not be proceeded with any further for it is introduced only to assert the House of Commons' right of passing legislation and deliberating without reference to the causes of summons expressed in the Governor General's speech.

§199. (1) There have been exceptions to this procedure. At the first sitting of the session of 1937, the Prime Minister did not introduce a pro forma Bill respecting the Administration of Oaths of Office. He introduced Bill No. 1, An Act respecting alteration in the law touching the succession to the Throne, which was read the first time and ordered for second reading at the next sitting of the House. *Journals,* January 14, 1937, p. 6.

(2) In the session of 1926, no bill was introduced prior to the motion for the debate of the Address, for as soon as the newly-elected Speaker reported that the House had been in the Senate Chamber and that he had made the usual claim of privileges which His Excellency had been pleased to confirm, the Leader of the House moved: "That in the opinion of this House, in view of the recent general elections, the Government was justified in retaining office and in summoning Parliament; and the Government is entitled to retain office unless defeated by a vote of this House equivalent to a vote of want of confidence." Debate was adjourned on this motion and never resumed. The Address in Reply to the Speech of the Governor General was moved the next day and the session went on with its work. As long as a majority, however small, supported the Government, there was no necessity to divide the House on that motion. *Journals,* January 8, 1926, p. 10.

Order of Business on First Day of the Session

§200. The Order of Business on the first day of the new session is as follows:

1. Prayers.
2. The Speaker communicates letter from Governor General's Secretary concerning the opening of Parliament.

3. Gentleman Usher of the Black Rod delivers Message. House proceeds to the Senate Chamber.

§201.   When the House returns from the Senate following the Speech from the Throne:

1. The Speaker gives the notification of Vacancies.
2. The Speaker announces the election of new Members.
3. New Members take their seats.
4. The Prime Minister moves for leave to introduce the pro forma Bill.
5. The Speaker reports that he has a copy of the Speech of His Excellency.
6. The Prime Minister moves that the Speech of His Excellency the Governor General be considered either this day or on some future day.
7. The Prime Minister moves the appointment of a Special Committee to strike the membership of the Standing Committees (in new Parliament only).
8. The Prime Minister tables the Minutes of the Privy Council and the Message from His Excellency respecting the appointment of Commissioners of Internal Economy which is read by the Speaker.
9. The Prime Minister moves the election of a Deputy Chairman of Committees and of an Assistant Deputy Chairman of Committees.

Consideration of the Address in Reply to the Speech From the Throne

§202.   (1) When the Governor General's Speech has been read, an Address in Reply thereto is moved in the House. Two Members, who are supporters of the Government but are not Ministers of the Crown, are selected by the Government to move and second the Address, as follows:

"That the following Address be presented to His Excellency the Governor General of Canada:

"'To His Excellency the Right Honourable ...., Chancellor and Principal Companion of the Order of Canada, Chancellor and Commander of the Order of Military Merit upon whom has been conferred the Canadian Forces' Decoration, Governor General and Commander-in-Chief of Canada:

"'MAY IT PLEASE YOUR EXCELLENCY:

"'We, Her Majesty's most loyal and dutiful subjects, the House of Commons of Canada, in Parliament assembled, beg leave to offer our humble thanks to Your Excellency for the gracious Speech which your Excellency has addressed to both Houses of Parliament.'"

(2) When the motion for the Address in Reply to the Speech from the

Throne has been adopted, a motion is moved to engross and present to His Excellency the Address.

THE OPENING OF A SITTING OF THE HOUSE

§203. A few minutes before the appointed hour for the opening of a sitting, on the day following his election, and every sitting day thereafter, the Speaker and his suite leave his library for the Chamber. They march in the following order: The Chief Constable and two sergeants, the Sergeant-at-Arms bearing the Mace, the Speaker, the Clerk of the House, the Clerks Assistant. A page, walking to the Speaker's right, carries documents to be read by the Speaker. They proceed to the Hall of Honour and the front corridor. At the Chamber door, the men who precede the Mace halt and stand at attention whilst the others enter the Chamber. Members, who may then be in their seats, rise as the Speaker walks to the Chair. The Sergeant-at-Arms stops at the end of the Table, waits until the Speaker has taken the Chair, then places the Mace on the Table, bows and goes to his desk. When there is a quorum present the Speaker reads Prayers (alternatively in English and French on successive days) the Clerk saying Amen at the end of each invocation.

5

Sittings of the House

5

Sittings of the House

Notices of times of meeting or adjournment of the House — Weekend Sittings — Secret Sittings — Quorum in the House — Messages brought by the Gentleman Usher of the Black Rod — Divisions — Speaker's casting vote — Pairing — Personal Interest — Questions of Order — Decorum in the House — Interruptions of Members — Disorder in the Galleries.

SITTINGS OF THE HOUSE

Notices of Times of Meeting or Adjournment of the House

§204. No notice is required for a motion relating to "the times of meeting or adjournment of the House". S.O. 42. The word "times" appears as "heures" in the French version of S.O. 42. It seems therefore that if a motion does not relate to the hour but to the day on which the House is to sit, a notice must be given. *Debates,* May 21, 1920, p. 2626.

Weekend Sittings

§205. Although no provision is made for it in the Standing Orders, the House may sit on Saturday or Sunday. The Special Order authorizing such a sitting will also normally specify the order of business for the day.

§206. Should the Special Order not provide for the order of business, a motion may be made, without notice, during routine proceedings. If a motion is not made, the order of business on a Saturday shall be the same as on a Friday. *Journals,* May 6, 1961, pp. 511-14.

Secret Sittings

§207. (1) The House may at any time hold a secret sitting; but when it desires to do so, it passes a motion which has been given the forty-eight hours' notice required under S.O. 42.

(2) On April 15, 1918, on a motion proposed by the Prime Minister, the House agreed, "That the sitting of Wednesday next, the seventeenth day of April, instant, shall be a secret session until the House shall then otherwise order, and that all strangers be ordered to withdraw during such secret session; provided, however, that this order shall not affect the privilege

enjoyed by members of the Senate of being present at debates in the House."
On the appointed day the House met at three o'clock. Hansard reporters were
not present. The Clerks at the Table and the Sergeant-at-Arms were in
attendance. The Speaker read Prayers but did not say: "Let the doors be
open." He immediately called the House to order and Routine Proceedings
were taken up. A petition was presented, the Speaker delivered a Message
from the Governor General, and the Chairman of the Select Standing
Committee on Banking and Commerce presented a report. A motion for the
Speaker to leave the Chair was then made and adopted and the House held its
secret session in Committee of Supply, after which progress was reported and
leave given to sit again "this day". At 5.05 o'clock p.m., a Minister of the
Crown moved that "The remainder of this day's sitting be open". This was
carried, the doors were opened and the House sat in the usual manner for the
rest of the day. A report of the proceedings was subsequently issued under the
authority of the Speaker.

(3) The Governor General in Council passed the following Regulation
prior to the secret sitting of February 24, 1942:

> "Whereas in the event of a secret session of the Senate or House of
> Commons being held it will be necessary to make provision for the
> preservation of the secrecy of such session.
>
> "Now therefore, His Excellency the Governor General in Council,
> on the recommendation of the Minister of Justice, and under the
> authority of the the War Measures Act, Chapter 206, Revised Statutes of
> Canada, 1927, is pleased to amend the Defence of Canada Regulations
> (Consolidation) 1941, and they are hereby amended by inserting
> immediately after Regulation 39A the following: —
>
> "'39AA. If the Senate or House of Commons, in pursuance of a
> resolution, holds a secret session, no person shall in any newspaper,
> periodical, circular or other publication, or in any public speech, publish
> any report or description of the proceedings at that session, except such
> report or description thereof as may be officially communicated through
> the Speaker of the House.'"

QUORUM IN THE HOUSE

§208. (1) Any Member may direct the Speaker's attention to the fact that
there is not a quorum present. The Clerk will proceed at once to count the
House and to take down the names. If there are not twenty Members present,
including himself, the Speaker will adjourn the House without question put,
until the usual hour of opening on the next sitting day.

(2) The only occasion when the Speaker takes the initiative in this matter
is at opening of the sitting, before Prayers or after the customary
interruptions. If he does not then see a quorum in the Chamber, he refrains
from calling the Members to order but asks the Clerk to count the House. If
there are not twenty Members present, he declares, without question put, that

the House stands adjourned until the next sitting day. This procedure must be duly recorded in the *Votes and Proceedings*.

§209. While the House is being counted the doors remain open and Members can comein during the whole time occupied by the counting. Sir John Bourinot, Parliamentary Procedure and Practice in the Dominion of Canada (4th ed., 1916), p. 218.

§210. A Member need not remain in the House after giving notice that a quorum is not present.

§211. (1) The Clerk should normally record only the names of those counted. *Journals,* December 17, 1974, pp. 217-18.

(2) When a count is taken, the original count is decisive and not the number of names later recorded by the Clerk. *Journals,* July 10, 1969, pp. 1329-30.

§212. If notice is taken by a Member that there is not a quorum present in the Committee of the Whole, the Chairman follows the course pursued by the Speaker in the House. If he ascertains that twenty Members are not present, he leaves the Chair, the House is resumed, and, on his report, the Speaker counts the House, and if there is not then a quorum, he must adjourn the House forthwith. Bourinot, pp. 217-18.

§213. If, after a division, it appears that the aggregate of the votes on each side, with the Speaker and the Members present who did not vote, do not make up a quorum, the question remains undecided and the House will have to be adjourned.

§214. A "count out" will always supersede any question that is before the House. If an Order of the Day for the reading or committal of a bill be under consideration at the time, and there is no quorum present, the House must be asked at a subsequent sitting to revive the question that may have lapsed in the way. Bourinot, p. 218.

§215. A message from the Governor General for the attendance of the House in the Senate, as, for example, for the purpose of giving Royal Assent to bills, makes a House without regard to the number present. Accordingly, when it is known that the attendance of the House in the Senate will be desired, the House meets at the time appointed. If twenty Members are not present, the Speaker takes the chair of the Clerk of the House; when the knock of Gentleman Usher of the Black Rod upon the outer door of the House is heard, the Speaker, although twenty Members are not present, takes the Chair, receives the message delivered by the Gentleman Usher of the Black Rod, and passes onward to the Senate. On his return, the Speaker resumes the Chair and makes his report to the House; as the House has been made, business may be proceeded with until, on notice taken, it is proved that twenty Members are not present.

MESSAGES BROUGHT BY THE GENTLEMAN USHER OF THE BLACK ROD

§216. (1) Messages brought in by the Gentleman Usher of the Black Rod should be received by the House in silence, but Members do not stand on such occasions.

(2) If Messages are signed by the Governor General's own hand and read by the Speaker or Clerk, they are heard by Members standing.

(3) If the House is sitting in Committee of the Whole on the arrival of the Gentleman Usher of the Black Rod, the Chairman leaves the Table and the Speaker takes the Chair. If the Message commands or desires the immediate attendance of the House in the Senate, it will be obeyed. On the return of the Members, the Speaker will announce the proceedings which took place in the Senate. He will then leave the Chair. The Committee of the Whole will resume at the point where the interruption had occurred.

DIVISIONS

§217. When the debate on a question is closed, and the House is ready to decide thereon, the Speaker says: "Is the House ready for the question?" If it is evident that no Member claims the right of speaking, the Speaker proceeds to put the question by reading the main motion, and then the amendment or amendments in their proper order. He then takes the sense of the Members of the last of these by saying: "Those who are in favour of the motion (or amendment) will say 'yea'. Those who are opposed to the motion will say 'nay'." When the supporters and opponents of the question have given their voices for and against, the Speaker says: "In my opinion, the yeas (or nays) have it." Should five or more Members rise to request a recorded vote, the Speaker says: "Call in the Members." The Sergeant-at-Arms ensures that the bells are rung; the Whips take steps to assemble their Members. Except under S.O. 9(2) there is no special time fixed for calling in the Members. It generally takes at least ten to fifteen minutes to get them, the Speaker remaining in the Chair, although order is not strictly maintained. The signal for taking the division is the return of the Government Whip and the Opposition Whip. The Whips march up the aisle and bow to the Speaker before returning to their seats. The Sergeant-at-Arms remains by the Bar, also bowing to the Speaker before resuming his seat. The Speaker then calls the House to order, rises and reads the question, adding: "The question is on the main motion (or amendment as the case may be). Those who are in favour of the motion (or amendment) will please rise." Led by the Party Leaders, Members starting from the front benches rise separately and a Clerk Assistant, standing, calls out their names. The Clerk records their votes on a printed list, repeating each name as he places a mark against it. The Members should sit down after they have heard their names distinctly repeated by the Clerk. Members are taken, by Party, in rows with the Party Leaders called out first as a matter of courtesy. When all the "yeas" have voted, the Speaker says: "Those who are opposed to the motion (or amendment) will please rise", and the votes are recorded as above. When the "yeas" and "nays" are taken down and counted, the Clerk rises, bows to the Speaker and declares the votes in both languages, saying: "Yeas, pour . . .; nays, contre . . ." The Speaker then says: "I declare the motion (or amendment) carried (or lost, as the case may be)." If a division takes place on an amendment to an amendment, the Speaker will immediately put the question on the first amendment, on which debate will be resumed or another division may be taken. The House may then resume debate or vote on the main motion. If the division took place on an amendment, when there was no second amendment, the Speaker will immediately put the question on the main motion, as amended, and again debate will be resumed or a division may follow.

§218. "Putting the Question" means the reading of the motion or amendment, from the Chair, seeking the pleasure of the House. When debate begins on a certain motion, amendments may be made; a Member who was present at the outset may leave the House only to return when the division is about to take place. The motion to be voted upon may then be different from the one he heard read, but it must be set forth by the Speaker who says: "The Question before the House is as follows." He reads the motion or amendment.

§219. A division on a question on which party lines are not recognized is commonly known as a free vote. When this occurs the method of counting the House may vary somewhat from the normal. The Speaker calls on Members to vote by rows beginning with the first row on the right and proceeding through all of the rows to his right before turning to those on his left. Both the "yeas" and "nays" are counted in this manner, beginning with the Members nearest to the Speaker and proceeding along the rows without regard to rank or party affiliation. *Debates*, June 22, 1976, pp. 14740-1.

§220. When a division is taken in a Committee of the Whole, the Members rise in rows and are counted by a Clerk Assistant. No names are recorded.

§221. The Speaker must put a question even when it affects himself personally. *Debates*, June 8, 1956, p. 4869.

§222. A division must take place if the Speaker is unable to decide from the Members' voices whether a motion is carried or lost. At such a time, the Speaker will call in the Members without being asked. *Journals*, May 15, 1928, pp. 407-8.

§223. (1) A Member must be within the House and hear the question put in its entirety, in one of the official languages, or his vote cannot be recorded. It is not sufficient for him to hear it while he is in a gallery or behind the curtains. *Debates*, August 26, 1891, pp. 4455-62. *Debates*, March 31, 1924, p. 889.

(2) A Member must be in his own seat should he wish to vote and should remain in his seat until the division is complete and the result announced. *Journals,* April 18, 1956, p. 416. *Debates,* February 16, 1976, p. 10986.

(3) If a Member who has heard the question put should inadvertently vote contrary to his intention, he may not be allowed to correct the mistake; but his vote must remain as first recorded. *Debates,* July 1, 1926, p. 5311.

(4) Any five Members may require a recorded division. They need not vote in any particular way in the division. Numerous examples may be found of unanimous recorded votes. *Journals,* December 20, 1966, pp. 1169-70.

(5) If a Member's name is entered incorrectly or is inadvertently left off the division list, he may have it rectified should the Clerk read out the names, or on the following day when he notices the error printed in the *Votes and Proceedings.* An error noted during a division may be corrected before the total is announced. *Debates,* August 9, 1977, p. 8173.

§224. A Member may not be compelled to vote. *Journals,* June 24, 1963, p. 130.

§225. When his attention has been called to a breach of order in the course of a division, the Speaker has directed that the division should proceed, and has dealt with the matter when the division was completed.

Speaker's Casting Vote

§226. Section 49 of the British North America Act reads: "Questions arising in the House of Commons shall be decided by a Majority of Voices other than that of the Speaker, and when the voices are equal, but not otherwise, the Speaker shall have a Vote."

§227. (1) When he has to give a casting vote, the Speaker is at liberty to vote like any other Member, according to his conscience, without assigning a reason; but in order to avoid the least imputation upon his partiality, it is usual for him, when practicable, to vote in such a manner as not to make the decision of the House final, and to explain his reasons which are entered in the *Journals.* He votes in such a manner as to leave the House another opportunity of deciding the question. *Debates,* April 15, 1920, p. 1265. *Debates,* March 26, 1928, p. 1681.

(2) If, in consequence of the subsequent revision of the votes, or otherwise, it is discovered that there was no occasion for a casting vote, but that the question was decided without it, the vote of the Presiding Officer is not reckoned with the others on the same side, but disregarded altogether as if it had never been given.

(3) When the voices are equal in a Committee of the Whole House, the Chairman, who does not otherwise vote, gives his casting vote, and in doing so is guided by the same principles as the Speaker of the House. Sir Erskine May,

Treatise on the Law, Privileges, Proceedings and Usage of Parliament (19th ed., 1976), p. 406.

Pairing

§228. Although there is no Standing Order in this regard, it has been customary for a Member who has to be absent to agree with another Member that he also shall be absent at the same time, or refrain from voting. Thus these Members are "paired" and a vote is neutralized on each side of the question.

§229. When pairs are employed, it has been the custom for a paired Member to rise in his place after the results of a division are announced and state how he would have voted had he not been paired. There is no parliamentary recognition of pairing, although it has never been expressly condemned; and it is therefore conducted privately by individual Members, or arranged by the Whips who are entrusted by their political parties with the office of collecting their respective forces on a division.

§230. A vote which is cast inadvertently and which breaks a pair cannot be rescinded except with the unanimous consent of the House. *Debates,* July 1, 1926, p. 5311.

Personal Interest

§231. (1) The personal interest of a Member in a subject before the House must be a direct pecuniary interest, and separately belonging to the persons whose votes were questioned, not in common with the rest of Her Majesty's subjects, or on a matter of state policy.

(2) Disallowance of a vote, on the score of personal interest, is restricted to cases of pecuniary interest and has not been extended to those occasions when the dictates of self respect, and of respect due to the House, might demand that a Member should refrain from taking part in a division. May, p. 411.

(3) The votes of Members on questions of public policy are allowed to pass unchallenged. Public bills are frequently passed, relative to matters such as Members' salaries, in which Members have an interest, but their votes, when questioned, have been allowed.

§232. (1) A Member's right to vote on a question in which he is personally interested is one of those matters that must be decided by the House and not by the Speaker. *Journals,* March 1, 1966, pp. 203-4.

(2) An objection to a vote on the grounds of personal interest must be taken by a substantive motion that the vote given be disallowed; it may not be raised as a point of order. *Debates,* May 22, 1956, pp. 4240-6.

(3) The Member whose vote is questioned, having been heard in his place, should withdraw before the question has been proposed. May, p. 411.

(4) An objection on the ground of personal interest raised in a Committee of the Whole must be determined by the Committee upon a motion made therein that the vote be disallowed. May, p. 410.

(5) The principle of the rule which disqualifies an interested Member from voting must always have been intended to apply as well to committees as to the House itself. May, p. 411.

QUESTIONS OF ORDER

§233. (1) Points of order are questions raised with the view of calling attention to any departure from the Standing Orders or the customary modes of proceeding in debate or in the conduct of legislative business and may be raised at virtually any time by any Member, whether he has previously spoken or not.

(2) A question of order concerns the interpretation to be put upon the rules of procedure and is a matter for the Speaker or, in a committee, for the Chairman to determine.

(3) Since the introduction of a time limit on the daily oral Question Period it has become the custom for the Speaker to recognize points of order only at the conclusion of the Question Period.

(4) Points of order or questions of privilege may not be raised when the House is debating a motion for the adjournment under S.O. 40. *Debates,* April 30, 1964, p. 2799.

§234. (1) If a point of order consists of asking a question to the Member speaking, it is a mere interruption, or if it is defective for other reasons, the Speaker will rule it out. A point of order cannot be raised on a point of order.

(2) A Member cannot rise on a point of order to move a motion. *Debates,* July 14, 1977, p. 7669.

(3) A Member should not rise on a point of order to deter or impede the progress of his own motion. He cannot raise a point of order against himself. *Journals,* May 26, 1961, p. 588.

§235. Any Member is entitled, even bound, to bring to the Speaker's immediate notice any instance of what he considers a breach of order. He may interrupt and lay the point in question concisely before the Speaker. He should do so as soon as he perceives an irregularity in the proceedings which are engaging the attention of the House. The Speaker's attention must be directed to a breach of order at the proper moment, namely the moment it occurred. A point of order may be taken after a debate is concluded and the Speaker is about to put the question to a vote or after the vote has been taken — in fact, at any time, but not so as to interrupt the Speaker when he is addressing the House. Even the provisions in Standing Orders that action must be taken "forthwith" or "forthwith without debate" with respect to certain proceedings do not bar a Member from raising a point of order when a serious irregularity occurs.

§236. If the Speaker's attention has been called to a breach of order in the course of a division, he has directed that the division be completed. In doubtful cases and in cases not provided for by practice or the Standing Orders, the Speaker refers the matter to the judgment of the House. It is the Speaker's duty to deal with minor offences, but the power to inflict punishment is left to the House.

§237. A point of order against procedure must be raised promptly and before the question has passed to a stage at which the objection would be out of place. *Journals,* February 20, 1911, p. 190.

§238. When a bill is under consideration, points of order should not be raised on matters which could be disposed of by moving amendments. The same may be said about Instructions which can only be moved if they are within the scope of the bill. It is more advantageous to proceed by amendments on the third reading when, if the House divides, every Member's attitude is clearly shown. Points of order are justified when there is some flagrant misuse of the rules, but they are unfortunate necessities which should not be regarded as usual phases of procedure and ought not to develop into long arguments with the Speaker who, being in a quasi-judicial position, should not be drawn into controversial discussions.

§239. (1) The Speaker decides questions of order only when they actually arise and not in anticipation. He is bound to call attention immediately to an irregularity in debate or procedure and not wait for the interposition of a Member.

(2) Hypothetical queries on procedure cannot be addressed to the Speaker from the floor of the House.

(3) When a Member asked the Speaker whether a motion was susceptible of amendment, as proposed, he said: "When the suggested amendment is proposed, I will give a ruling upon it, and unless an immediate decision is required, I shall be glad to consider it." *Debates,* October 17, 1932, p. 290.

§240. The Speaker will not give a decision upon a constitutional question nor decide a question of law, though the same may be raised on a point of order or privilege. *Journals,* July 8, 1969, pp. 1319-20.

§241. In all matters of doubt, the Speaker will consider attentively the opinions of Members. Sometimes, instead of expressing his opinion on either side, he may ask instructions from the House or reserve his decision on the point of discussion, or suggest that the House may, if it thinks proper, dispense with the Standing Order in a particular case. In doubtful cases, he will be guided largely by circumstances.

§242. When a Member moves that a certain matter be referred to a committee, any other Member may, if he thinks it more convenient, suggest that the reference be to another committee; but it is not within the Speaker's duties to make such a suggestion, and if he does he plainly goes out of his jurisdiction.

§243. The Speaker or the Chairman of a Committee of the Whole ought not to consider the consequences of the adoption or rejection of a motion or an amendment, nor is it his concern whether Ministers of the Crown or private Members are proceeding fast enough with their bills or motions. All he has to do is to see that the rules of procedure are observed. The House will decide what course to follow after the Members who sponsor measures have introduced and explained them. Vague motions, if properly worded, cannot be ruled out if they are relevant.

DECORUM IN THE HOUSE

§244. The Standing Orders of the House are virtually silent on the subject of Members' dress. S.O. 28 requires that a Member who wishes to speak must rise in his place uncovered. While the wearing of hats in the Chamber has a respectable historical tradition, Speakers in recent years have frowned on unorthodox headgear. Beyond this, Speakers have enforced conservative, contemporary standards in the House.

§245. The concern of the Speaker for the appearance of the Chamber, during debate, extends further than the dress of Members. While Members are entitled to refresh themselves with glasses of water during debates, the consumption of any other food in the House is strictly forbidden. Smoking has never been permitted in the Commons' Chamber.

§246. While a degree of informality in debate may be encouraged, it has been ruled improper for a Member to rest his foot on his chair while addressing the House. While a Member will be allowed to rest his notes on a pile of books on his desk, the use of a lectern has been forbidden.

Interruptions of Members

§247. S.O. 12(3) states that a Member speaking shall not be interrupted except on a point of order. This prohibition is commonly ignored. It is accepted practice for a Member to be asked to explain further some point he has made in debate or to answer specific questions arising from his speech. The acceptance of such interruptions is entirely at the discretion of the Member concerned; he may answer at the time, suggest that questions should be left to the end of his speech or refuse outright to answer.

§248. Other forms of interruption have traditionally been accepted as proper. Applause provided by Members banging on the tops of their desks is common and a wide range of brief, shouted remarks either expressing approval or disapproval have been overlooked. If the interruptions are excessive, the Member speaking may appeal to the Speaker for help, which will be forthcoming, or the Speaker may intervene on his own authority to restore order in the House.

§249. Although difficult to enforce on occasion, Speakers have also consistently attempted to discourage loud private conversations in the Chamber, and have urged those wishing to carry on such exchanges to do so outside the House. It has also been suggested that Members should not sit on chair arms or on desks with their backs to the House when conversing privately.

Disorder in the Galleries

§250. It is rare for a Member to attempt to have the galleries of the House cleared by moving a motion under S.O. 13. General authority to maintain decorum in the galleries is exercised by the Sergeant-at-Arms and the Protective Service who act in most circumstances without specific direction or orders from the House.

6

Business of the House

6

Business of the House

PROCEEDINGS OF THE HOUSE

§251. Motions, amendments, references to committees, and the three readings of bills come under the term of "proceedings in Parliament". They are the means used to the end that a matter may be considered and disposed of by the House. The word "proceeding" is derived from the verb "to proceed" which means "to advance" or "to carry on a series of actions". Members take part in the proceedings usually by making speeches; however, many proceedings take place without any debate. Speeches are not essential; they either help or hinder a proceeding, but they are not a proceeding. The verbatim report of Members' speeches is in Hansard but this is not an official record of the House proceedings. The official record of proceedings is found in minutes of the sittings which are printed and distributed daily under the title of *Votes and Proceedings* and are published after prorogation under the title of *Journals of the House of Commons.*

§252. When a Committee of the Whole is given leave to sit again "this day" and the House adjourns before the Committee resumes its sittings, the Order is considered as one which has not been disposed of and is postponed until the next sitting day without a motion to that effect. S.O. 19(3).

§253. The expressions "next sitting", "next sitting day" and "next sitting of the House", when used to state the time until which a question is ordered to stand over, mean the future sitting at which this question shall come up according to the precedence given to it by the Standing Order.

ARRANGEMENT OF BUSINESS

§254. The proceedings of the House must be taken up in accordance with the order of business given in the *Order Paper. Journals,* March 18, 1926, p. 163.

Prayers

§255. (1) When there is a quorum of Members present, the Speaker reads the Prayers in English and in French on alternative days.

(2) No strangers are admitted into the galleries until the Prayers are read.

§256. Should the Speaker be unavoidably absent, an announcement to that effect is made by the Clerk as soon as the Mace has been placed on the Table and before Prayers are read; the Speaker's place is then taken by the Deputy Speaker.

Proceedings pursuant to Standing Order 43

§257. These motions are of an urgency and pressing necessity that the mover asks the leave of the House to dispense with the required notice. See Chapter 10 (Notices).

Oral Question Period

§258. The oral Question Period lasts for forty-five minutes. This is discussed in greater detail in Chapter 9 (Questions, Returns and Reports).

THE DAILY ROUTINE OF BUSINESS

§259. (1) In accordance with S.O. 15(2), the daily routine of business indicating the relative order of precedence between the various classes of business is set out as follows:

PRESENTING REPORTS FROM STANDING OR SPECIAL COMMITTEES
TABLING OF DOCUMENTS
STATEMENTS BY MINISTERS
INTRODUCTION OF BILLS
FIRST READING OF SENATE PUBLIC BILLS
GOVERNMENT NOTICES OF MOTIONS
MOTIONS (except those permitted before Oral Questions)

(2) A full description of the various classes is given later for the purpose of explaining the action which may be taken at each order of business.

Presenting Reports from Standing or Special Committees

§260. This topic is covered in Chapter 15 (Standing, Special and Joint Committees).

Tabling of Documents

§261. Tabling of documents is covered in Chapter 9 (Questions, Returns and Reports).

Statements by Ministers

§262. Statements by Ministers have now been given a recognized place in Routine Proceedings. The Standing Order is specific but considerable latitude has been left to the Speaker to set limits on the participants. The Speaker has emphasized that both the Government and Opposition contributions should be brief and factual. The purpose of the ministerial statement is to convey information, not to encourage debate.

§263. A brief question and answer period may follow the Minister's statement and Opposition comments. The length of this period is left to the discretion of the Speaker by the Standing Order. Questions asked in this period should be related to the statement and not deal with the general policy of the department. *Debates,* June 10, 1977, p. 6545.

§264. The option of a Minister to make a statement either in the House or outside it may be the subject of comment, but is not the subject of a question of privilege. *Debates,* March 18, 1977, p. 4122.

§265. Tradition and convenience have also established a somewhat different type of ministerial statement. Each Thursday, before the Orders of the Day are called and usually in response to a question from the Opposition, the House Leader announces what Government business will be considered in the succeeding week. Short questions for the purpose of clarification are normally permitted.

Introduction of Bills

§266. This subject is covered in Chapter 17 (Proceedings on Public Bills).

First Reading of Senate Public Bills

§267. (1) Senate bills are not transferred from the *Notice Paper* but are placed under the Routine Proceedings directly that a message is received from the Senate asking the House to pass the bill. When it has received first reading it is transferred to Government Orders.

(2) In the case of a private Member's bill from the Senate, it is given first reading and appointed for second reading, and transferred directly to Private Members Business (Private Bills).

Government Notices of Motions

§268. The Government may, from time to time, put on the *Notice Paper* notices of motions concerning the business of the House. When these items are called they are deemed transferred to Government Orders on the *Order Paper*. S.O. 21(2).

Motions

§269.   The motions allowed under Routine Proceedings are those relating to the business of the House or to the discussion of committee reports.

§270.   (1) Motions respecting changes in the time of meetings or adjournments deal with the business of the House rather than government affairs and are moved by the Government House Leader who is responsible for the arrangements of the business of the session and the order in which ministerial measures are introduced and debated. These motions are taken up under Routine Proceedings as provided in S.O. 32(1)(*p*). *Journals,* September 4, 1950, p. 27. *Journals,* December 10, 1951, p. 291. *Journals,* December 20, 1951, pp. 345-6. *Journals,* February 3, 1954, p. 260.

(2) A motion to extend the hours of sitting of the House is not classified as Government Business and may be properly moved under Routine Proceedings. *Journals,* June 18, 1970, pp. 1029-30. A similar motion to extend the hours of sitting of the House moved under S.O. 6(5) may be moved during debate.

§271.   A motion by a private Member for the appointment of a committee to prepare and bring in a bill may be considered only under private Members business and not under Routine Proceedings on the *Order Paper. Journals,* November 10, 1969, pp. 73-5.

§272.   Motions to concur in any committee report shall be listed, when notice is required, called and disposed of under "Motions" on the *Order Paper. Journals,* January 20, 1970, pp. 327-9.

BUSINESS BEFORE CALLING THE ORDERS OF THE DAY

Ceremonial Speeches

§273.   Before the Speaker calls upon the Clerk to read the Orders of the Day, and occasionally at other times during the day, ceremonial speeches have been allowed. Originally confined to commemorating, on their deaths, the public services of distinguished statesmen who were, or had been, Members of the House, in recent times the practice has extended to other occasions of rejoicing or mourning.

Recognition of Distinguished Visitors

§274.   It has been the custom for the Speaker or a Minister of the Crown to draw the attention of Members to the presence of distinguished visitors in the galleries. Such visitors are generally leading figures from other jurisdictions. However, the Speaker has discouraged similar recognition of constituency and other groups by private Members.

ORDERS OF THE DAY

§275. (1) It is a fundamental rule that, with the exception of certain matters dealt with under Routine Proceedings, no question can be considered by the House unless it has been previously appointed either by a notice or a regular Order of the House. The paper known as *Order Paper and Notices* is the official agenda printed on the responsibility of the Clerk of the House, containing all the proposed questions set out in accordance with the Standing Orders. All the proposed proceedings of the House are recorded in abbreviated form in that paper. To add to, or suppress from it, any proposal which the House has ordered would constitute a serious infringement on the privileges of the House of Commons. If any serious errors are made they may be corrected by the House only in open sitting with the Speaker in the Chair. When an Order of the Day has been read, it must thereupon be proceeded with, appointed for a future day, or discharged.

(2) An Order of the Day is a proceeding which may only be dealt with as an outcome of a previous Order made in the House itself, except for measures requiring the immediate consideration provided for in S.O. 42(2).

(3) The successive stages of bills are Orders of the Day since the House at each stage makes an Order and appoints a date for the consideration of the next stage, and without such Order, the bill cannot be further advanced. A question or motion becomes an Order of the Day if the debate upon it be adjourned and the House orders the continuance of it on a subsequent date.

(4) It is one of the fundamental principles of parliamentary procedure that when nothing is done respecting an order of business, it is struck out and cannot make further progress until the procedure regulating its passage has been regulated by the House. Neither the Speaker nor any officer of the House have the power to move it forward.

§276. A motion to proceed to another Government Order may be moved only by the Government House Leader (or a Member acting on his behalf). *Journals,* October 23, 1968, pp. 156-7.

§277. Should the House with consent agree to proceed with private Members' business before the normal hour of 4:00 p.m. on Friday, proceedings under that heading shall occupy no more than sixty minutes and shall not continue until the normal 5:00 p.m. interruption. *Debates,* April 30, 1976, pp. 1353-4.

Proceedings on the Orders of the Day

§278. (1) All items standing under Private Members business must normally be moved in their proper order, though the House may sometimes consent to vary this.

(2) No control is conceded to a Minister over Orders standing in the names of private Members which are governed by the ordinary rules of priority, though the consideration of those Orders may be stood at the request of the Government.

(3) When the House has appointed a day for the consideration of a bill or other matter, no earlier day may afterwards be substituted except, of course, with unanimous consent.

(4) To replace an Order of the Day, which may have been cut short by a count out, a motion is made without notice under Routine Proceedings, before the commencement of the Orders of the Day, to appoint the Order either for the current sitting or for a future day.

(5) When the sponsor of a bill does not want his bill to be proceeded with, he may request, when it is called for second reading, "That the Order be discharged and the bill withdrawn". Such a motion, which may be made without notice, is not debatable and requires unanimous consent.

§279. A Private Bill disappears from the *Order Paper* when a committee reports that the preamble is "not proven".

§280. (1) The Government, being largely interested in the progress of the business of the House, is responsible for allowing a question or motion to stand if the Member is absent or does not proceed when it is called. If a question or motion disappears from the *Order Paper,* it may be reinstated only after a new notice. But, if the House is adjourned before an Order of the Day under consideration is disposed of, it is not treated as a dropped Order, but, being superseded, must be revived before it again takes its place with Orders.

(2) The discharge of an Order is the indispensable preliminary to the making of a different Order with regard to the same subject. Thus the Order for a paper to lie upon the Table is sometimes discharged, whereupon another order that the paper be withdrawn is made by the House. Similarly the House has discharged the Order for the second reading of a bill; this procedure has been followed by an Order for the withdrawal of the bill. On other occasions an Order has been discharged without further action, e.g., for printing a paper or for a return. Part of an Order has also been discharged. Sir Erskine May, Treatise on the Law, Privileges, Proceedings and Usage of Parliament (19th ed., 1976), pp. 382-3.

§281. In the absence of a Member in whose name an undebatable motion for the production of papers stands on the *Order Paper,* another Member may, if no one objects, make the motion, provided he has been authorized to do so.

He says: "Mr. Speaker, the Honourable Member for .... being unable to be present today, I move on his behalf...." If objection is taken, the question cannot be put by the Speaker.

Motions to Pass to the Orders of the Day

§282.   When an Order of the Day is under debate, a motion "That the Orders of the Day be now read" is a nullity as the House has already reached that stage of its proceedings. *Journals,* June 28, 1971, p. 759.

MOTIONS TO ADJOURN THE HOUSE

§283.   (1) A motion "That the House do now adjourn" is always in order but no second motion to the same effect may be made until some intermediate proceeding has taken place.

(2) A Member may not use a point of order to secure the floor in order to move the adjournment of the House.

(3) A motion to adjourn the House may not have conditions attached, otherwise it becomes a substantive motion which may be moved only after notice.

(4) There must be some question before the House for a Member to move a motion to adjourn the House.

§284.   (1) The term "intermediate proceedings" used in S.O. 25, means a proceeding that can properly be entered on the *Journals.* The true test is that if any parliamentary proceeding takes place, the second motion is regular and the Clerk ought to enter the proceedings to show that the motion in question is regular.

(2) It has never been understood in the House of Commons that the word "proceedings" covered speeches; it is not applied to arguments but it covers such things as utterances bearing directly on making motions, moving amendments, presenting reports, putting the questions, answering questions placed on the *Order Paper,* voting, naming a Member; it is construed as relating to procedure and not to debates.

MOTIONS TO ADJOURN THE HOUSE UNDER STANDING ORDER 26

§285.   Standing Order 26 gives considerable discretion to the Speaker in deciding if a subject is a proper matter to be brought before the House in this way. The Standing Order appears clear that the question be specific and must require urgent consideration. It must deal with a matter within the administrative competence of the Government and there must be no other reasonable opportunity for debate. *Journals,* January 22, 1969, p. 610. But most decisions based on these conditions are bound to be subjective and few clear cut decisions can be made. In making his ruling, the Speaker may, on occasion, take into account the general wish of the House to have a debate. *Journals,* June 25, 1970, p. 1121.

§286. The "specific and important matter requiring urgent consideration", for the discussion of which the adjournment of the House may be moved under S.O. 26, must be so pressing that public interest will suffer if it is not given immediate attention.

§287. "Urgency" within this rule does not apply to the matter itself, but means "urgency of debate", when the ordinary opportunities provided by the rules of the House do not permit the subject to be brought on early enough and public interest demands that discussion take place immediately.

§288. The Speaker is bound to apply to motions made under S.O. 26 the established rules of debate, and to enforce the principle that subjects excluded by those rules cannot be brought forward thereon, such as a matter under adjudication by a court of law, or matters already discussed or appointed for consideration during the current session, whether upon a substantive motion, upon an amendment, or upon an Order of the Day.

§289. Matters arising out of the debates of the same session, or the term of a bill before the Senate, matters of privilege or order, or matters debatable only upon a substantive motion, cannot be submitted to the House under this Standing Order.

§290. Leave to make a motion for the adjournment of the House, for the purpose of discussing a specific and important matter requiring urgent consideration, is out of order if the matter proposed to be discussed has been moved as an amendment to the Address in Reply to the Speech from the Throne which has not yet been disposed of. *Journals,* March 31, 1931, p. 50.

§291. (1) A general question of the maladministration of a department cannot be considered a genuine emergency under S.O. 26. *Debates,* March 27, 1974, p. 906.

(2) A motion under S.O. 26 should not be essentially a censure or no-confidence motion. *Journals,* September 16, 1971, pp. 801-2.

§292. (1) The Speaker's duty with regard to a motion to adjourn the House under S.O. 26 is confined to determining as to whether, in the first instance, a motion so proposed is in order. There his responsibility ends. There is a further question as to the propriety, or desirability of discussing a matter of such grave importance. That is for the House to decide.

(2) After the Speaker decides that the matter is proper to be brought before the House, the mover of the motion requires the leave of the House to introduce his motion. If there is no unanimity, twenty Members must rise before the Speaker may put the motion. *Debates,* February 22, 1978, p. 3129.

§293.   When setting the time for a debate on a motion under S.O. 26, the Speaker may seek the advice of the House Leaders before specifying the hour of the debate. *Journals,* June 25, 1970, p. 1121.

§294.   The debate on the urgent matter referred to in S.O. 26 cannot be adjourned, as the motion actually before the Chair is "that the House do now adjourn".

7

Rules of Debate

7

Rules of Debate

RULES OF DEBATE

Process of Debate

§295. (1) The proceedings between the rising of a Member to move a motion and the ascertainment by the Speaker of the decision of the House constitute a debate, and this process affords an opportunity for, and usually involves, discussion although a decision may be reached without discussion.

(2) The interval between the proposing and the putting of the question, which is usually used for discussion, gives an opportunity for further proceedings such as the moving of an amendment; and this may give rise to a subsidiary debate, with its own question and decision, within the principal debate. Sir Erskine May, Treatise on the Law, Privileges, Proceedings and Usage of Parliament (19th ed., 1976), p. 364.

(3) Debate arises when a question has been proposed by the Speaker and before it has been fully put. A question is fully put when the Speaker has taken the voices of the "yeas" and the "nays". May, p. 415.

§296. It is a paramount principle that no Member may speak except when there is a question before the House. Among the few exceptions to this principle are the following: questions put before the commencement of public business to Ministers or other Members of the House, questions of privilege, personal explanations and statements made by the Ministers of the Crown regarding public affairs with other Members commenting on such statements.

Language of Debate

§297. The British North America Act guarantees that a Member may address the House in either English or French; the simultaneous interpretation system ensures that debate may flow freely and intelligently. Examples may be found of other languages being used in debate, but in recent years the Speaker has tended to discourage the use of anything but the two official languages. *Debates,* December 8, 1964, p. 10926.

Decorum in Debate

§298. (1) Members may sit in their respective places with their heads covered, but when they desire to speak, they must rise and remove their hats. They are not to cross between the Chair and a Member who is speaking or between the Chair and the Table, or between the Chair and the Mace when the Mace is taken off the Table by the Sergeant-at-Arms. When they cross the House, or otherwise leave their places, they should make obeisance to the Speaker.

(2) When the Speaker is in the Chair, a Member must be in his place to:

    (a)   raise a point of order;

    (b)   ask a question in debate;

    (c)   make a significant contribution to the debate.

Relevance and Repetition

§299. (1) Relevancy is not easy to define. In borderline cases the Member should be given the benefit of the doubt.

(2) The rule against repetition is difficult to enforce as the various stages of a bill's progress give ample opportunity and even encouragement for repetition. In practice, wide discretion is used by the Speaker and the rule is not rigidly enforced. *Journals,* May 24, 1955, p. 616.

DEBATABLE MOTIONS

§300. (1) Formerly all motions were debatable unless some rule or other parliamentary usage could be quoted to the contrary. But at present the rule is reversed. All motions are to be decided without debate or amendment, except those specifically recognized as debatable under S.O. 32.

(2) Examples of motions which come under S.O. 32(1)(*p*) and are debatable are motions:

    (a)   relating to the time of sitting and the business of the House;

    (b)   approving appointments, transfers, dismissals or retirement of certain officers of the House;

    (c)   expressing sympathy for the death of some prominent person;

    (d)   acknowledging any gift made to the House;

    (e)   accepting or making any invitation;

    (f)   making an important correction in the *Debates, Votes and Proceedings* and *Journals* of the House;

(g) for the election of the Chairman of committees of the Whole House;

(h) for the appointment of the Striking Committee;

(i) questions of privilege when raised under Routine Proceedings also come within that category.

LIST OF MEMBERS DESIRING TO SPEAK

§301. There is no official list of speakers with an order of precedence in the House of Commons. Any Member who wishes to speak may rise and endeavour to catch the speaker's eye. He who is seen first has the right to speak. By old parliamentary usage, a Member who wishes to make his maiden speech enjoys the privilege of being seen first by the Speaker, if he rises at the same time as other Members; but the privilege will not be conceded unless claimed within the Parliament to which the Member was first returned. Under all circumstances, the succession of speakers is left entirely to the Speaker. It is customary for the Speaker to try to arrange for speakers, for and against the motion, in a reasonable rotation.

§302. (1) When a motion that a Member "be now heard" is defeated, it is assumed that the Member originally recognized by the Speaker has the floor. It is impossible to move a succession of these motions to delay a Member's speech indefinitely. *Debates,* May 24, 1956, p. 4310.

(2) A motion that a Member "be now heard" must be moved before the Member recognized has begun speaking.

§303. (1) In order to be allowed to speak more than forty minutes, under S.O. 31, a Member who speaks in reply immediately after a Minister has moved a government measure must speak in opposition to the motion. *Journals,* June 23, 1952, p. 560.

(2) It should be noted that there are now numerous exceptions in other Standing Orders to the forty minute limitation provided in S.O. 31.

SECONDING OF MOTIONS

§304. (1) The Member who makes a motion may give the name of his seconder who will, if necessary, indicate his consent, and the seconder will then be allowed to speak on the question. But if the seconder should rise and say only a word or two, for instance, "I second the motion", he is precluded from again addressing the House.

(2) Having moved the adjournment of the debate, a Member has spoken on the question and cannot make a second motion during the same debate. *Journals,* September 23, 1891, p. 526.

(3) By moving or seconding an amendment a Member, if he utters a few words, actually speaks to the main motion. It is only after the amendment has been put by the Speaker that it is considered a new question. Sir John

Bourinot, Parliamentary Procedure and Practice in the Dominion of Canada (4th ed., 1916), p. 346.

(4) A Member who speaks in seconding an amendment is unable to speak again on the original question after the amendment has been withdrawn or otherwise disposed of. Bourinot, p. 346.

(5) If a Member does not speak in moving an amendment, he will be allowed to address himself to the main question by withdrawing his amendment. Bourinot, p. 346.

(6) A Member who has already spoken to a question has no right to propose an amendment, though he may speak to an amendment when moved by another Member. Bourinot, pp. 345-6.

(7) A Member who has already spoken to a question has no right to move or second an adjournment of the debate or of the House.

(8) A Member who has moved or seconded the adjournment of the debate cannot afterwards (during the same debate) rise to move the adjournment of the House. Bourinot, p. 346.

(9) After an amendment has been moved and seconded, the question on the amendment is proposed, and any Member who speaks after that question has been proposed speaks to it and not to the main question. When the amendment has been disposed of and the main question is again proposed, any Member may speak who has not already spoken on the main question, whether or not he spoke on the amendment. The mover and seconder of the amendment having spoken to the main question cannot speak again to it. The same rule applies, of course, to the case of an amendment to an amendment. The mover and seconder of an amendment are not penalized as compared with other Members, because, in their one speech, they speak both to the main question and to the amendment which they are moving or seconding.

(10) Every amendment is a question by itself. A Member who has spoken only on an amendment is entitled to speak on the main motion after the amendment is disposed of. *Journals,* March 14, 1928, p. 154.

RIGHT OF REPLY

§305. (1) It is plain, from S.O. 37(2), that a reply is allowed only to the mover of a substantive motion but that the House has extended this rule to include the mover of the motion for the second reading of a bill.

(2) Should a Member propose a motion on behalf of another Member, a later speech by either will close the debate. *Journals,* February 7, 1961, p. 226.

(3) When amendments are moved and voted on, the Member who proposed the main motion is entitled to make his reply before the Speaker puts the final question: "Shall the motion (or the motion as amended, as the case may be) carry?"

(4) If a Member, who moves an Order of the Day, should rise and say only a word or two, for instance, "I move the order", he is precluded from

again addressing the House except if the Order of the Day be a substantive motion or the second reading of a bill, in which case he will be allowed a reply.

§306. A Member who, during a debate, has spoken to a question may again be heard to offer explanation of some material part of his speech which has been misunderstood; but he must not introduce new matter or endeavour to strengthen, by new arguments, his former position which he alleges to have been misunderstood, or to reply to other Members. Here again, a greater latitude is permitted in cases of personal explanation, where a Member's character or conduct has been impugned in debate. The proper time for explanation is at the conclusion of the speech which calls for it, but it is a common practice for the Member desiring to explain, to rise immediately the statement is made to which his explanation is directed. If the Member in possession of the House gives way and resumes his seat, the explanation is at once received; but the explanation cannot then be offered if the Member speaking declines to give way. May, p. 418.

§307. A Member who has already spoken may rise and speak again, on a point of order or privilege, if he confines himself to that subject and does not refer to the general tenor of the debate.

§308. Following the adoption of S.O. 6 and S.O. 31, which provide for the adjournment of the House at fixed times and for limiting the length of speeches to forty minutes, if a Member has not concluded his speech at the time of interruption, he is allowed to move the adjournment of the debate or call attention to the clock. Unless he rises to speak first on the resumption of the debate, he will be debarred from subsequently joining in the debate, for his speech must be continuous if it is to last forty minutes. Otherwise, he would be making two speeches, which is prohibited by S.O. 37.

READING SPEECHES

§309. (1) It is a rule in both Houses of Parliament that a Member must address the House orally, and not read from a written, previously prepared speech. Bourinot, p. 335.

(2) On April 19, 1886, a resolution was adopted by the House, which reads:

"That the growing practice in the Canadian House of Commons of delivering speeches of great length, having the character of carefully and elaborately prepared written essays, and indulging in voluminous and often irrelevant extracts, is destructive of legitimate and pertinent debate upon public questions, is a waste of valuable time, unreasonably lengthens the sessions of Parliament, threatens by increased bulk and cost to lead to the abolition of the official report of the debates, encourages a discursive and diffuse, rather than an incisive and concise style of public speaking, is a marked contrast to the practice in regard to debate that prevails in the British House of Commons, and tends to repel the public from a careful and intelligent consideration of the proceedings of Parliament." *Journals,* April 19, 1886, p. 167.

§310. Tradition has established exceptions to this principle, and these have been recognized by the Speaker from time to time. Ministers of the Crown, Leaders of Opposition Parties (and those speaking on their behalf), a Member speaking in a language that is not his own, and a Member making his maiden speech or using technical data or statistics are allowed a written text. In addition, those participating in the general debates of a session, such as the debate on the Address in Reply to the Speech from the Throne, are exempt. *Journals,* January 31, 1956, pp. 93-102.

§311. Under no circumstances may a Member merely table a speech for printing in Hansard. With minor exceptions, what appears in the record of debates has actually been spoken in the House. On rare occasions a Member may receive the consent of the House to have printed as part of his speech long lists, statistics or similar material. Such consent should rarely be asked for and is rarely granted. The House may also give its consent to have documents, or exchanges of letters, printed as a formal appendix to Hansard for the use and information of Members.

CONTENT OF SPEECHES

§312. The proceedings of a committee may not be referred to in debate before they have been laid upon the Table.

§313. A Member may not speak against or reflect upon any determination of the House, unless he intends to conclude with a motion for rescinding it.

§314. The rule that allusions to debates in the other House of the current session are out of order, prevents fruitless arguments between members of two distinct bodies who are unable to reply to each other, and guards against recrimination and offensive language in the absence of the party assailed; but it is mainly founded upon the understanding that the debates of the other House are not known. May, p. 424.

§315. (1) It is a wholesome restraint upon Members that they cannot revive a debate already concluded; and it would be little use in preventing the same question from being offered twice in the same session if, without being offered, its merits might be discussed again and again.

(2) It is irregular to reflect upon, argue against, or in any manner call in

question in debate the past acts or proceedings of the House, on the obvious ground that, besides tending to revive discussion upon questions which have already been once decided, such reflections are uncourteous to the House and irregular in principle inasmuch as the Member is himself included in and bound by a vote agreed to by a majority; and it seems that, reflecting upon or questioning the acts of the "majority" is equivalent to reflecting upon the House. May, p. 424.

(3) Reference to debates of the current session is discouraged even if such reference is relevant, as it tends to re-open matters already decided. The same result is often obtained by indirect methods. Direct reference is permitted, however, when a Member wishes to complain of something said or to clear up misrepresentation or make a personal explanation, but only such of the previous speech should be brought up as is necessary for such purposes.

§316. Besides the prohibitions contained in S.O. 35, it has been sanctioned by usage that a Member, while speaking, must not:

(a) refer to any debate of the same session on any question not then under discussion;

(b) refer to any debate in the Senate, but he may refer to the official printed records of the Senate though they have not been formally communicated to the House of Commons;

(c) refer to the presence or absence of specific Members;

(d) anticipate discussion on a motion set down for future consideration;

(e) impute bad motives or motives different from those acknowledged to a Member;

(f) make a personal charge against a Member;

(g) use the Sovereign's name for the purpose of influencing a debate;

(h) cast reflections upon the conduct of Judges of Superior Courts, unless such conduct is based upon a substantive motion;

(i) reflect upon the past acts and proceedings of the House;

(j) read from a printed document or book commenting on any speech made in Parliament during the session;

(k) discuss messages or reports which are not regularly before the House; or

(l) read petitions referring to debates in the House.

INTERRUPTIONS IN DEBATE

§317. If a Member desires to ask a question during debate, he must first obtain the consent of the Member who is speaking. If the latter ignores the request, the former cannot insist, even if he thinks he is being misrepresented. He cannot make a denial during the speech, but he must wait until the Member has resumed his seat and then he may ask leave to make a statement, or he must wait until his turn comes to address the House.

§318. There are words of interruption such as the cries of "question", "order, order", "hear, hear", or "resign", which have been sanctioned by long parliamentary usage and if used in moderation, are not unparliamentary, but when frequent and loud, cause serious disorder.

REFERRING TO MEMBERS IN DEBATE

§319. (1) It is the custom in the House that no Member should refer to another by name. Members should be referred to in the third person as "the Honourable Member for ...." A Minister of the Crown is normally designated by the portfolio he holds as "the Honourable Minister of ...." Other office holders are similarly identified by their offices. The two main party leaders are generally referred to as "the Prime Minister" and "the Leader of the Opposition", and other party leaders are identified with their parties. Parliamentary Secretaries are normally identified by the posts they hold. More rarely, the Party Whips may also be referred to by their offices.

(2) When a Member belongs to the Imperial Privy Council, or is otherwise entitled to the designation, he is referred to in the House as "the Right Honourable ...."

(3) In the House of Commons a Member will not be permitted by the Speaker to indulge in any reflections on the House itself as a political institution; or to impute to any Member or Members unworthy motives for their actions in a particular case; or to use any profane or indecent language; or to question the acknowledged and undoubted powers of the House in a matter of privilege; or to reflect upon, argue against or in any manner call in question the past acts and proceedings of the House, or to speak in abusive and disrespectful terms of an Act of Parliament. Bourinot, pp. 360-1.

§320. (1) It has been ruled unparliamentary to refer to a Member as:

(a) a parliamentary pugilist and political bully .... *Debates,* March 19, 1875, p. 786.

(b) abusing his position in the House .... *Debates,* March 1, 1877, p. 386.

(c) a bag of wind .... *Debates,* February 15, 1878, p. 267.

(d) scarcely entitled to be called gentlemen.... *Debates,* April 17, 1876, p. 2060.

(e) a servile follower of the government .... *Debates,* April 25, 1878, p. 2191.

(f) honourable only by courtesy .... *Debates,* April 30, 1880, p. 1902.

(g) inspired by forty-rod whiskey .... *Debates,* January 27, 1881, p. 744.

(h) sitting for his constituency by the grace of the leader of the Government .... *Debates,* February 20, 1884, p. 448.

(i)   coming into the world by accident .... *Debates*, May 4, 1886, p. 1071.

(j)   insolent and impertinent .... *Debates*, February 7, 1890, p. 378.

(k)   a parliamentary babe and suckling .... *Debates*, March 26, 1890, p. 2476.

(l)   a blatherskite .... *Debates*, May 7, 1890, p. 4538.

(m) disgracing the House .... *Debates*, January 17, 1896, p. 224.

(n)   talking twaddle .... *Debates*, February 21, 1898, p. 855.

(o)   living politically by deceit .... *Debates*, July 28, 1899, p. 8810.

(p)   grovelling in the dirt in order to get an office .... *Debates*, March 2, 1900, p. 1241.

(q)   a cowardly slanderer and a bully .... *Debates*, February 21, 1907, p. 3434.

(r)   misrepresenting his constituency .... *Debates*, February 23, 1909, p. 1537.

(s)   the political sewerpipe from Carleton County .... *Debates*, September 14, 1917, p. 5871.

(t)   seeking cheap notoriety .... *Debates*, April 30, 1919, p. 1937.

(u)   a trickster .... *Debates*, March 18, 1919, p. 580.

(v)   lacking in intelligence .... *Debates*, March 8, 1934, p. 1281.

(w) hysterical .... *Debates*, March 17, 1943, p. 1341.

(x)   stooping to pretty low motives .... *Debates*, February 2, 1956, p. 820.

(y)   attempting to distort the facts as he had in the past .... *Debates*, June 26, 1956, p. 5382.

(z)   a dim-witted saboteur .... *Debates*, August 13, 1956, p. 7500.

(2) Since 1958, it has been ruled unparliamentary to use the following expressions:

ANIMAL
sick animal .... *Debates*, March 10, 1966, p. 2523

ASS
ass .... *Debates*, February 18, 1970, p. 3760
pompous ass .... *Debates*, December 4, 1967, p. 5030

ATTITUDE
dictatorial attitude .... *Debates*, June 22, 1961, p. 6918
to hell with parliament attitude .... *Debates*, June 22, 1961, p. 6918

BULLSHIT
bullshit .... *Debates*, September 19, 1973, p. 6736

CHEAP
small and cheap .... *Debates*, November 25, 1960, p. 222
cheap political way .... *Debates*, December 2, 1960, p. 453

CONDUCT

shameful conduct .... *Debates*, August 8, 1960, p. 7767

CROOK

crook .... *Debates*, September 23, 1971, p. 8127
                              Debates, September 24, 1971, p. 8137

DECEIVE

deceive .... *Debates*, March 22, 1977, p. 4206
                              Debates, March 23, 1977, p. 4257
deceived .... *Debates*, January 27, 1960, p. 395
deliberately deceived .... *Debates*, August 5, 1960, p. 7640
                              Debates, June 1, 1961, p. 5746
                              Debates, June 22, 1961, p. 6889
                              Debates, March 22, 1971, p. 4468
intentional deceit .... *Debates*, June, 15, 1961, p. 6401

DEMAGOGUE

demagogue .... *Debates*, June 16, 1963, p. 10194

DISHONEST

dishonest .... *Debates*, April 22, 1959, p. 2937
                              Debates, February 1, 1960, p. 586
                              Debates, July 15, 1961, p. 8013
                              Debates, January 25, 1962, p. 188
                              Debates, August 17, 1964, p. 6934
                              Debates, November 25, 1964, p. 10540
                              Debates, December 10, 1964, p. 11010
dishonest answers .... *Debates*, February 27, 1968, p. 7024
dishonest insinuations .... *Debates*, March 10, 1960, p. 1935
dishonest performance .... *Debates*, April 2, 1960, p. 3171

DISTORT

deliberate distortion .... *Debates*, December 5, 1968, p. 3517
deliberately distorted .... *Debates*, May 26, 1972, p. 2589

EVIL

evil genius .... *Debates*, January 23, 1962, p. 138

FABRICATION

fabrication .... *Debates*, January 27, 1959, p. 385
fabricated a statement .... *Debates*, January 30, 1961, p. 1542

FALSE

false .... *Debates*, June 15, 1961, p. 6404
                              Debates, April 10, 1964, p. 1997
                              Debates, March 10, 1965, p. 12190
                              Debates, January 19, 1966, p. 23
false representations .... *Debates*, October 20, 1975, p. 8364

FALSE, cont.

false statement .... *Debates,* May 20, 1961, p. 5100
Debates, January 25, 1962, p. 203
deliberate falsehood .... *Debates,* June 29, 1961, p. 7283
falsehood .... *Debates,* December 3, 1976, p. 1640
falsify .... *Debates,* March 24, 1964, p. 1431

FRAUD

fraud .... *Debates,* May 5, 1960, p. 3606
Debates, December 16, 1960, p. 878
fraudulent character .... *Debates,* April 9, 1962, p. 2644

GANG

B and B gang .... *Debates,* June 18, 1964, p. 4439

GUTS

has not got the guts .... *Debates,* May 27, 1959, p. 4078

HONOUR

devoid of honour .... *Debates,* July 27, 1960

HYPOCRITES

hypocrites .... *Debates,* July 8, 1961, pp. 7737-7738
hypocritical .... *Debates,* February 21, 1961, p. 2264
Debates, June 22, 1961, p. 6916
Debates, July 5, 1961, p. 7559

IDIOT

idiot .... *Debates,* March 6, 1962, p. 1521
Debates, December 16, 1966, p. 11233

IGNORAMUS

ignoramus .... *Debates,* May 18, 1961, p. 5017

ILLEGAL

illegal .... *Debates,* November 14, 1977, p. 817
illegal (actions) .... *Debates,* March 22, 1976, p. 11999

INSOLENT

insolent and irresponsible reply .... *Debates,* December 5, 1962, p. 2346

IRRESPONSIBLE

irresponsible members .... *Debates,* May 8, 1969, p. 8476
irresponsible reply .... *Debates,* December 5, 1962, p. 2346

JOKER

joker is a joker in this house ..... *Debates,* May 11, 1960, p. 3797

KANGAROO COURT

kangaroo court .... *Debates,* August 8, 1960, p. 7766

LIE

deliberately mis-stated the truth ... *Debates,* March 28, 1960, p. 2503

MISLEAD, cont.

Debates, May 19, 1960, p. 4026
Debates, June 19, 1964, p. 4489
Debates, March 11, 1966, p. 2583

deliberately misleading .... *Debates,* January 26, 1977, p. 2401
Debates, December 2, 1977, p. 1517

deliberately misled .... *Debates,* May 20, 1959, p. 3837
Debates, June 29, 1966, p. 7019
Debates, February 6, 1967, p. 12685
Debates, June 19, 1969, p. 10403
Debates, May 7, 1970, p. 6712
Debates, May 19, 1970, p. 7086
Debates, November 24, 1971, p. 9847
Debates, December 22, 1971, p. 10711
Debates, March 15, 1972, p. 848-849
Debates, June 28, 1972, p. 3598
Debates, February 7, 1973, p. 1033
Debates, May 10, 1973, p. 3608
Debates, November 19, 1973, p. 7913
Debates, March 5, 1974, p. 168
Debates, April 18, 1974, p. 1537

wilfully misled .... *Debates,* May 7, 1970, p. 6712
Debates, March 5, 1974, p. 168

misleading the public .... *Debates,* February 1, 1960, p. 591

MISREPRESENT
attempted to misrepresent .... *Debates,* January 30, 1961, p. 1555

MURDERERS
members...have aligned themselves with
the murderers in Quebec .... *Debates,* October 20, 1970, p. 402

MUSSOLINI
Canadian Mussolini .... *Debates,* June 25, 1964, 4715

NAZI
Nazi .... *Debates,* February 22, 1962, p. 1145

NEFARIOUS
nefarious .... *Debates,* May 5, 1960, p. 3615

OBSTRUCT
...obstruct the operation of
government .... *Debates,* November 19, 1957, p. 1295
obstructionist .... *Debates,* May 6, 1961, p. 4459

OFFENSIVE
offensive .... *Debates,* June 10, 1964, p. 4148

PERVERT
deliberately trying to pervert ...... *Debates,* March 7, 1960, p. 1822

RENEGED PROMISES
reneged promises .... *Debates,* October 25, 1962, p. 936

SCURRILOUS
scurrilous .... *Debates,* February 10, 1961, p. 1930

SEAL
trained seal .... *Debates,* March 6, 1961, p. 2703

SILLY
silly reason .... *Debates,* January 26, 1961, p. 1426

SLANDEROUS
slanderous accusations .... *Debates,* August 8, 1960, p. 7777

SPINELESS
does not have a spine .... *Debates,* December 22, 1971

STEAL
stealing .... *Debates,* February 23, 1960, p. 1349

THEFT
theft .... *Debates,* July 19, 1960, p. 6553
                                 Debates, October 22, 1963, p. 3885

TREASON
treason .... *Debates,* November 19, 1957, p. 1248
                                 Debates, July 14, 1959, p. 6015

TRICKERY
trickery .... *Debates,* May 25, 1959, p. 3972

UNDERHANDED
underhanded .... *Debates,* February 10, 1961, p. 1931

UNTRUE
untrue statement .... *Debates,* July 11, 1961, p. 7883
                                 Debates, March 20, 1962, p. 1967
                                 Debates, April 18, 1967, p. 15051
above the truth .... *Debates,* February 22, 1962, p. 1141
not the complete truth .... *Debates,* June 19, 1964, pp. 4489, 4521

VIOLATE
violated his oath .... *Debates,* November 10, 1967, p. 4123

(3) Since 1958, it has been ruled parliamentary to use the following expressions:

ARROGANT
arrogant .... *Debates,* May 19, 1970, p. 7087

ASHAMED
ashamed of their past actions ..... *Debates,* September 8, 1964, p. 7751

ASPERSIONS
aspersions .... *Debates,* June 30, 1959, p. 5306

BLACK SHEEP
black sheep .... *Debates,* September 9, 1964, p. 7811

BLACKMAIL
blackmail .... *Debates,* September 27, 1971, p. 8173
Debates, November 16, 1977, p. 941

CHANGE
change one's mind .... *Debates,* May 19, 1964, p. 3346
change sides .... *Debates,* May 19, 1964, p. 3346

CLOWNERY
clownery .... *Debates,* April 16, 1975, p. 4926

COVER-UP
cover-up .... *Debates,* November 16, 1977, p. 941

COWARD
coward .... *Debates,* April 1, 1976, pp. 12386, 12409-10

CULPABILITY
culpability .... *Debates,* November 16, 1977, p. 941

CYNIC
cynics .... *Debates,* December 20, 1975, p. 10232

DEBASED
debased .... *Debates,* April 29, 1960, p. 3438

DECEIVE
deceive .... *Debates,* February 23, 1970, p. 3953
Debates, May 19, 1970, p. 7087

DELAYING
delaying the House .... *Debates,* April 6, 1973, p. 3049

DEPRIVING
depriving .... *Debates,* February 23, 1960, p. 1349

DISHONEST
dishonest .... *Debates,* February 6, 1959, p. 788

FALSE
false .... *Debates,* May 8, 1961, p. 4523
Debates, April 13, 1964, p. 2067
Debates, April 14, 1964, p. 2125
Debates, May 10, 1966, p. 4971
Debates, March 28, 1969, p. 7253
falsehoods .... *Debates,* November 14, 1977, p. 859

FALSE, cont.
barefaced falsehood .... *Debates,* May 26, 1971, p. 6140

FILIBUSTER
filibuster .... *Debates,* January 18, 1958, p. 3364
stupid filibuster .... *Debates,* July 11, 1969, p. 11105

FORGED
forged .... *Debates,* November 14, 1967, p. 4238

FRAUD
fraudulent .... *Debates,* November 9, 1964, p. 9880

HYPOCRITE
hypocrites .... *Debates,* December 20, 1975, p. 10232
hypocrisy .... *Debates,* October 25, 1966, p. 9109

INDECENT
indecent .... *Debates,* December 1, 1964, p. 10733

INSINCERE
insincere .... *Debates,* June 19, 1964, p. 4505

INSINUATIONS
insinuations .... *Debates,* March 26, 1965, p. 12842

MALICIOUS
malicious attack .... *Debates,* December 16, 1960, p. 886

MENTAL
momentary mental relapse .... *Debates,* February 1, 1960, p. 591

MISINFORM
misinforming .... *Debates,* June 24, 1964, p. 4671

MISLEAD
misleading .... *Debates,* April 12, 1960, p. 3175
misled .... *Debates,* March 7, 1974, p. 257

MISREPRESENT
misrepresentations .... *Debates,* March 7, 1974, p. 257

MOUTHPIECE
mouthpieces .... *Debates,* January 10, 1974, p. 9256

OBSCENE
obscene .... *Debates,* February 19, 1971, p. 3565

OBSTRUCTION
obstruction .... *Debates,* March 29, 1962, p. 2317
                                Debates, May 26, 1975, p. 6097

PARTIAL
partiality .... *Debates,* August 26, 1964, p. 7296

PHONY
phony . . . . *Debates,* July 7, 1959, p. 5624
                            Debates, July 11, 1959, p. 5849
                            Debates, May 19, 1960, p. 4051
                            Debates, April 21, 1967, p. 15206

PIG
the pig has nothing left but a
squeak . . . . *Debates,* December 7, 1977, p. 1647

REFLECTIONS
cast reflections . . . . *Debates,* May 31, 1972, p. 2720

ROTTEN
rotten speech . . . . *Debates,* December 1, 1964, p. 10747

SCANDALOUS
scandalous . . . . *Debates,* April 29, 1960, p. 3438

SEPARATIST
separatist . . . . *Debates,* September 3, 1964, p. 7652

SMOKESCREEN
smokescreen . . . . *Debates,* May 19, 1960, p. 4027

SPURIOUS
spurious charge . . . . *Debates,* October 13, 1966, p. 8598
                            Debates, October 18, 1966, p. 8784

STINKER
stinker . . . . *Debates,* April 2, 1969, p. 7420

STUPID
stupid . . . . *Debates,* August 27, 1964, p. 7393
stupid statement . . . . *Debates,* May 19, 1970, p. 7087

SUBTERFUGE
subterfuge . . . . *Debates,* May 25, 1961, p. 5370

TRICKERY
trickery . . . . *Debates,* February 22, 1968, p. 6919

TRUTH
not telling the truth . . . . *Debates,* February 9, 1970, p. 3342

UNFAIR
from dishonest to unfair . . . . *Debates,* December 12, 1957, p. 2259

UNSCRUPULOUS
unscrupulous . . . . *Debates,* February 15, 1966, p. 1226

UNTRUE
untrue . . . . *Debates,* June 21, 1977, p. 6972

UNTRUE, cont.

untruthful .... *Debates,* November 16, 1977, p. 941

WORST

worst President of the Privy

Council .... *Debates,* April 1, 1976, p. 12387

PROTECTED PERSONS

§321. (1) All references to judges and courts of justice of the nature of personal attack and censure have always been considered unparliamentary, and the Speaker has always treated them as breaches of order. Members have been interrupted in Committee of the Whole by the Chairman when they have cast an imputation upon a judicial proceeding.

(2) When a judge has been employed as a Royal Commissioner, it is proper in the House to criticize his report but not its author.

(3) The Speaker has traditionally protected from attack a group of individuals commonly referred to as "those of high official station". The extent of this group has never been defined. Over the years it has covered senior public servants, ranking officers of the armed services, the United Kingdom High Commissioner in Canada, a Minister of the Crown who was not a Member of either House, and the Prime Minister before he won a seat in the House.

STATEMENTS BY MEMBERS

§322. It has been formally ruled by Speakers that a statement by a Member respecting himself and particularly within his own knowledge must be accepted, but it is not unparliamentary temperately to criticize statements made by a member as being contrary to the facts; but no imputation of intentional falsehood is permissible. On rare occasions this may result in the House having to accept two contradictory accounts of the same incident.

UNPARLIAMENTARY LANGUAGE

§323. (1) Unparliamentary words may be brought to the attention of the House either by the Speaker or by any Member. When the question is raised by a Member it must be as a point of order and not as a question of privilege.

(2) The proper time to raise such a point of order is when the words are used and not afterwards.

(3) Unparliamentary language offending against the proprieties of the House, when the Speaker is in the Chair, cannot be withdrawn in Committee of the Whole. *Journals,* May 1, 1936, p. 281.

§324. (1) It is impossible to lay down any specific rules in regard to injurious reflections uttered in debate against particular Members, or to declare beforehand what expressions are or are not contrary to order; much depends upon the tone and manner, and intention, of the person speaking; sometimes upon the person to whom the words are addressed, as, whether he is a public officer, or a private Member not in office, or whether the words are meant to be applied to his public conduct, or to his private character; and sometimes upon the degree of provocation, which the Member speaking had received from the person he alludes to; and all these considerations must be attended to at the moment, as they are infinitely various and cannot possibly be foreseen in such a manner that precise rules can be adopted with respect to them. *Journals,* March 19, 1976, pp. 1135-7.

(2) An expression which is deemed to be unparliamentary today does not necessarily have to be deemed unparliamentary next week. *Debates,* July 23, 1955, p. 6638.

§325. When the Speaker takes notice of any expression as personal and disorderly, and tending to introduce heat and confusion, and calls upon the offending Member to explain, it is the duty of the latter immediately to explain or retract the offensive expressions, and to apologize to the House for the breach of order, in terms large and liberal enough both to satisfy the House, and the Member of whom the offensive expressions were used. The Speaker's demand usually produces the required explanation, at once; if not, the Speaker then repeats the call for explanation, and informs the Member, that if he does not immediately respond to it, it will become the duty of the Speaker to name him to the House; if the Member should still refuse, the Speaker would then name him to the House, upon which proceedings would immediately ensue for the purpose of censuring or punishing such Member for his disorderly conduct.

§326. (1) Threatening language is also unparliamentary. When a Member has intimated that he would move the adjournment unless certain explanations were given, the Speaker has interposed and called him to order for using language menacing to the House. Bourinot, p. 364.

(2) Words may not be used hypothetically or conditionally, if they are plainly intended to convey a direct imputation. Putting a hypothetical case is not the way to evade what would be in itself disorderly. Bourinot, p. 364.

DOCUMENTS CITED

§327. (1) A Minister of the Crown is not at liberty to read or quote from a despatch or other state paper not before the House, unless he be prepared to lay it upon the Table. This restraint is similar to the rule of evidence in courts of law, which prevent counsel from citing documents which have not been produced in evidence. The principle is so reasonable that it has not been contested; and when the objection has been made in time, it has been generally acquiesced in. May, p. 431.

(2) It has been admitted that a document which has been cited ought to be laid upon the Table of the House, if it can be done without injury to the public interest. The same rule, however, cannot be held to apply to private letters or memoranda. May, pp. 431-2.

(3) A public document referred to but not cited or quoted by a Minister need not be tabled. *Journals,* November 16, 1971, p. 922.

(4) Only the document cited need be tabled by a Minister. A complete file need not be tabled because one document in it has been cited. *Debates,* April 17, 1913, pp. 7925-45.

(5) To be cited, a document must be quoted or specifically used to influence debate. The admission that a document exists or the reading of the salutation or address of a letter does not constitute citing. *Debates,* April 3, 1957, p. 3008. *Debates,* March 4, 1975, p. 3755.

(6) If a Minister cites or quotes an official document in debate, he should be prepared to table it. A private Member has neither the right nor the obligation to table an official, or any other, document. *Journals,* April 6, 1971, pp. 475-6.

(7) When a letter, even though it may have been written originally as a private letter, becomes part of a record of a department, it becomes a public document, and if quoted by a Minister in debate, must be tabled on request. *Journals,* February 22, 1972, p. 15.

Quotations

§328.   A Member may read extracts from documents, books or other printed publications as part of his speech provided in so doing he does not infringe on any point of order. A speech should not, however, consist only of a single long quotation, or a series of quotations joined together with a few original sentences.

§329.   (1) A Member cannot read a letter referring to anything that has taken place in a debate in the House.

(2) An unsigned letter should not be read in the House. *Debates,* May 16, 1928, p. 3073.

(3) It is against the general principles which govern debate to read to the House an imaginary letter supposed to have been written by one of the sitting Members of Parliament. *Debates,* May 12, 1921, pp. 3260-1.

(4) When quoting a letter in the House, a Member must be willing either to give the name of the author or to take full responsibility for the contents himself.

§330.   Telegrams should not be quoted in the House as there is no way of ensuring the authenticity of the signature.

§331.   A Member cannot read before the House documentary evidence and letters relating to a charge referred on a previous occasion to a committee for investigation. This would be bringing into the House for discussion evidence that must come from the committee in support of the charge. *Journals,* May 15, 1873, p. 349.

§332.   (1) On March 17, 1933, a Member quoting a newspaper in debate was ruled out of order by the Deputy Speaker who said: "The rule is quite clear, that the quoting of a newspaper, an author or a book which reflects upon debate before the House, either directly or indirectly is entirely out of order, because Members are here to give their own opinions and not to quote the opinions of others . . . [Members] may quote an article or a book stating facts, but a commentary on any proceeding or any discussion in the House, with the object of swinging an opinion to one side or the other, is out of order." *Debates,* March 17, 1933, pp. 3103-4.

(2) It is in order to quote a newspaper reflecting on proceedings in the House if the quotation is followed by a privilege motion.

(3) When a complaint is made of a newspaper, it is the practice in the House of Commons for the Member to rise on a question of privilege and point out that he has been libelled or misrepresented. He may read as much of the article as is necessary to prove his case but he cannot go further. He is bound to confine himself strictly to the question of privilege. *Debates,* April 5, 1933, p. 3729.

Exhibits

§333.   Speakers have consistently ruled that it is improper to produce exhibits of any sort in the Chamber. Thus during the flag debate of 1964, the display of competing designs was prohibited. At other times boxes of cereal, detergent and milk powder have been ruled out of order. *Debates,* June 16, 1969, p. 10156.

CLOSURE

§334.   (1) Closure is a method of procedure which brings debate to a conclusion and enables the House to secure a decision upon the subject under discussion. Closure was introduced as a rule to the Standing Orders in 1913. *Journals,* April 24, 1913, p. 508.

(2) If debate is on an amendment under closure, and a division takes place on that amendment before one o'clock in the morning, a new amendment may then be proposed, but the speeches thereon will be limited to one for each Member who has not already spoken and shall not be longer than twenty minutes. A division may again take place on this new amendment, and another one be again proposed, and so on until one o'clock.

(3) If a Member has taken the floor at 12:55 o'clock a.m., he is entitled to speak for twenty minutes, but no Member shall rise to speak after one o'clock a.m.

(4) Should a Member rise to speak shortly before one o'clock and a motion be made and rejected that a second Member "be now heard", the original Member may speak for his full twenty minutes regardless of the fact that his speech will begin after one o'clock a.m. *Journals,* December 14, 1964, p. 1000.

(5) A motion for closure applies not only to the main motion under debate but also to such amendments as may be moved to that motion. *Journals,* July 24, 1969, pp. 1393-6.

(6) A motion for closure applies to all the formal subsidiary motions consequent on the main motion.

(7) "Consideration" of a clause or other item may be achieved by as little as one speech when the item is called.

(8) Precedents conflict as to whether closure may be moved on a clause which has not yet been called and postponed in a Committee of the Whole. On four occasions (1913, 1917 (twice) and 1919) all clauses had been postponed before closure was moved. On two occasions (1932 and 1956) closure was used on clauses which had not been called.

THE SUB-JUDICE CONVENTION

§335.   Members are expected to refrain from discussing matters that are before the courts or tribunals which are courts of record. The purpose of this sub-judice convention is to protect the parties in a case awaiting or undergoing trial and persons who stand to be affected by the outcome of a judicial inquiry. It is a voluntary restraint imposed by the House upon itself in the interest of justice and fair play.

§336.   (1) The sub-judice convention has been applied consistently in criminal cases. *Debates,* June 29, 1942, p. 3745. *Debates,* January 29, 1948, p. 710. *Debates,* February 27, 1968, p. 7020.

(2) The precedents in criminal cases are consistent in preventing reference to court cases before a judgment is rendered; however, the convention ceases to apply after the judgment is given. *Debates,* February 10, 1928, p. 366. Nevertheless, the convention is applied again when an appeal is launched. *Journals,* May 2, 1966, pp. 491-3.

§337.   (1) No settled practice has been developed in relation to civil cases, as the convention has been applied in some cases but not in others.

(2) In civil cases the convention does not apply until the matter has reached the trial stage. *Debates,* February 11, 1976, p. 10844.

§338.   (1) Matters before a royal commission are not subject to the convention. *Journals,* May 2, 1966, pp. 491-3.

(2) When an appeal is taken to the Governor-in-Council, it cannot be considered sub-judice while the appeal is pending because the Governor-in-

Council then acts in an administrative and not a judicial capacity, and therefore such matters may be debated in the House of Commons. *Journals,* April 17, 1923, pp. 268-70.

(3) The convention applies to motions, references in debates, questions and supplementary questions, but does not apply to bills. *Journals,* October 4, 1971, pp. 847-8.

(4) The reference of a bill to the Supreme Court of Canada withdraws that bill temporarily from the jurisdiction of Parliament. If the constitutional situation of human rights is submitted to the Supreme Court, it thereby becomes sub-judice and cannot be considered by a committee of the House until the Court has given its decision. The question cannot be before two public bodies at the same time. *Journals,* April 12, 1948, p. 344.

§339. The Special Committee on the Rights and Immunities of Members recommended that the responsibility of the Speaker during the question period should be minimal as regards the sub-judice convention, and that the responsibility should principally rest upon the Member who asks the question and the Minister to whom it is addressed. However, the Speaker should remain the final arbiter in the matter but should exercise his discretion only in exceptional cases. In doubtful cases he should rule in favour of debate and against the convention. *Journals,* April 29, 1977, pp. 720-9.

THE RULE OF ANTICIPATION

§340. (1) The rule of anticipation, a rule which forbids discussion of a matter standing on the *Order Paper* from being forestalled, is dependent upon the same principle as that which forbids the same question from being raised twice within the same session.

(2) The rule against anticipation is that a matter must not be anticipated if it is contained in a more effective form of proceeding than the proceeding by which it is sought to be anticipated, but it may be anticipated if it is contained in an equally or less effective form. May, p. 371.

(3) The British practice in reference to this rule is sufficiently clear; the same cannot be said about Canadian precedents where attempts have been made to apply the rule to our own Canadian practice. The difficulty stems from the fact that the British Commons' Standing Orders include a specific rule on this subject.

§341. (1) In determining whether a discussion is out of order on the grounds of anticipation, the Speaker must have regard to the probability of the matter anticipated being brought before the House within a reasonable time.

(2) In applying the anticipation rule, preference is given to the discussions which lead to the most effective result, which has established a descending scale of values for discussions, such as Bills which have priority

over Motions, which in turn have priority over Amendments. *Journals,* February 24, 1936, p. 68.

§342. (1) There is nothing in the rules and no precedent to prevent the setting down of more than one bill or motion dealing with the same subject. *Journals,* July 3, 1969, pp. 1289-90.

(2) Debate on a government motion effectively blocks debate on a notice of motion for the consideration of the report of a committee which deals with essentially the same subject. Had the motion for consideration of the committee report been moved, it would have had precedence over the government motion and blocked debate on it. Once a motion has been transferred for debate under Government Orders it becomes the government's decision and the government's responsibility to decide whether it will proceed with its motion. It is at that point that the anticipation rule might become operative in the sense that the government motion, if proceeded with, might block consideration of the committee report. *Journals,* July 7, 1969, pp. 1316-18.

THE PREROGATIVES OF THE CROWN

Clemency

§343. (1) Parliament does not appear to have any part to play in the matter of clemency, which is a prerogative of the Crown that should not be interfered with by proceedings of the House of Commons while the subject is under consideration by His Excellency and his advisers. *Journals,* May 2, 1917, pp. 158-9.

(2) Speakers have consistently refused to allow questions or debate, on the subject, until after a decision has been made.

Disallowance

§344. Disallowance of provincial laws is a function of the executive and not of Parliament. There appears to be no constitutional reason why the House can not express its opinion before the Government acts, and indeed, on one occasion has done so. It is clear, however, that any such decision of the House can have no legal validity.

Agreements

§345. Although the Government may propose a motion for approval of the ratification of an Agreement, it does not mean that the Government is abdicating its prerogative in the realm of treaty making. A motion of this type does not allow amendments dealing with the terms of that treaty. *Journals,* May 6, 1966, p. 515.

8

Address in Reply to His Excellency's Speech

8

Address in Reply to His Excellency's Speech

The Speech from the Throne — The Address in Reply to His Excellency's Speech — Amendment in the Address — Transaction of Public Business.

THE SPEECH FROM THE THRONE

§346. The Speech from the Throne is generally a statement of the government's policies and the debate, broadly, is a debate on that policy.

THE ADDRESS IN REPLY TO HIS EXCELLENCY'S SPEECH

§347. (1) The motion in this debate is in the form that the House expresses its thanks to the Queen, if she delivered the Speech personally, or to the Governor General for the most gracious speech addressed to both Houses of Parliament.

(2) The motion moved is usually in the following form:

"That the following address be presented to His Excellency the Governor General of Canada:

"'To His Excellency the Right Honourable ...., Chancellor and Principal Companion of the Order of Canada, Chancellor and Commander of the Order of Military Merit upon whom has been conferred the Canadian Forces' Decoration, Governor General and Commander-in-Chief of Canada:

"'MAY IT PLEASE YOUR EXCELLENCY:

"'We, Her Majesty's most loyal and dutiful subjects, the House of Commons of Canada, in Parliament assembled, beg leave to offer our humble thanks to Your Excellency for the gracious Speech which your Excellency has addressed to both Houses of Parliament.'"

(3) The mover and seconder of this motion are appointed by the Government from their supporters who do not hold office.

AMENDMENTS TO THE ADDRESS

§348. Amendments to the Address in Reply to the Speech from the Throne are used by the Opposition for the purpose of challenging government policies or actions. A sub-amendment may be moved provided it is relevant, but if it proposes to add to the main amendment words of commendation for the Government, then it is equivalent to an expanded negative and destroys the whole effect of the Opposition's amendment. *Journals,* January 30, 1959, p. 56.

§349. Debate on the Address in Reply is very wide-ranging. It is one of the few opportunities for backbenchers to bring forward topics of their own choosing.

§350. Members should be extremely careful in moving amendments on the Address in Reply. If, later in the session, amendments which touch those very points on which the House has given its judgment are moved to other motions, then these new amendments should be declared to be out of order. *Journals,* May 3, 1955, pp. 545-6.

§351. An amendment to the Address in Reply to the Speech from the Throne is a motion of "no-confidence". But a sub-amendment is not a new motion of "no-confidence"; it is intended to strengthen or weaken the amendment to which it must be relevant and upon which it is dependent. The moving of a sub-amendment does not entitle the Member to speak longer than forty minutes, as this privilege has already been exercised by the mover of the amendment.

§352. The purpose of a sub-amendment is to alter the amendment; it should not enlarge upon the scope of the amendment but should deal with matters that are not covered by the amendment; if it is intended to bring up matters foreign to the amendment, the Member should wait until the amendment is disposed of and move a new amendment. *Journals,* January 24, 1966, pp. 43-4.

§353. Any Member may introduce an amendment up until the moment when the final vote has to be taken. *Journals,* January 30, 1959, p. 56.

§354. At the hour appointed for the interruption of proceedings, when the Speaker puts the question, a Member who is speaking at that time is considered as concluding his speech even though he has not spoken for his full allotted time. He may, however, speak on any subsequent amendment or sub-amendment. *Journals,* January 19, 1956, p. 32.

TRANSACTION OF PUBLIC BUSINESS

§355. (1) The transaction of public business is carried on while proceedings on the Address are in progress.

(2) Debate upon the Address in Reply to the Speech from the Throne does not have any particular precedence over the transaction of business of the House.

9

Questions, Reports and Returns

9

Questions, Reports and Returns

QUESTIONS

§356. The House recognizes two broad categories of questions — the written question, which is designed to provide information for a Member, and the oral question, which the Standing Orders recognize as dealing with matters of urgency. While under the rules all oral questions could properly be placed on the *Order Paper,* not all written questions (e.g., those addressed to more than one Minister) could properly be asked during the daily Question Period.

Written Questions

§357. (1) The traditional restrictions on questions are those listed in Beauchesne's Fourth Edition at citation 171, which is as follows:

"171. In putting a question a member must confine himself to the narrowest limits.

"In making a question, observations which might lead to debate cannot be regarded as coming within the proper limits of a question.

"The purpose of a question is to obtain information and not to supply it to the House.

"A question oral or written must not:

(*a*)   be ironical, rhetorical, offensive, or contain epithet, innuendo, satire, or ridicule.

(*b*)   be trivial, vague, or meaningless.

(*c*)   multiply, with slight variations, a similar question on the same point.

(*d*)   repeat in substance a question already answered, or to which an answer has been refused.

"(e)   inquire whether statements made in a newspaper are true.

"(f)   contain an expression of opinion.

"(g)   be hypothetical.

"(h)   contain inferences.

"(i)   contain imputations.

"(j)   be framed so as to suggest its own answer.

"(k)   be a speech, however short; nor be of unreasonable length.

"(l)   seek, for purposes of argument, information on matters of past history.

"(m)   ask solution of a legal proposition, such as interpretation of a Statute, a Minister's own powers, etc.

"(n)   reflect on or relate to character or conduct of persons other than in a public capacity.

"(o)   refer discourteously to a friendly foreign country.

"(p)   be asked which might prejudice a pending trial in a Court of law.

"(q)   contain or imply charges of a personal character.

"(r)   refer to debate or answers to questions of the current Session.

"(s)   embody a series of questions which should be moved for an Address or Order.

"(t)   impugn the accuracy of information conveyed to the House by a Minister.

"(u)   suggest amendments to bills.

"(v)   anticipate an Order of the Day or other matters.

"(w)   raise a matter of policy too large to be dealt with in the limits of an answer to a question.

"(x)   deal with an action of a Minister for which he is not responsible to Parliament, or with matters not within his official knowledge.

"(y)   raise matters under control of local authorities not responsible to Government or Legislature.

"(z)   refer to speeches made outside the House; but in the case of Cabinet Ministers, it is permissible to ask the Prime Minister whether such speech represents policy of Government.

"(aa)   seek information about the internal affairs of foreign countries or the Dominions.

"(bb)   ask the Government's opinion on matters of policy.

"(cc)   ask what advice a Minister proposes to give Crown, (but may ask what advice he has given).

"(dd)   deal with matters not officially connected with Government or Parliament, or which are of a private nature.

"(ee)   relate to communications alleged to have passed between a Member and a Minister.

"(ff)   seek information set forth in documents equally accessible to the questioner, as Statutes, published reports, etc.

"(gg)   seek information about matters which are in their nature secret, such as decisions or proceeding of Cabinet, advice given to Crown by Law Officers, etc.

"(*hh*) seek information about proceedings in a Committee which has not yet made its report to the House.

"(*ii*) introduce name of, or contain reflection on, the Sovereign or Royal Family, or refer to influence of the Crown.

"(*jj*) be addressed to the Leader of the Opposition inquiring the course he intends to adopt regarding a motion by the Government.

"(*kk*) critize decisions of the House.

"(*ll*) seek from an ex-Minister information with regard to transactions during his term of office.

"(*mm*)reflect on the character or conduct of the Speaker, the Deputy Speaker, members of either House of Parliament and Judges of High Courts. These can only be dealt with on a substantive motion.

"(*nn*) relate to matters which passed outside the walls of the House and do not relate to any Bill or motion before the House."

(2) Many of the traditional limitations on questions are now applied more strictly to written questions than to oral questions. In the words of one Speaker: "... one need only look at citation 171 of Beauchesne's Fourth Edition, in which will be found numerous, and in many cases, inoperable, restrictions covering the form and content of questions. I suggest that if each and every one of these restrictions were applied in every case, very few questions would ever reach the *Order Paper*". *Journals,* March 30, 1965, pp. 1193-4.

Oral Questions

§358. In 1964, the Special Committee on Procedure recommended the following guidelines, which were subsequently concurred in by the House, to be used by Members in asking or answering oral questions:
answering oral questions:

(1) Such questions should:

(a) be asked only in respect of matters of sufficient urgency and importance as to require an immediate answer;

(b) not inquire whether statements made in a newspaper are correct;

(c) not require an answer involving a legal opinion;

(d) not be asked in respect of a matter that is sub-judice;

(e) not be of a nature requiring a lengthy and detailed answer;

(f) not raise a matter of policy too large to be dealt with as an answer to a question. *Journals,* April 20, 1964, p. 225.

(2) Answers to questions should be as brief as possible, should deal with the matter raised, and should not provoke debate. *Journals,* April 20, 1964, p. 225.

§359. The Speaker expressed some general principles in order to clarify the regulations and restrict the negative qualifications which traditionally have guided the Question Period:

"A brief question seeking information about an important matter of some urgency which falls within the administrative responsibility of the government or of the specific Minister to whom it is addressed, is in order.

"(1) It must be a question, not an expression of an opinion, representation, argumentation, nor debate.

"(2) The question must be brief. A preamble need not exceed one carefully drawn sentence. A long preamble on a long question takes an unfair share of time and provokes the same sort of reply. A supplementary question should need no preamble.

"(3) The question ought to seek information and, therefore, cannot be based upon a hypothesis, cannot seek an opinion, either legal or otherwise, and must not suggest its own answer, be argumentative or make representations.

"(4) It ought to be on an important matter, and not be frivolous.

"(5) The matter ought to be of some urgency. There must be some present value in seeking the information during the Question Period rather than through the *Order Paper* or through correspondence with the Minister or the department.

"(6) A question must be within the administrative competence of the Government. The Minister to whom the question is directed is responsible to the House for his present Ministry and not for any decisions taken in a previous portfolio.

"(7) A question must adhere to the proprieties of the House, in terms of inferences, imputing motives or casting aspersions upon persons within the House or out of it.

"(8) A question that has previously been answered ought not to be asked again.

"(9) A question cannot deal with a matter that is before a court. Refer to the detailed explanation of the Sub-judice Rule in Chapter 7 (Rules of Debate).

"(10) A question ought not to refer to a statement made outside the House by a Minister.

"(11) A question which seeks an opinion about government policy is probably out of order in that it asks for an opinion and not information. A question asking for a general statement of government policy may be out of order in that it requires a long answer that should be made on motion or in debate. Other questions inevitably deal with government policy and the general restrictions regarding such questions have never been applied.

"(12) Questions should not anticipate a debate scheduled for the day, but should be reserved for the debate." *Journals,* April 14, 1975, pp. 439-41.

§360. Some further limitations seem to be generally understood. A question may not:

(1) ask a solution of a legal question, such as the interpretation of a statute.

(2) seek information about matters which are in their nature secret, such as decisions or proceedings of Cabinet or advice given to the Crown by the Law Officers.

(3) seek information about proceedings in a committee which has not yet made its report to the House.

(4) criticize decisions of the House.

(5) reflect on the character or conduct of the Speaker or other occupants of the Chair, Members of either House of Parliament and members of the judiciary.

(6) relate to communications alleged to have passed between a Member and a Minister.

§361. A question may not be asked of a Minister in another capacity, such as being responsible for a province, or part of a province, or as spokesman for a racial or religious group. *Journals,* October 16, 1968, pp. 132-4.

§362. Reading telegrams, letters or extracts from newspapers as an opening to an oral question is an abuse of the rules of the House. It is not good parliamentary practice to communicate written allegations to the House and then to ask Ministers either to confirm or deny them. It is the Member's duty to ascertain the truth of any statement before he brings it to the attention of Parliament.

Replies to Questions

§363. (1) A Minister may decline to answer a question without stating the reason for his refusal, and insistence on an answer is out of order, with no debate being allowed. A refusal to answer cannot be raised as a question of privilege, nor is it regular to comment upon such a refusal. A Member may put a question but has no right to insist upon an answer.

(2) An answer to a question cannot be insisted upon, if the answer be refused by the Minister on the ground of the public interest; nor can the question be replaced on the *Notice Paper*. The refusal of a Minister to answer on this ground cannot be raised as a matter of privilege. *Debates,* April 29, 1942, p. 1974.

§364. If a question is made an Order of the House for a Return under S.O. 39(4), it is understood that the answer will be in the form of a Return and may not necessarily answer every portion of the original question. *Journals,* November 16, 1962, pp. 285-7.

§365. No questions of any sort may be addressed to the Speaker. If information relating to matters under the jurisdiction of the Speaker is required, it must be obtained privately.

§366. Questions may be asked of private Members only under strict limitations. Virtually the only question possible would refer to a committee of which the Member is the Chairman. A question asking, for example, if a Member intended to introduce certain legislation, is out of order.

§367. A question may not be asked of a former Minister seeking information with regard to transactions during his term of office.

§368. The Speaker, in common with his duties of supervision over the proceedings of the House, may rule out any question which violates the rules or practice of Parliament in the same way as he deals with irregularities in motions and amendments. He may make an alteration in the question or refer it back to the Member for correction. *Journals,* October 15, 1962, pp. 70-1.

§369. A question of privilege or point of order raised during the oral Question Period ought to be taken up after the oral Question Period, unless the Speaker considers it to be an extremely grave matter.

Questions by Parliamentary Secretaries

§370. Those such as Parliamentary Secretaries who are clothed with the responsibility of answering for the Government ought not to use the time of the Question Period for the privilege of asking questions of the Government. *Debates,* November 5, 1974, pp. 1059-64.

Supplementary Questions

§371. Although there may be no debate on an answer, further questions, as may be necessary for the elucidation of the answers that have been given, within due limits, may be addressed to a Minister. The extent to which supplementary questions may be asked is in the discretion of the Speaker. Sir Erskine May, Treatise on the Law, Privileges, Proceedings and Usage of Parliament (19th ed., 1976), pp. 334-5.

ADJOURNMENT PROCEEDINGS
UNDER STANDING ORDER 40

§372. The time limits established under S.O. 40 are strictly adhered to. Unlike ordinary debates, extensions of the time by unanimous consent are neither asked for nor granted. No point of order or question of privilege will be recognized during this thirty-minute period. *Debates,* April 30, 1964, p. 2799.

§373. A notice of intention to raise, after ten o'clock p.m., the subject-matter of a question that the Speaker has ruled out of order, on grounds other than those listed in S.O. 39(6), is inadmissible. *Debates,* April 27, 1964, p. 2582.

§374. The period allotted between 10 o'clock p.m. and 10:30 o'clock p.m. is for the purpose of dealing with three questions. If the full time is not used, the remaining time lapses. *Debates,* May 15, 1964, p. 3301.

REPORTS OR PAPERS TABLED

§375. The text of a Minister's statement of the kind normally made under S.O. 15 cannot be tabled pursuant to S.O. 41. *Journals,* June 28, 1973, pp. 445-6.

§376. S.O. 41 provides a way for Ministers to table documents in the House. It does not impose an obligation on Ministers to do so. *Debates,* April 16, 1974, p. 1455.

§377. A Minister may not answer a series of oral questions by tabling a document under S.O. 41(2). *Journals,* February 3, 1969, pp. 655-7.

§378. S.O. 41(2) is intended to enlarge the class of papers which can be tabled by the Government without notice and without leave beyond those mentioned in S.O. 41(1). So long as the report or paper deals with a matter which comes within the administrative responsibility of the Government, and that paper is an official document for which the Minister or his Parliamentary Secretary accepts responsibility, it may be tabled pursuant to S.O. 41(2). *Journals,* February 3, 1969, pp. 655-7.

PRODUCTION OF PAPERS

§379. (1) Papers are laid before the House in pursuance of:

(a) provisions of an Act of Parliament;
(b) an Order of the House;
(c) an Address to the Crown; or
(d) Standing Orders of the House.

(2) Papers may be laid before the House voluntarily under S.O. 41(2).

§380. (1) There are two cases where the House calls for the production of documents. One is for public papers from a department of the Government and the other is for communications made by the Government as a whole. *Journals,* May 6, 1959, p. 407.

(2) The general rule is that information to be obtained from any department, constituted or regulated by statute, is obtained by means of an

Order, while information to be obtained from the Governor-in-Council is obtained by means of an Address.

Papers tabled by Acts of Parliament

§381. The papers brought down in pursuance of Acts of Parliament are mostly reports, accounts and other documents which, under statutory provisions, are required to be laid before Parliament.

Papers tabled by Order of the House

§382. Papers may be ordered directly when they relate:

(1) to matters under the immediate control and direction of the different departments; or

(2) to the business of the House.

Papers tabled by Addresses to the Crown

§383. (1) Addresses are moved for:

(a) correspondence between the Federal and foreign governments;

(b) correspondence between the Federal and provincial governments;

(c) correspondence between the Federal Government and any company, corporation or individual;

(d) Orders-in-Council;

(e) information respecting a royal commission;

(f) instructions to the Governor General for papers relating to the government of the territories;

(g) petitions not in the possession of the House but addressed to the Governor-in-Council and including statements of public aid;

(h) returns of petitions of right and cases before the Supreme and Federal Courts of Canada;

(i) returns relative to the administration of justice and the judicial conduct of judges; or

(j) papers relative to the exercise of the prerogatives of the Crown.

(2) If recommendations or reports of a Crown agency pursuant to statute are submitted to the Governor-in-Council and a Minister of the Crown is only the vehicle whereby the agency deals with the Governor-in-Council, then these documents should properly be asked for by way of an Address. *Journals,* February 15, 1960, pp. 137-9.

(3) A motion for the production of papers is directed to a Minister who has responsibility for a department.

(4) A Minister without portfolio has no department of Government and is, therefore, excluded from the responsibility of producing documents from a department. On the other hand, he is a Privy Councillor, a Minister of the Crown, and a Member of the Government and, therefore, in respect of acts in

his official capacity of a Member of the Government, he is presumably amenable to the jurisdiction of the House with regard to the production of documents, subject to the limitation of public policy and so on, which pass through him in that capacity. Therefore, motions for the production of papers, if issued, would have to be read as though they limited themselves to communications made on behalf of the Government. *Journals,* May 6, 1959, p. 407.

Papers tabled by Standing Orders

§384. Papers which must be laid before the House in pursuance of any Standing Order of the House are usually brought down without any formality by being deposited with the Clerk of the House as if they had been laid on the Table.

NOTICES OF MOTIONS FOR PRODUCTION OF PAPERS

§385. When Notices of Motions for the Production of Papers are called on Wednesdays, a representative of the Government may state that certain Notices of Motions are acceptable to the Government, some are acceptable subject to certain reservations and that others are unacceptable. He will then seek the permission of the House to allow the remaining Notices of Motions to stand. *Journals,* April 15, 1964, p. 213.

§386. (1) The responsibility of the Speaker is to see that the motion is before the House in the proper form; that is, whether it is the appropriate motion to do what is sought to be done. *Journals,* February 15, 1960, pp. 137-8.

(2) In the absence of a Member in whose name a motion for the production of papers stands on the *Order Paper,* another Member may, if no one objects, make the motion, provided he has been authorized to do so. He says: "Mr. Speaker, the Honourable Member for ...., being unable to be present today, I move on his behalf . . ." If objection is taken, the question cannot be put by the Speaker.

§387. (1) Notices of Motions for Production of Papers when called on Wednesdays before the Orders of the Day are not debatable or amendable. *Journals,* February 27, 1961, p. 296.

(2) If a Notice of Motion for the Production of Papers is to be debated, it is transferred by the Clerk to the order, "Notices of Motions (Papers)".

(3) A representative of the government may state that a Notice of Motion for the Production of Papers is unacceptable to the Government and ask that the Member withdraw his Notice of Motion. In some circumstances the Member may withdraw it.

(4) There has been a well-recognized practice that a Minister, who does not wish to be found by an unqualified Order of the House to produce documents, may rise and state his objection so that his objection will be a

matter of record. This statement is, to some extent, a protection of the Minister against the unqualified Order of the House calling upon him to produce the documents mentioned. It is a practice which has commended itself to the House and which has been well established. *Journals,* February 27, 1961, p. 296.

§388.   There is a general rule that papers should be ordered only on subjects which are of a public or official character. May, p. 256.

§389.   The House shall decide after debate, if desired, whether it will order a document to be laid upon the Table. *Journals,* February 15, 1960, pp. 137-8.

§390.   In 1973, the Government of the Day tabled in the House of Commons its view on the general principles governing Notices of Motions for Production of Papers — principles, although not formally approved by the House, but which have been followed since:

(1) To enable Members of Parliament to secure factual information about the operations of Government to carry out their parliamentary duties and to make public as much factual information as possible, consistent with effective administration, the protection of the security of the state, rights to privacy and other such matters, government papers, documents and consultant reports should be produced on Notice of Motion for the Production of Papers unless falling within the categories outlined below, in which case an exemption is to be claimed from production.

(2) The following criteria are to be applied in determining if the government papers or documents should be exempt from production:

(a)   Legal opinions or advice provided for the use of the government.

(b)   Papers, the release of which would be detrimental to the security of the State.

(c)   Papers dealing with international relations, the relase of which might be detrimental to the future conduct of Canada's foreign relations; (the release of papers received from other countries to be subject to the consent of the originating country).

(d)   Papers, the release of which might be detrimental to the future conduct of federal-provincial relations or the relations of provinces *inter se*: (the release of papers received from provinces to be subject to the consent of the originating province).

(e)   Papers containing information, the release of which could allow or result in direct personal financial gain or loss by a person or a group of persons.

(f)   Papers reflecting on the personal competence or character of an individual.

(g)   Papers of a voluminous character or which would require an inordinate cost or length of time to prepare.

(h)   Papers relating to the business of the Senate.

(i) Papers, the release of which would be personally embarrassing to Her Majesty or the Royal Family or official representatives of Her Majesty.

(j) Papers relating to negotiations leading up to a contract until the contract has been executed or the negotiations have been concluded.

(k) Papers that are excluded from disclosure by statute.

(l) Cabinet documents and those documents which include a Privy Council confidence.

(m) Any proceedings before a court of justice or a judicial inquiry of any sort.

(n) Papers that are private or confidential and not of a public or official character.

(o) Internal departmental memoranda.

(p) Papers requested, submitted or received in confidence by the Government from sources outside the Government.

(3) Ministers' correspondence of a personal nature, or dealing with constituency or general political matters, should not be identified with government papers and therefore should not be subject to production in the House.

(4) In the case of consultant studies, the following guidelines are to be applied:

(a) Consultant studies, the nature of which is identifiable and comparable to work that would be done within the Public Service, should be treated as such (the reports and also the terms of reference) when consideration is being given to their release.

(b) Consultant studies, the nature of which is identifiable and comparable to the kind of investigation of public policy for which the alternative would be a Royal Commission, should be treated as such and both the terms of reference for such studies and the resulting reports should be produced.

(c) Prior to engaging the services of a consultant, Ministers are to decide in which category the study belongs and, in cases of doubt, are to seek the advice of their colleagues.

(d) Regardless of the decision as to which category ((a) or (b) above) the consultant report will belong, the terms of reference and contract for the consultant study are to ensure that the resulting report comprises two or more volumes, one of which is to be the recommendations, while the other volume(s) is (are) to be the facts and the analysis of the study. The purpose of this separation is to facilitate the release of the factual and analytical portions (providing that the material is not covered by the exemptions listed above) enabling the recommendations (which, in the case of studies under category (a), would be exempt from the production) to be separated for consideration by Ministers. *Debates,* March 15, 1973, p. 2288.

RETURNS

§391. If one House desires any Return relating to the business or proceedings of the other, neither courtesy nor custom allows such a Return to be ordered; but an arrangement is generally made by which the Return is moved for in the other House; and after it has been presented, a message is sent to request that it may be communicated. *Journals,* March 20, 1919, p. 80.

§392. Upon occasion, Orders for Returns have not been completed before the end of a session. In this event, the Government tables a supplementary Return in the following session. *Journals,* February 27, 1974, p. 6.

§393. A Return to an Order of the House is not in proper form if it requires the use of a mechanical device for its interpretation. *Journals,* February 25, 1970, p. 489.

10

Notices

10

Notices

NOTICES

§394. (1) The distinction between orders and resolutions must be considered in the interpretation of S.O. 42 which limits the giving of forty-eight hours notice to "leave to present a bill, resolution or Address, the appointment of any committee and the placing of a question on the *Order Paper*". It does not mention "orders", and it is specific in saying that the rule shall not apply to bills after their introduction, or to the times of meeting or adjournment of the House.

(2) Such notices are laid on the Table in order that they may be printed in the *Notice Paper* which is appended to the *Order Paper*.

ORAL NOTICES

§395. (1) Oral notices for future proceedings do not generally exist in the House of Commons. It is useless for a Member to say: "Mr. Speaker, I give notice that I will move a certain motion tomorrow." This would not give him any precedence on the next day and he would not thereby acquire the right to speak on matters not standing on the *Order Paper*. An exception must be made in respect of certain routine proceedings dealing with the observance of properties of the House, the maintenance of its authority, the conduct of its officers, the management of its business, the correctness of its records or any other similar matter brought forward by the Government House Leader and settled without the passage of any motion. A Minister may also announce from his seat that he will later make an official statement on some important matter but he does so as a courtesy to the Members. These indications of the Government's intentions are not the type of notices required under S.O. 42 which must be printed in the *Votes and Proceedings*.

(2) Standing Orders 33 and 75C provide for a Minister of the Crown to give oral notice of his intention to move a motion. This type of notice is not covered by the terms of S.O. 42(1). *Debates*, December 1, 1971, p. 10050.

IRREGULAR NOTICES

§396. As the *Notice Paper* is published by authority of the House, a notice of motion, or of a question to be put to a Member, containing unbecoming expressions, infringing its rules, or otherwise irregular, may, under the Speaker's authority, be corrected by the Clerks at the Table. These alterations, if necessary, are submitted to the Speaker or to the Member who gave the notice. A notice wholly out of order, as, for instance, containing a reflection on a vote of the House, may be withheld from publication on the *Notice Paper*; if the irregularity be not extreme, the notice is printed but reserved for future consideration.

AMENDED NOTICES

§397. (1) A modification of a notice of motion standing upon the *Notice Paper* is permitted, if the amended notice does not exceed the scope of the original notice. Sir Erskine May, Treatise on the Law, Privilege, Proceedings and Usage of Parliament (19th ed., 1976), p. 367.

(2) A new notice must be given in the *Votes and Proceedings*, under S.O. 42, when a material change is to be made to a notice of motion before it is taken into consideration by the House.

WITHDRAWAL OF NOTICES

§398. There are only two ways in which a notice can be withdrawn from the *Order Paper*: first, by the Member giving a written notice to the Clerk of the House or second, by the Member, from his place in the House, informing the Speaker that he desires the question to be dropped or withdrawn. *Journals,* January 13, 1910, p. 154.

PUBLICATION OF NOTICES

§399. The exact time at which notices should be handed to the Clerk at the Table is of minor importance. *Journals,* April 14, 1913, p. 461.

§400. (1) The publication of a proposed motion, once in the *Notice Paper* and the next day on the *Order Paper,* is sufficient to cover two days' notice under S.O. 42.

(2) If Saturday is a sitting day, notices handed in on that day will appear on the *Order Paper* on Monday. Sir John Bourinot, Parliamentary Procedure and Practice in the Dominion of Canada (4th ed., 1916), p. 296. *Journals,* May 8, 1961, p. 516.

MOVING MOTIONS FOR WHICH NOTICE HAS BEEN GIVEN

§401. No notice is required for a motion to change the sponsor of a public or private bill after its introduction. *Journals,* March 14, 1884, p. 238.

§402. Merely formal motions for the adoption of reports or for certain papers, to which there is no objection, are usually permitted to be made in the absence of the Member who has placed the notice on the *Order Paper.*

§403. If the Member who has given notice of an amendment to a private bill is not in his seat when the bill is called for third reading, no other Member can move the amendment on his behalf. *Debates,* May 25, 1928, p. 3379.

MOTIONS NOT REQUIRING NOTICE

§404. In the absence of Standing Orders to the contrary, such motions as the following may be made without notice:

(a) for the correctness of the records of the House;
(b) for the adjournment of the House or debate;
(c) for the observance of the proprieties of the House of Commons such as accepting a gift or any exchange of courtesies;
(d) for the fixing of sitting days and the time of meeting or adjournment;
(e) for the previous question;
(f) for reading the Orders of the Day;
(g) for proceeding to another Order;
(h) for postponing the question to a day certain; or
(i) for amending the question.

SUSPENSION OF NOTICE

§405. Under the terms of S.O. 43, a motion may, in case of urgent and pressing necessity previously explained by the mover, be made by unanimous consent of the House without notice having been given under S.O. 42.

§406. The unanimous consent involved in S.O. 43 refers only to the setting aside of the notice provision of S.O. 42. It does not affect the ordinary rules applicable to the form and content of motions. *Journals,* May 16, 1972, p. 299.

§407. In assessing whether a Member has unanimous consent under S.O. 43 the Speaker need hear only one negative voice to prevent the motion from being put. *Debates,* May 24, 1977, pp. 5883, 5885.

§408. A Member, when proposing a motion under S.O. 43, should restrict his comments to the necessity or desirability of suspending the notice provision for a motion. *Journals,* October 28, 1971, p. 895.

§**409.**   Before accepting a motion for submission to the House under S.O. 43 the Speaker may rule whether it fulfills the conditions of urgency and pressing necessity laid down in the Standing Order. *Debates,* May 16, 1977, p. 5656. *Debates,* May 17, 1977, p. 5715.

§**410.**   Motions proposed under S.O. 43 are not immune from the strictures against unparliamentary or opprobrious language. *Debates,* November 15, 1977, p. 863.

11

Motions; Amendments; Notices of Motions; The Previous Question

11

Motions; Amendments; Notices of Motions; The Previous Question

Process of Debate — Dividing Motions — The Question being once made — Type of Motions — Notices of Motions — Motions — Amendments — Form and Content of Amendments — Sub-Amendments — Form and Content of Sub-Amendments — Member amending his own Motion — Withdrawal of Motions and Amendments — Order of Proceeding in Putting the Question — Rescinding Resolutions — The Previous Question.

PROCESS OF DEBATE

§411. (1) Every matter is determined in the House of Commons upon a question put by the Speaker, on a proposition submitted by a Member, and resolved either in the affirmative or negative as the case may be. This proposition, called a motion, is a proposal moved by one Member, in accordance with certain well-established rules, that the House do something or order something to be done or express an opinion with regard to some matter.

(2) The judgment or will of the House of Commons is that which is evidenced by the consent or agreement of the majority of Members present and voting. In order to ascertain this agreement, the method of proceeding consists of the submission of a proposition upon which the Members express their opinion by a simple affirmative or negative. This method has been expanded into a system of rules whereby the judgment of the House may be ascertained with facility and precision.

(3) Every motion that is duly moved and seconded is placed before the House by the Speaker as a question for the decision of the House. All motions must be presented to the Speaker in writing in either of the two official languages. No motion is regularly before the House until it has been read from the Chair. Then it may be debated, amended, superseded, adopted, negatived or withdrawn, as the House may decide. There can be but one question pending at the same time, though there may be numerous matters of business in various stages of progress standing on the *Order Paper* for consideration during the session. The only exception from this citation occurs at the report stage of a bill, when the Standing Orders confer upon the Speaker the power to combine amendments or clauses for discussion and decision.

§412. (1) The *question* is the subject matter of the motion, and on the merits of that subject matter the House has to give a decision either unanimously or by the majority of the members present. Every question when agreed to assumes the form either of an *order* or a *resolution* of the House. By its orders the House directs its committees, its members, its officers, the order of its own proceedings and the acts of all persons they concern; by its resolutions the House declares its own opinions and purposes.

(2) When a motion is adopted, it becomes the resolution or order of the House. Therefore, its form must consequently be so framed, and its language so expressed that, if it meets the approbation of the House, it may at once become the resolution or order of the House which it purports to be.

§413. If a motion finds no seconder, it is dropped immediately. When it has been seconded, it should at once be proposed from the Chair.

§414. If a motion is ruled out on the grounds that its wording is objectionable or its allegations are irregular, the mover is not thereby deprived of the right to move it again after having made the necessary corrections and given a new notice. If the irregularities are trivial or without bearing on the main purpose of the motion, the House may agree to rectify them, but the mover himself cannot amend his own.

Dividing Motions

§415. (1) A motion which contains two or more distinct propositions may be divided so that the sense of the House may be taken on each separately. The Speaker has a discretionary power to decide whether he should divide a motion. *Journals,* June 15, 1964, p. 427.

(2) It is only in exceptional circumstances and when there is little doubt that the Speaker may intervene and, of his own initiative, amend the motion proposed by a Member. *Journals,* March 23, 1966, p. 334.

The Question Being Once Made

§416. (1) An old rule of Parliament reads: "That a question being once made and carried in the affirmative or negative, cannot be questioned again but must stand as the judgment of the House." Unless such a rule were in existence, the time of the House might be used in the discussion of a motion of the same nature and contradictory decisions would be sometimes arrived at in the course of the same session. Sir John Bourinot, Parliamentary Procedure and Practice in the Dominion of Canada (4th ed., 1916), p. 328.

(2) This rule also applies to decisions taken by the House on amendments to the Address in Reply to the Speech from the Throne and to the Budget Motion.

TYPES OF MOTIONS

§417. Motions may be divided into several categories:

(1) *Substantive* motions are self-contained proposals, not incidental to any proceeding, amendable and drafted in such a way as to be capable of expressing a decision of the House.

(2) *Privileged* motions, which must not be mistaken for questions of privilege, deal with situations arising from the subject-matter of, or the debate on, the original question either in consequence or in anticipation of a vote or through the necessity of resorting to new proceedings. They must be given the right of way when proposed during a debate. They are divided into amendments and superseding motions.

(a) *Amendments* are discussed in detail later in this chapter.

(b) *Superseding* motions, though independent in form, are moved in the course of debate on questions which they seek to set aside. They may only be moved when a question is under debate, and cannot be moved by a Member rising on a point of order. *Journals,* December 30, 1971, p. 1014. Superseding motions cannot be applied to one another; for example, if a motion to postpone consideration of the original question is moved, a motion to read the Orders of the Day or for the previous question cannot be moved to suppress that motion. Superseding motions are divided into two classes; namely, the previous question and dilatory motions.

(i) *The Previous Question* is discussed in detail later in this chapter.

(ii) *Dilatory* motions are designed to dispose of the original question either for the time being or permanently. They are usually of the following type:

"That consideration of the question be postponed to .... (date)".

"That the Orders of the Day be read."

"That the House proceed to (name another Order)".

"That the House proceed to the next business."

"That the debate be now adjourned."

"That the House do now adjourn."

Adjournment motions are in this class because they may sometimes be used to stop a debate which will never be resumed. However, when a Government Order is under debate, a motion "That the Orders of the Day be now read" is a nullity as the House has already reached that stage of its proceedings. *Journals,* June 29, 1971, p. 759.

(3) *Incidental* motions are those which arise out of, and are connected with, other motions to which they relate as, for instance, motions for reading Papers immediately after they have been laid on the Table, to withdraw a

motion or an amendment, or for obtaining unanimous consent to dispense
with a rule, for the time being, in order to expedite business.

(4) *Subsidiary* motions are used to move questions forward in different
stages of procedure through which they must pass before their final adoption.
Motions for the readings of bills are in this class.

NOTICES OF MOTIONS

§418.   It is a long established practice that there can be more than one notice
on the same subject appearing on the *Order Paper. Journals,* September 14,
1973, p. 555.

§419.   (1) A notice of motion by a private Member for the appointment of a
committee to prepare and bring in a bill may be considered only under Private
Members business and not under Routine Proceedings on the *Order Paper.
Journals,* November 10, 1969, p. 73.

(2) In debate on a private Member's motion it is not in order to move
that the subject-matter be referred to a Committee, as this is not an
amendment but a new motion which would require notice. *Journals,*
November 5, 1971, p. 912.

§420.   A debate on a motion effectively blocks debate on another notice of
motion when both deal with essentially the same subject matter. *Journals,*
July 7, 1969, p. 1316.

§421.   Motions for concurrence in committee reports are placed under
Motions on the *Order Paper.*

§422.   When the Government introduces notices of motions they are placed
under Government Notices of Motions on the *Order Paper.* When called by
the Speaker during Routine Proceedings, they are transferred by virtue of
S.O. 21(2) for consideration under Government Orders.

MOTIONS

§423.   A motion should be neither argumentative, nor in the style of a
speech, nor contain unnecessary provisions or objectionable words. It is
usually expressed in the affirmative, even where its purpose and effect are
negative.

§424.   (1) When a Member hands a motion to the Speaker after having
spoken in support of it, the Speaker may, before putting the question to the
House, make such corrections as are necessary or advisable in order that it
should conform with the usages of the House. *Journals,* April 28, 1924, pp.
186-8.

(2) A motion is not irregular on account of its vagueness. *Journals,* March 31, 1870, p. 127.

(3) It is the Speaker's duty to call the attention of the mover and of the House to the irregularity of a motion; whereupon the motion is usually withdrawn or so modified as to be no longer objectionable. If the motion is of such a nature that objection cannot be removed, the Speaker may refuse to put the motion to the House. He treats it as a nullity.

(4) The Speaker has the unquestioned authority to modify motions with respect to form. *Journals,* April 28, 1924, p. 186.

(5) Any irregularity of any portion of a motion shall render the whole motion irregular. *Journals,* May 31, 1954, p. 674.

(6) If a motion is not objectionable it is the right of the mover to have his motion proposed in the very words in which it is made.

(7) A motion dealing with the same subject-matter as a bill, standing on the *Order Paper* for second reading, cannot be considered. *Journals,* May 31, 1923, p. 420.

(8) If a private Member neglects or declines to proceed with his motion, the House cannot force him to do so; however, he has the right to allow it to be dropped from the *Order Paper.* In addition, the motion may be dropped from the *Order Paper* under the terms of S.O. 49.

AMENDMENTS

§425. The object of an amendment may be either to modify a question in such a way as to increase its acceptability or to present to the House a different proposition as an alternative to the original which must, however, be relevant to the subject of the questions. Sir Erskine May, Treatise on the Law, Privilege, Proceedings and Usage of Parliament (19th ed., 1976), p. 387.

§426. It is an imperative rule that every amendment must be relevant to the question on which the amendment is proposed. Every amendment proposed to be made, either to a question or to a proposed amendment, should be so framed that, if agreed to by the House, the question or amendment as amended would be intelligible and consistent with itself. May, pp. 388-9.

§427. After a decision has been made on an amendment to any part of a question, an earlier part of the question cannot be amended. In like manner, when an amendment to any part of a question has been proposed from the Chair, an earlier part of the question cannot be amended unless the proposed amendment is rejected or withdrawn. May, p. 390.

§428. (1) A motion may be amended by: (a) leaving out certain words; (b) leaving out certain words in order to insert other words; (c) inserting or adding other words.

(2) When an amendment is irregular in one particular, the whole of it is

not admissible and must be ruled out of order. *Journals,* April 29, 1970, p. 732.

Form and Content of Amendments

Admissible Amendments

§429. An amendment cannot be ruled out because of its vagueness. *Journals,* March 30, 1870, p. 124-6.

§430. An amendment already negatived may be put a second time if it contains additional particulars.

§431. An amendment to alter the main question, by substituting a proposition with the opposite conclusion, is not an expanded negative and may be moved. *Journals,* June 6, 1923, p. 437.

Inadmissible Amendments

§432. An amendment which is substantially the same as one moved on the Address in Reply to the Speech from the Throne is not in order because an amendment must not raise a question substantially identical with one on which the House has given a decision in the same session. *Journals,* February 13, 1913, p. 247.

§433. (1) No amendment is allowed to the motion "that the House do now proceed to the Orders of the Day". *Journals,* May 8, 1873, p. 300.

(2) It is not in order to move as an amendment to another question a motion which is on the *Order Paper* as a notice of motion. *Journals,* April 1, 1889, p. 214.

§434. (1) An amendment proposing that a motion be considered "this day six months" is out of order, as the six months hoist only applies to "readings" or other proceedings which take place on an appointed date. It has no application to motions for direct adoption. *Debates,* March 20, 1924, p. 519.

(2) In similar manner, reasoned amendments may only be applied against readings of bills.

§435. (1) It is not an amendment to a motion to move that the question go to a committee. *Journals,* March 22, 1926, p. 171.

(2) On the motion to refer a contract to a committee, a Member cannot move, as an amendment, that the contract should be cancelled as this amendment is an expanded negative and, moreover, it raises a question which can only be considered on a motion after proper notice. *Journals,* February 7, 1939, p. 74.

§436. (1) An amendment proposing a direct negative, though it may be covered up by verbiage, is out of order. *Journals,* February 20, 1913, p. 277. *Journals,* October 16, 1970, p. 28.

(2) An amendment which would produce the same result as if the original motion were simply negatived is out of order. *Journals,* June 23, 1920, p. 435.

(3) An amendment approving part of a motion and disapproving the remainder is out of order. *Journals,* October 20, 1932, pp. 47-8.

§437. (1) An amendment setting forth a proposition dealing with a matter which is foreign to the proposition involved in the main motion is not relevant and cannot be moved. *Journals,* February 26, 1923, p. 122.

(2) An amendment may not raise a new question which can only be considered as a distinct motion after proper notice. *Journals,* October 16, 1970, p. 28.

SUB-AMENDMENTS

§438. (1) The purpose of a sub-amendment (an amendment to an amendment) is to alter the amendment; it should not enlarge upon the scope of the amendment but it should deal with matters that are not covered by the amendment; if it is intended to bring up matters foreign to the amendment, the Member should wait until the amendment is disposed of and move a new amendment. *Journals,* January 24, 1966, p. 43. *Journals,* July 11, 1969, p. 1334.

(2) A sub-amendment must attempt to explain the substance of the amendment and may not substitute an entirely new proposal. *Journals,* January 11, 1973, p. 28.

§439. To an amendment, when proposed from the Chair, an amendment may be moved; but only two amendments can be proposed at the same time to a question. Some limit is necessary; the usage has grown into law that an amendment to an amendment is allowable, but that no motion to amend further can be entertained until one of the two amendments is disposed of. There is no limit, however, to the number of amendments to a question provided they come within the principle.

§440. As the proposal of an amendment to an amendment originates a fresh subject for consideration, the new question thus created must, to prevent confusion, be disposed of by itself. An amendment, when undergoing alteration, is therefore treated throughout as if it were a substantive motion upon which an amendment has been moved. The original motion is accordingly laid aside; and the amendment becomes for the time a separate question to be dealt with, until its terms are settled.

Form and Content of Sub-Amendments

§441. (1) A sub-amendment cannot be moved if it proposes to leave out all the words of the proposed amendment. In such a case the first amendment must be negatived. *Journals,* March 8, 1937, p. 208. *Journals,* November 29, 1944, p. 934. *Journals,* March 14, 1947, p. 198.

(2) A sub-amendment must be relevant to the amendment it purports to amend and not to the main motion. *Journals,* January 18, 1973, p. 49.

(3) A sub-amendment which proposes an alternative to the original amendment is in order provided it is relevant to the question. *Journals,* June 23, 24, 1926, pp. 465, 468.

(4) When the House has negatived a sub-amendment to strike out certain other words in a proposed amendment, it is in order to move another sub-amendment to insert other words than those offered in the original sub-amendment. *Debates,* June 19, 1925, p. 4554.

MEMBER AMENDING HIS OWN MOTION

§442. (1) A Member, having proposed an amendment, and subsequently desiring to amend the same can do so only if the House allows his original amendment to be withdrawn, at which time he may then propose a new amendment. *Debates,* February 20, 1935, p. 1033.

(2) The rule that no Member may amend his own motion is often relaxed for the benefit of a Minister of the Crown.

WITHDRAWAL OF MOTIONS AND AMENDMENTS

§443. (1) The Member who has proposed a motion may withdraw it only with the unanimous consent of the House.

(2) An amendment may be withdrawn with the unanimous consent of the House, but neither a motion nor an amendment can be withdrawn in the absence of the Member who moved it.

§444. Where an amendment has been proposed to a question, the original motion cannot be withdrawn until the amendment has been first disposed of by being agreed to, withdrawn or negatived, as the question on the amendment stands before the original motion. May, p. 376.

§445. In asking leave to withdraw a motion, a Member is not entitled to make a speech.

§446. A Member who has been given leave to withdraw an amendment may move it again at a later date. *Journals,* April 7, 1941, p. 260.

§447. Occasionally a motion or amendment is, by leave, withdrawn, and another motion or amendment substituted, in order to meet the views of the House as expressed in debate; but that course can only be taken with the consent of the House.

ORDER OF PROCEEDING IN PUTTING THE QUESTION

§448. When a motion, an amendment and an amendment to the amendment have been proposed, the Speaker will first take the sense of the House on the last by saying: "Is it the pleasure of the House to adopt the amendment to the amendment?" After this has been disposed of, another may be moved as soon as the Speaker has proposed the question: "Is it the pleasure of the House to adopt the amendment (or the amendment as amended) to the main motion?" After this has been disposed of, the Speaker will propose: "Is it the pleasure of the House to adopt the motion (or the motion as amended)?" Then a Member may move another amendment.

RESCINDING RESOLUTIONS

§449. (1) A resolution may be rescinded and an order of the House discharged, notwithstanding the rule that a question, being once made and carried in the affirmative or negative, cannot be questioned again, but must stand as a judgment of the House.

(2) Technically indeed, the rescinding of a vote is the matter of a new question; the form being to read the resolution of the House and to move that it be rescinded; and thus the same question which had been resolved in the affirmative is not again offered, although its effect is annulled. May, p. 384.

§450. (1) To rescind a negative vote, except on the different stages of bills, is a proceeding of greater difficulty because the same question would have to be offered again. The only means, therefore, by which a negative vote can be revoked is by proposing another question similar in its general purport to that which has been rejected but with sufficient variance to constitute a new question; the House would determine whether it were substantially the same question or not.

(2) Upon a motion which practically rescinded a resolution of the House, reference is permitted to the debate upon that resolution.

§451. Sometimes the House may not be prepared to rescind a resolution, but may be willing to modify its judgment by considering and agreeing to another resolution relating to the same subject.

THE PREVIOUS QUESTION

§452. (1) The previous question is moved when the original question is under debate in order to force a direct vote on it, thereby preventing any amendments to the original question to be proposed. The form of the motion is "That the question be now put." Once it is proposed, the debate may continue on the original question. Bourinot, p. 327.

(2) If the previous question be carried, the Speaker will immediately put

the question without further debate. But, if the previous question is resolved in the negative, then the Speaker cannot put the main motion, which is consequently superseded, but which, however, may be revived on a future day, as the negative of the previous question merely binds the Speaker not to put the main question at that time. Bourinot, p. 326.

(3) The previous question may be moved by a Member who does not want it to carry; his object being to prevent the Speaker from putting the original question.

§453. (1) Members who have spoken to the main motion or amendments may speak again to the previous question.

(2) The debate on the previous question is subject to closure. *Journals,* March 2, 1926, p. 123.

§454. The Members proposing and seconding the previous question generally vote in its favour, but there is no rule to prevent them voting against their own motion if their intention is to supersede the question. Bourinot, p. 327.

§455. No amendment can be proposed to the previous question.

§456. The previous question cannot be moved upon a motion relating to the transaction of public business or to sittings of the House. May, p. 379.

§457. A motion for the previous question is not admitted in a Committee of the Whole or in any committee of the House. Bourinot, p. 328.

§458. The motion for the previous question may be interrupted by a motion to adjourn or for the reading of the Orders of the Day. But such a motion cannot be made if the House resolves that the question shall now be put under this rule. It is also in order to move the adjournment of the debate on the previous question, but not if the House decides that the question be put. Bourinot, pp. 327-8.

§459. The previous question has been moved upon the various stages of a bill, but it cannot be moved upon an amendment; however, after the amendment has been adopted, the previous question can be put on the main question as amended. May, p. 379.

§460. When the previous question is moved on the third reading of a bill and voted in the negative, the main motion must be dropped, as the reading of a bill cannot be placed on the *Order Paper* unless a day has been appointed therefor by the House. The bill is not lost by this procedure but may be taken up again at a later date. The decision of the House is only that the question be not now put. Another day may be appointed for its consideration.

12

Committee of the Whole House

12

Committee of the Whole House

COMMITTEE OF THE WHOLE HOUSE

§461. The function of a Committee of the Whole House is deliberation, not enquiry. All matters concerning the imposition of taxes must be considered in a Committee of the Whole and any other questions which, in the opinion of the House, may be more fitly discussed in this Committee, are dealt with in a Committee of the Whole. The provisions of public bills are considered, from time to time, in a Committee of the Whole House. The proceedings of a Committee of the Whole are recorded verbatim in the *Debates* but not in the *Votes and Proceedings*.

Appointment

§462. (1) A Committee of the Whole is, in fact, the membership of the House itself presided over by a Chairman instead of by the Speaker. Whenever an Order of the Day is read for the House to go into a Committee of the Whole, the Speaker is directed by S.O. 54 to leave the Chair without putting any question.

(2) The chief accompanying circumstances in the passage from the House to Committee of the Whole are:

(a) The Presiding Officer is changed. In place of the Speaker, the Chairman of Committees presides, sitting in the Clerk's chair at the Table. The Speaker's Chair remains empty.

(b) The Mace is placed on the rack at the lower end of the Table.

(c) A Clerk Assistant becomes the Clerk of the Committee of the Whole.

(3) Whenever the Chairman, from illness or other cause, finds it necessary to leave the Committee, he may call upon the Deputy Chairman or Assistant Deputy Chairman to preside for the remainder of the sitting. However, if neither of these Members is present, the Chairman (or the

Speaker before he leaves the Chair) may call upon any other Member of the House to preside over a Committee of the Whole.

(4) The quorum in a Committee of the Whole is the same as that of the House, namely, twenty.

PROCEEDINGS ON PUBLIC BILLS

§463. The Standing Orders and precedents setting forth the procedure to be followed in a Committee of the Whole on public bills are detailed in Chapter 17 (Proceedings on Public Bills).

Motion to Report Progress

§464. A Committee of the Whole House has no power either to adjourn its own sittings or to adjourn its consideration of any matter to a future sitting. If its consideration of a matter is not concluded, or if all the matters referred to it have not been considered, the Chairman is directed to report progress and ask leave to sit again. Sir Erskine May, Treatise on the Law, Privilege, Proceedings and Usage of Parliament (19th ed., 1976), p. 608.

§465. (1) If a Member wishes to supersede a question, he will move "That the Chairman do now leave the Chair", and if this motion, which is not debatable, is resolved in the affirmative, the Chairman will at once leave the Chair, and with no report having been made to the House, the bill or question disappears from the *Order Paper*.

(2) Two motions to report progress cannot immediately follow one another; some intermediate proceedings must occur after the putting of the first motion to report progress.

§466. If a Committee of the Whole has agreed to certain clauses of a bill, but is unable to conclude the discussion of other clauses, it is customary to direct the Chairman to report the former and to seek leave to sit again.

§467. (1) When the public bill before a Committee of the Whole has been agreed to, the Chairman asks: "Shall I report the bill?" If no one objects he takes it for granted that he is ordered to make a report to the House. He therefore leaves the Chair, without question put, and reports the bill with or without amendments.

(2) Until such a report has been made, the House cannot refer to the bill or to the proceedings of a Committee of the Whole.

INTERRUPTIONS

§468. A message from the Governor General, or his representative, summoning the House to attend him in the Senate will require a Committee of the Whole to rise and the Speaker to resume the Chair immediately.

§469. When an outbreak of disorder occurs in a Committee of the Whole, the Speaker may take the Chair immediately, without awaiting the ordinary forms.

§470. If any occasion of public business arises in which the House is concerned, the Speaker resumes the Chair, at once, without receiving any report from the Committee of the Whole. When the incident which has occasioned the interruption of the sitting has been dealt with, the House forthwith resolves itself again into a Committee of the Whole.

ORDER AND DECORUM

§471. (1) The Chairman maintains order in the Committee of the Whole, deciding all questions of order subject to an appeal to the Speaker. No debate is permitted on any decision.

(2) In cases of an appeal to the Speaker, it is the duty of the Chairman to leave the Chair immediately and report the point of order which he has decided. The Speaker must then rule upon the matter. No discussion is allowed on the appeal. Should the Speaker be absent, the Chairman takes the Chair of the House and another Member makes the report of appeal to the acting Speaker who will at once rule upon the question.

(3) If a Member wishes at any time to call in question the conduct of the Chairman in the execution of his duties, his proper course is to give notice of a motion to that effect. Sir John Bourinot, Parliamentary Procedure and Practice in the Dominion of Canada (4th ed., 1916), p. 397.

DIVISIONS

§472. (1) When a division is taken in a Committee of the Whole, the Members rise and are counted by the Clerk Assistant, who will then declare the numbers voting for or against the question.

(2) The names of the Members voting are not recorded nor are the bells rung.

(3) As in the House during a recorded division, no Member may enter the Committee of the Whole while a division is in progress. *Debates,* April 17, 1962, p. 3080.

(4) Members are not required to be at their allocated desks during a division.

(5) In the event of a tie, the Chairman has a casting vote and, in giving it, he is governed by the same rules as the Speaker under similar conditions.

ROLE OF THE SPEAKER

§473. Although the Speaker is restrained by usage while he is in the Chair in the exercise of his independent judgment, he is not precluded by the Standing

Orders from speaking or voting in a Committee of the Whole. Under modern practice, however, he has generally abstained from the exercise of this right.

§474.   Since 1974, the Speaker has defended the Budgetary Estimates of the House of Commons when they are studied by the appropriate Committee.

13

Business of Supply and Ways and Means

13

Business of Supply and Ways and Means

The Business of Supply — Allotted Days — Estimates — Presentation — Purpose — Form of Estimates — Contents of the Estimates — Supplementary Estimates — Interim Supply — Procedure in Committee — Amendments in Committee — Committee Reports on Estimates — Procedure on Last Allotted Day — Notices of Objections — The Appropriation Bill — Business of Ways and Means — Ways and Means Motions — Relation of Bills to the Ways and Means Resolution — Second Reading Stage of Ways and Means Bills — Committee Stage of Ways and Means Bills — Provisions for Reducing Existing Charges — Increase in Charges and Classes — Amendments to Schedules — Report Stage of Ways and Means Bills — Third Reading Stage of Ways and Means Bills.

THE BUSINESS OF SUPPLY

§475.   The Business of Supply consists of the consideration of main, or supplementary Estimates, including motions to restore or reinstate any item in the Estimates, interim Supply, the passage at all stages of any bill based thereon, and opposition motions considered on allotted days.

§476.   The action taken by the House of Commons, upon the request for aids and supply for the Public Service made in the Speech from the Throne, is for the appointment, pursuant to S.O. 58(1), of a continuing Order of the Day for the consideration of the business of Supply.

§477.   The Estimates of a department or agency of the Government are referred to and considered in the various standing committees, where the Members have an opportunity to agree to, negative, withdraw, reduce or supersede each Vote of the Estimates.

ALLOTTED DAYS

§478.   (1) Under the terms of S.O. 58(5), twenty-five days are allotted to the business of Supply in each year. Although technically the business under discussion is government business, motions given precedence on these allotted days may be moved only by Members in opposition to the Government. To this extent, there is a distinction between the business of supply and other government business with respect to S.O. 18.

(2) For the purpose of Supply, the parliamentary session is divided into three periods ending on December 10, March 26 and June 30 respectively. During each of these periods, not more than two opposition motions, which are considered votes of "no-confidence" in the Government, may come to a division. *Journals,* December 6, 1968, p. 430.

(3) When any day or days allotted to the Address Debate or to the Budget Debate are not used for those debates, such day or days may be added to the number of allotted days in the period in which they occur. S.O. 58(6).

§479. (1) The choice of subjects to be raised on allotted days rests with the Opposition; hence, the interchangeable terminology "allotted" or "opposition" day.

(2) The Opposition prerogative is very broad in the use of the allotted day and ought not to be interfered with except on the clearest and most certain procedural grounds. *Journals,* November 14, 1975, pp. 861-2.

§480. On an Opposition Day, when a no-confidence motion may be proposed on a subject to be chosen by the mover, the Speaker should not intervene to prevent debate unless the motion is clearly and undoubtedly irregular. When the procedural aspect is open to reasonable argument, it is the duty of the Speaker to accept the motion and to allow the House to make a decision on the question of confidence. *Journals,* March 6, 1973, pp. 165-7.

§481. The similarity of the subject-matter of an Opposition motion can not prejudice in any way the progress of a bill under discussion which deals with approximately the same matter. *Journals,* November 14, 1975, p. 861.

§482. On an allotted day, during consideration of the business of Supply, an amendment must not provide the basis for an entirely different debate than that proposed in the original motion. *Journals,* March 16, 1971, p. 416. *Journals,* June 1, 1972, p. 348.

ESTIMATES

Presentation

§483. (1) The Estimates for the year are tabled by the President of the Treasury Board submitting them to the House with a message from the Governor General. This message is read by the Speaker as the Members of the House of Commons stand in their places. The Minister may move either then or at a later day that the Estimates be referred to the various standing committees.

(2) In accordance with S.O. 58(14), in every session the main Estimates to cover the incoming fiscal year for every department of government shall be referred to standing committees on or before March 1 of the then expiring fiscal year. Each such committee shall consider and shall report, or shall be

deemed to have reported, the same back to the House not later than May 31 in the then current fiscal year.

Purpose

§484. The purpose of the Estimates is to present to Parliament the budgetary and non-budgetary expenditure proposals of the Government for the next fiscal year. These Estimates include Votes, which Parliament is asked to approve through Appropriation Acts, as well as other items called statutory items, for which the required expenditures have already been approved through existing legislation and are included only for information purposes. The proposals with respect to items which the House may vote upon are conveyed formally in these Estimates in the wording and amount of the Votes which, when included in Appropriation Acts, become the governing conditions under which the expenditures may be made.

Form of Estimates

§485. (1) Items in the Estimates which are clearly intended to amend existing legislation should come to the House by way of an amending bill rather than as an item in the Estimates. *Journals,* December 10, 1973, p. 737. *Journals,* December 7, 1977, pp. 184-6.

(2) As a result of a motion adopted by the Standing Committee on Miscellaneous Estimates on March 20, 1973, the Treasury Board submits to each committee detailed explanations for One Dollar Votes listed in the Estimates.

§486. If a Vote in the Estimates relates to a bill not yet passed by Parliament, then the authorizing bill must become law before the authorization of the relevant Vote in the Estimates by an Appropriation Act. *Journals,* January 25, 1973, p. 68. *Journals,* February 5, 1973, pp. 94-5.

Contents of the Estimates

§487. (1) The Estimates are limited to setting out only the sums which it is calculated will be required in the current year, and do not show the value of assets held or the liabilities outstanding from the previous financial year or to be spread over future years.

(2) The principle underlying the classification of Estimates is that each class of Estimates is designed to correspond to a separate programme; as far as possible, connected services appear together and all the Estimates for the services controlled by a particular department are mainly grouped in the same class.

(3) Each class is divided into a number of Votes, on which the standing committees of the House may decide separately. Votes are units of appropriation and are usually drawn up on a departmental basis.

SUPPLEMENTARY ESTIMATES

§488. Supplementary Estimates may be presented either:

(1) for a further grant to an existing service, in addition to the sum already appropriated,

(2) for a new expenditure on behalf of a newly-enacted statute,

(3) to meet the cost created by an unexpected emergency,

(4) to transfer funds from one Vote to another, or;

(5) to extend the purposes of a Vote.

INTERIM SUPPLY

§489. Interim Supply provides the Government with money to meet its obligations during the time before the main Estimates are approved. Interim Supply is normally requested in the first supply period for the first three months of the new fiscal year for all departments of government. In addition, Interim Supply is requested for other items in the Estimates depending upon the need in each case. The main Estimates and the bill based thereon are not disposed of until the last allotted day for the Supply period ending June 30.

§490. (1) The motion to concur in Interim Supply is expressed in twelfths of the total Estimate for the year, depending upon the number of months for which Interim Supply is needed.

(2) Interim Supply is usually granted on the last day of the Supply period ending on March 26.

PROCEDURE IN COMMITTEE

§491. The procedure to be followed by the standing committees while studying the Estimates follows the ordinary usage of a standing committee. No amendments can be moved which are not relevant to the Vote under consideration. The Votes should be considered in the order in which they stand; but any Vote may be passed over and not moved. Once it is moved, a motion to postpone it cannot be entertained. Each resolution for a Vote forms a distinct motion which can only be dealt with by being agreed to, reduced, negatived, superseded or withdrawn. The committee may reduce the amount of a Vote by the omission or reduction of the items of expenditure of which the Vote is composed. Here the power of the committee ceases. Sir Erskine May, Treatise of the Law, Privilege, Proceedings and Usage of Parliament (19th ed., 1976), p. 735.

§492. It is not allowable to attach a condition or an expression of opinion to a Vote or to change the destination of a grant. Sir John Bourinot, Parliamentary Procedure and Practice in the Dominion of Canada (4th ed., 1916), p. 428.

§493. A proposed motion may be allowed to stand over until another occasion by a majority decision of the committee.

§494. The whole management of a department may be discussed in a general way when the committee is considering the first item of the Estimates of that department, which reads as follows: "Vote 1 — Administration"; but the discussion must not be extended to any particular item mentioned in the Estimates of that department. If, however, the words "General Administration" cover all the expenses to be incurred during the year by that department, it is relevant to discuss every phase of the department totally or in detail.

§495. The conduct of any employee of the Government, insofar as his behaviour outside of office hours is concerned, cannot be inquired into by a Member of the House, unless that employee is alleged to have done or published something prejudicial to the public interest. If that be the case, it is competent for the House to secure all the details. *Debates,* May 20, 1918, p. 2279.

Amendments in Committee

§496. When two or more amendments upon the same Vote are proposed at the same time to the committee, the Chairman puts first the amendment which proposes the largest reduction, and then, if that is not accepted, the lesser amendments; still, as reductions are moved upon a Vote independently the one of the other, a succession of reductions may be moved alternating between larger or smaller amounts, as may seem expedient to the movers, subject to the authority of the Chairman, who may intervene to determine the most convenient order in taking the amendments offered. May, p. 737.

§497. (1) Amendments moved for the reduction of a Vote are proceeded with under the general rules governing amendments. A proposal to reduce an Estimate is expressed in the form, "That (the Estimate) be reduced by ($)". The amendment takes the form of the original motion offering, in lieu of the sum thereby proposed, a reduced sum for the acceptance of the committee.

(2) Rejection of the amendment leaves room for the proposal, without limit, of amendments in the same form and of ever-varying amounts.

(3) The reduction must be of a substantial and not trifling amount.

§498. Statutory items which are included in the Estimates for informational purpose may be amended only by the introduction of amending legislation.

§499. (1) A committee may not go beyond the bounds of the Royal Recommendation by substituting a financial provision in a Vote of the Estimates for one that has been recommended by His Excellency. *Journals,* March 24, 1970, p. 636.

(2) Amendments proposing to substitute a loan for a subsidy; to change

the destination, purpose and conditions of a subsidy; attaching a condition to a subsidy; affecting the ends and provisions of a subsidy, can be moved only by a Minister of the Crown with the recommendation of the Governor General. *Journals,* June 3-4, 1913, pp. 763-5. *Journals,* June 1, 1921, p. 420-1.

Committee Reports on Estimates

§500. (1) The report of a committee both in its form and as to its substance ought to correspond with the authority with which it was invested. *Journals,* June 18, 1973, p. 419.

(2) A motion to move concurrence in a committee report on Estimates may be moved only on an allotted day. *Journals,* December 6, 1973, p. 726.

PROCEDURE ON LAST ALLOTTED DAY

§501. When the last allotted day in a Supply period has been designated by a Minister of the Crown, notice is given by the President of the Treasury Board of a motion or motions to concur in the Estimates. He may also give notice of a motion to reinstate any Votes of the Estimates that may have been reduced, negatived, superseded or withdrawn at any earlier stage of the Supply proceedings.

§502. (1) The procedure for the consideration of Supply is identical whether on an Opposition day or on a Government day under S.O. 58(18). *Journals,* February 7, 1973, pp. 102-3.

(2) On an allotted day, the business of Supply has precedence over all other government business. If a Member does not proceed with his motion, the House will proceed to the next supply motion and, failing that, to other government business. S.O. 58(8), S.O. 58(12).

§503. It is not possible to debate or amend motions once the guillotine rule has been applied under the terms of S.O. 58(10).

Notices of Objections

§504. (1) Forty-eight hours' written notice shall be given of motions to concur in Supply, to restore or reinstate any items in the Estimates. Twenty-four hours' written notice shall be given of a notice to oppose any item in the Estimates. Members may give notice to oppose any Vote or part of a Vote in the Estimates, less any amounts already voted in the Interim Appropriation Act, if applicable.

(2) Whenever a notice of objection appears on the *Notice Paper,* concurrence in that particular Vote is separated from the general motion to concur in the Estimates given previously by the President of the Treasury Board, to allow a specific decision by the House on that item. *Journals,* December 10, 1973, p. 735.

§505. Once the notice of objection is given, the Vote of the Estimates relating to that notice is put in the form of a motion to the House, at which time Members have the right to vote for or against it. *Journals,* June 22, 1972, p. 402.

§506. When a notice of objection to part of a Vote in the Estimates is given, the House proceeds to decide for or against the whole Vote and not just that part objected to. *Journals,* June 26, 1973, pp. 435-6.

§507. A notice of objection to an item in the Estimates is not a question to which the House may address itself. To enable a decision to be taken, the Estimate objected to is separated from the remainder and is put as a distinct question. *Journals,* March 24, 1976, p. 1144.

§508. A notice of objection under S.O. 58(4) should not include argument and should not attempt indirectly to reduce a Vote in the Estimates which is not actually before the House. *Journals,* December 10, 1973, pp. 735-6.

THE APPROPRIATION BILL

§509. (1) The concurrence by the House of the Estimates is an Order of the House to bring in a bill, known as the Appropriation Bill, based thereon.

(2) Because of the guillotine procedure involved in passing the Appropriation Bill, the House has agreed to a departure from its regular practice by distributing copies of the proposed Appropriation Bill to all Members in advance of its actual consideration. *Debates,* June 23, 1977, p. 6994.

§510. There is a historical justification for including in a supply bill based upon the main Estimates, and even one based upon Interim supply, a clause which relates to the borrowing power of the Government. An Appropriation Bill based upon supplementary Estimates, however, may not include a clause which gives the Government power to borrow money. *Journals,* December 9, 1975, p. 924.

§511. Since 1968, some Appropriation Bills have been debated at the second reading stage and in a Committee of the Whole. *Debates,* February 13-16, 19, 20, 1973. *Debates,* October 24, 25, 1974. *Debates,* March 24, 1977.

§512. After receiving its three readings, the Appropriation Bill is sent to the Senate. Following its passage there, it is given Royal Assent, as in the case of all legislation.

§513. Upon returning to the House following Royal Assent to an Appropriation Bill, the Speaker informs the House that he had addressed the

Honourable the Deputy of His Excellency the Governor General as follows:

"MAY IT PLEASE YOUR HONOUR:

"The Commons of Canada have voted Supplies required to enable the Government to defray certain expenses of the public service.

"In the name of the Commons I present to Your Honour the following Bill:

"'An Act for granting to Her Majesty certain sums of money for the public service for the financial year ending the 31st March, 19 ...'

"To which Bill I humbly request Your Honour's Assent."

BUSINESS OF WAYS AND MEANS

§514. (1) The consideration of the financial statement made by the Minister of Finance is the most important business of Ways and Means. This statement, familiarly known as "the Budget Speech", is made when the Minister has completed his estimate of the probable income and expenditure for the financial year. In it, the Minister of Finance develops his views of the resources of the country, communicates his calculations of probable income and expenditure, and declares whether the burdens upon the people are to be increased or diminished. The economic aspect of this Budget is important and taxes are imposed for their economic effects as well as for raising revenue to meet the expenditure for the year. May, pp. 785-6.

(2) In Canada, a Budget is presented whenever the Minister of Finance moves the motion "That this House approves in general the budgetary policy of the Government".

§515. There is no necessity to have a budget presentation before the introduction of Ways and Means legislation. *Journals,* March 20, 1972, p. 202.

WAYS AND MEANS MOTIONS

§516. (1) A Ways and Means motion is a necessary preliminary to the imposition of a new tax, the continuation of an expiring tax, an increase in the rate of an existing tax, or an extension of the incidence of a tax so as to include persons not already payers.

(2) The principle that the sanction of the Crown must be given to every grant of money drawn from the public revenue, applies equally to the taxation levied to provide that revenue. No motion can therefore be made to impose a tax, save by a Minister of the Crown, unless such tax be in substitution, by way of equivalent, for taxation at that moment submitted to the consideration of Parliament; nor can the amount of a tax proposed on behalf of the Crown be augmented, nor any alteration made in the area of imposition. In like manner, no increase can be considered either of an existing, or of a new or temporary tax for the service of the year, except on the initiative of a Minister,

acting on behalf of the Crown; nor can a Member other than a Minister move for the introduction of a bill framed to effect a reduction of duties, which would incidentally effect the increase of an existing duty, or the imposition of a new tax, although the aggregate amount of imposition would be diminished by the provisions of the bill.

§517. (1) The Minister of Finance will generally table Ways and Means motions relating to the changes announced in the Budget either on Budget night or shortly thereafter.

(2) A Minister of the Crown designates a day for consideration of the Ways and Means motion under the terms of S.O. 60(2).

(3) On the designated day, the Ways and Means motion is decided upon without debate or amendment. If the motion is adopted by the House (it then becomes known as a Ways and Means Resolution), then a bill is introduced based upon the provisions of any such resolution, given first reading, printed and ordered for second reading and referral to a Committee of the Whole at the next sitting of the House. S.O. 74(3).

(4) The authority of the Speaker in respect to dividing questions is extremely limited and has never been exercised in relation to a Ways and Means notice. *Journals,* December 13, 1973, pp. 746-7.

RELATION OF BILLS
TO WAYS AND MEANS RESOLUTIONS

§518. (1) A bill, related to a Ways and Means resolution, must be based on, but need not be identical with, the resolution. The taxing power of the Crown is limited by such resolutions, but relatively minor widening of exemptions from taxation may be allowed. *Journals,* December 18, 1974, p. 224.

(2) The most desirable practice is for the bill to adhere strictly to the provisions of the resolution, and departures if any, ought to be subject to the strictest interpretation. *Journals,* July 14, 1975, p. 707. *Journals,* May 19, 1978, pp. 784-786.

§519. If any of the provisions of the bill should be found to go beyond the Ways and Means resolutions as agreed to by the House:

(a) a further motion must be passed by the House before those provisions in the bill are considered in committee;

(b) or the bill must be amended so as to conform to the motions to which the House has agreed. *Journals,* December 18, 1974, p. 224. *Journals,* July 14, 1975, p. 706. *Journals,* May 19, 1978, pp. 784-786.

SECOND READING STAGE
OF WAYS AND MEANS BILLS

§520. Debate and amendment on the second reading of bills based upon

Ways and Means resolutions are governed by the ordinary rules of relevancy and usage applicable to bills generally.

§521. Bills related to Ways and Means resolutions are referred to a Committee of the Whole House.

COMMITTEE STAGE
OF WAYS AND MEANS BILLS

§522. Amendments in committee on bills introduced upon Ways and Means resolutions are governed by the ordinary rules applicable to bills generally. May, p. 792.

§523. Amendments must not exceed the scope, increase the amount or extend the incidence of any charge upon the public, defined by the terms of the Ways and Means resolutions, by which the provisions proposed to be amended are authorized. May, p. 793.

§524. The motion by which a tax is proposed in the House is now treated as an effective expression of the financial initiative of the Crown, and therefore, as the standard in relation to which the admissibility of amendments is determined. Accordingly, an amendment is debarred, not only from increasing the rate of a tax, but also from extending its incidence to new classes, even while proposing to relieve other classes of payers. May, p. 716.

§525. The committee is not bound by the terms of the provisions which the Ministers have inserted in the bill; and, when no amount has been mentioned in the resolution, any Member may propose to increase the grants specified in the bill or to extend the application of the provisions of the bill, whatever may be the cost resulting therefrom, so long as the power conferred by the Royal Recommendation is not exceeded.

Provisions for Reducing Existing Charges

§526. Reductions can be made in committee on the bill, but no grant can be increased except upon recommendation of the Crown.

§527. So long as an existing tax is not increased, any modification of the proposed reduction may be introduced in the committee on the bill, and is regarded as a question not for increasing the charge upon the people but for determining to what extent such charge shall be reduced.

§528. In the past, amendments have been allowed proposing to substitute another tax of equivalent amount for the tax embodied in a resolution moved by the Government. In admitting such an amendment it was no doubt felt that the financial initiative of the Crown was not infringed since the amount of

Ways and Means, designed to be yielded by the tax, had been demanded on behalf of the Crown, and this amount the amendment did not propose to increase. According to modern practice such an amendment is out of order. Even if the exact equivalence of the amount of the yield could be guaranteed (which is manifestly impossible), the objection, that the incidence of the tax proposed would be extended to persons previously exempt, would be fatal to such an amendment. May, p. 785.

§529. When a tax is imposed in a bill, subject to alleviations of any kind which were not expressed in the Ways and Means resolution authorizing the tax, or for a shorter period than the period (if any) specified in that motion, amendments are in order in committee on the bill to omit the alleviation or extend the period up to the limit laid down by the resolution. May, p. 793.

Increase in Charges and Classes

§530. No augmentation of a tax or duty asked by the Crown can be proposed to the committee, nor tax imposed, save upon the motion of a Minister of the Crown; nor would an amendment to extend the imposition of a tax to persons enjoying an exemption therefrom be now permitted.

§531. When the Ways and Means bill imposing a tax is in a Committee of the Whole, an amendment to the effect that certain taxpayers be paid a rebate on a tax and that in lieu thereof the general tax be increased, is out of order on the ground that it involves an increase of taxation which should be moved by a Minister of the Crown. *Debates,* May 22, 1941, p. 3048.

§532. A motion for the imposition of an import duty has been ruled out of order because such a proposition should emanate from the Government. *Journals,* June 14, 1869, p. 242.

§533. (1) A private Member may move that certain specified taxes be readjusted and that the scope of tax exemptions be enlarged. *Journals,* April 28, 1924, pp. 186-8. It is in order to move an abstract proposition respecting the revision of the tariff. *Journals,* February 18, 1976, p. 69.

(2) An amendment to enlarge a class of articles on which duties are levied cannot be moved to the Tariff Act by a private Member. *Journals,* May 17, 1929, p. 425.

Amendments to Schedules

§534. When a schedule of duties has been agreed to by the House, the committee on the bill cannot increase such duties or add any articles not previously voted; but if the duties so voted are less than those payable under the existing law, it is competent for the committee on the bill to increase them provided such increases be not in excess of the existing duties. Sir Erskine

May, Treatise on The Law, Privileges, Proceedings and Usage of Parliament (13th ed., 1924), pp. 511-12.

REPORT STAGE OF WAYS AND MEANS BILLS

§535.   In accordance with S.O. 75(4), the consideration of report stage of bills from a Committee of the Whole is disposed of forthwith without amendment or debate.

§536.   An amendment agreed to in a Committee of the Whole on a bill has been ruled out of order by the Speaker, on his own initiative, when the Order was called for receiving the committee's report, because it contemplated a larger expenditure than was provided for in the original motion which had been recommended by the Governor General prior to the introduction of the bill. *Journals,* May 19, 1914, p. 505.

THIRD READING STAGE
OF WAYS AND MEANS BILLS

§537.   Debate and amendment on the third reading stage of bills based upon Ways and Means resolutions are governed by the ordinary rules of relevancy and usage applicable to bills generally.

§538.   On the third reading of a bill to authorize the levying of a tax, a private Member cannot move an amendment, even with the approval of the Government, that the bill be referred back to a Committee of the Whole with the object of having the tax increased. *Journals,* August 17, 1917, p. 567.

14

Financial Relations between the Crown and Parliament

14

Financial Relations between the Crown and Parliament

Financial Relations between the Crown and Parliament — The Royal Recommendation — Signification of Recommendation by a Minister of the Crown — Requirements for the Use of the Royal Recommendation — Conditions Respecting the Use of the Royal Recommendation — Legislation not Requiring the Royal Recommendation — Abstract Motions — Motions Emanating from Private Members — Reports Emanating from Committees — Granting of Aids and Supplies by Parliament.

FINANCIAL RELATIONS BETWEEN THE CROWN AND PARLIAMENT

§539. (1) The Parliamentary principles surrounding the financial relations between the Crown and Parliament in Canada are the same as those which are applicable in the United Kingdom.

(2) The Sovereign, being the executive power, is charged with the management of all the revenue of the State and with all payments for the public service. The Crown, therefore, acting with the advice of its responsible ministers, makes known to the Commons the pecuniary necessities of the Government; the Commons, in return, grants such aids or supplies as are required to satisfy these demands; and they provide by taxes, and by the appropriation of other sources of the public income, the ways and means to meet the supplies which they have granted. Thus the Crown demands money, the Commons grants it, and the House of Lords assents to the grants: but the Commons do not vote money unless such taxation be necessary for the Public Service, as declared by the Crown through its constitutional advisers. Sir Erskine May, Treatise on The Law, Privileges, Proceedings and Usage of Parliament (19th. ed., 1976), p. 695.

THE ROYAL RECOMMENDATION

§540. The guiding principle in determining the effect of an amendment upon the financial initiative of the Crown is that the communication, to which the Royal Recommendation is attached, must be treated as laying down *once for all* (unless withdrawn and replaced) not only the amount of the charge, but also its objects, purposes, conditions and qualifications. In relation to the standard thereby fixed, an amendment infringes the financial initiative of the Crown not only if it increases the amount but also if it extends the objects and purposes, or relaxes the conditions and qualifications expressed in the communication by which the Crown has demanded or recommended a charge. And this standard is binding not only on private Members but also on Ministers whose only advantage is that, as advisors of the Crown, they can present new or supplementary estimates or secure the Royal Recommendation to new or supplementary resolutions.

SIGNIFICATION OF RECOMMENDATION BY A MINISTER OF THE CROWN

§541. The Governor General's Recommendation is communicated to the House and is included on the *Notice Paper* with the item of parliamentary business. When required, the Royal Recommendation is printed in a bill and when that bill is given first reading, the text of the Message and Recommendation of the Governor General is printed in the *Votes and Proceedings*.

§542. No cases can be found of any private Member receiving the authority of the Crown, through a Minister, to propose a bill or motion involving either the expenditure of public money or the incidence of taxation.

REQUIREMENTS FOR THE USE OF THE ROYAL RECOMMENDATION

§543. (1) If any motion or bill or proceeding is offered to be moved, whether in the House or in a committee which requires, but fails to receive, the recommendation of the Crown, it is the duty of the Speaker to announce that no question can be proposed upon the motion, or to direct the withdrawal of the bill, or to say that the problem may be rectified by the proposer obtaining a Royal Recommendation.

(2) In like manner, after the question has been proposed on an amendment, and it has appeared that the amendment would vary the incidence of taxation or increase the charge upon the Consolidated Revenue Fund, the Speaker has declined to put the question.

§544. The principle that the sanction of the Crown must be given to every grant of money drawn for the public revenue applies equally to the taxation levied to provide that revenue.

§545. The recommendation of the Crown is needed for such measures as bills relating to the extension of time for the repayment of the deposit which has become liable to forfeiture in the case of a private bill; the release or compounding of sums due to the Crown; the repeal of an exemption from an existing duty, as the burden of the duty is thereby augmented; a proposal to repeal existing drawbacks on exports.

§546.   Under S.O. 62(1), a Royal Recommendation is required in the session in which an expenditure is proposed, but the expenditure need not be in the same fiscal year. *Journals,* June 25, 1973, p. 437.

§547.   Section 54 of the British North America Act and S.O. 62 relate only to appropriations and do not refer to the imposition of taxation. The only condition imposed on a taxation measure is that it be introduced by a Minister of the Crown. *Journals,* April 24, 1878, p. 200. *Journals,* November 20, 1969, p. 108.

§548.   Amendments to bills are out of order if they attempt to substitute an alternative scheme to that proposed with the Royal Recommendation. *Journals,* April 11, 1939, p. 325.

CONDITIONS RESPECTING THE USE OF THE ROYAL RECOMMENDATION

§549.   The Royal Recommendation is not part of a bill; therefore, its subject-matter cannot be referred to a committee. *Journals,* January 20, 1971, p. 270.

§550.   It is not necessary that all of the objectives of a bill be recited in a Royal Recommendation, but rather it is the financial charges or expenditures that must be covered in it. *Journals,* May 21, 1970, p. 837.

§551.   A private Member cannot introduce a public bill based on a Royal Recommendation previously received in respect of a government bill which has been withdrawn. *Journals,* December 7, 1970, pp. 181-2.

§552.   The previous recommendation of the Crown is not required for the introduction of a bill consolidating or amending revenue laws when the imposition of new burdens is not contemplated. *Journals,* July 8, 1908, p. 608.

§553.   A possible error in the Royal Recommendation preceding a bill should not preclude the introduction of the bill. *Journals,* December 16, 1974, pp. 212-13.

§554.   A bill from the Senate which constitutes an amendment to an Appropriation Act, by bestowing on the Governor-in-Council the right to dispose of money in a manner not authorized by the Appropriation Act, infringes the privileges of the House under S.O. 62 (1). *Journals,* November 12, 1969, p. 79.

§555.   A bill from the Senate, certain clauses of which would necessitate some public expenditure, is in order if it is provided by a clause of the said bill that no such expenditure shall be made unless previously sanctioned by Parliament. *Journals,* April 5, 1870, p. 155.

§556.   It may happen that the Royal Recommendation sanctions some expenditures without fixing the maximum amount to be spent. If, for instance, the Royal Recommendation states that adequate salaries be paid to a newly constituted body and the amounts of the salaries are fixed in the bill based on that Royal Recommendation, the committee, while studying the bill, has the right to increase those amounts because, in doing so, it does not go beyond the scope of the Royal Recommendation.

LEGISLATION NOT REQUIRING ROYAL RECOMMENDATION

§557.   A bill, which does not involve a direct expenditure but merely confers upon the government a power for the exercise of which public money will have to be voted by Parliament, is not a money bill, and no Royal Recommendation is necessary as a condition precedent to its introduction.

§558.   A bill, designed to furnish machinery for the expenditure of a certain sum of public money, to be voted subsequently by Parliament, may be introduced in the House without the recommendation of the Crown. *Journals,* January 16, 1912, pp. 118-19.

ABSTRACT MOTIONS

§559.   Motions which take the form of merely advocating public expenditure or the imposition of a charge can be entertained and agreed to by the House. Resolutions of this nature are permissible because, being only expressions of opinion by the House, no grant is made or burden imposed by their adoption. May, p. 766.

§560.   The tendency in the House of Commons has been to rule out all motions purporting to give the Government a direct order to do a thing which cannot be done without the expenditure of money.

§561.   (1) Abstract motions should use the words, "that the Government consider the advisability of. . . ." *Journals,* April 10, 1973, pp. 257-8.
   (2) When these words are used, it leaves the Government free, after considering the advisability of doing something, to come to the conclusion

that it should not do so. There would not, therefore, necessarily be an expenditure of public money involved. *Journals,* February 10, 1959, p. 104.

(3) An abstract motion does not finally bind the House to make the grant, and it imposes upon the Government the responsibility of either accepting or rejecting the recommendation.

Motions Emanating From Private Members

§562.   Private Members may introduce motions that do not directly involve the expenditure of public money and have no operative effect but simply express an abstract opinion on a matter which may necessitate a future grant. These motions merely involve an expression of opinion on the part of the House, and they do not affect the constitutional method of placing upon the Government the responsibility of initiating all legislation which has for its object the expenditure of money. *Journals,* March 16, 1921, pp. 100-1.

§563.   A motion that certain commissioners should be appointed to examine the feasibility of some public improvements and report the results of their investigations to the House is in order, as it is an abstract proposition that does not necessarily bind the House in any way. *Journals,* May 11, 1874, p. 214.

Reports Emanating From Committees

§564.   It is a long-established practice of this House that Reports coming from a committee and requiring expenditure of money include the traditional words, "that the Government give consideration to the advisability of" spending moneys. *Journals,* April 10, 1973, p. 257.

GRANTING OF AIDS AND SUPPLIES BY PARLIAMENT

§565.   The Senate may take exception if a message from the Crown for pecuniary aid is sent exclusively to the Commons. The legal right of the Senate, as a co-ordinate branch of the Legislature, to withhold their assent from any bill whatever, to which their concurrence is desired, is unquestionable. They may throw out any money bill, and their vote is irrevocable during the session.

§566.   A supply bill should be passed as a matter of course by the Senate in almost any conceivable circumstances if it contains nothing but supply. If other matters are inserted in the bill or "tacked to it", these should be struck out and be made into a separate bill or bills. Memorandum submitted to the Senate by the Honourable Senator W.B. Ross, May 15, 1918.

§567.   (1) When the House receives a Message from the Senate stating that it has amended a tax bill, the House may concur in the amendments but disapprove of any infraction of its privileges or rights by the other House. In this case, the House waives its claim to insist upon such rights and privileges, but the waiver of the said rights and privileges is not to be constituted as a precedent.

(2) This method involves more than just a question of agreement. It involves a question of the privileges of the House which have been enshrined in a rule — S.O. 63. But if the House, in its wisdom, feels that the circumstances are such that it should waive its asserted privileges it does so, in effect, by suspending S.O. 63. Therefore, unless a motion proposes to suspend S.O. 63, it would require the unanimous consent of the House to pass the amendments which are proposed. A proposed motion in effect amounts to a waiver of S.O. 63, which would require notice as Standing Orders can only be suspended by an Order of the House made on proper notice or by unanimous consent. The purport of that Standing Order is that a money bill is unalterable by the Senate and unless that Order is suspended, such Senate alterations of a money bill cannot be brought before the House for approval. *Journals*, July 14, 1959, pp. 707-9.

(3) The House may concur in amendments proposed by the Senate in whole or in part. Objections to Senate amendments have been stated directly in the motion for disposing of these amendments. *Journals*, September 2, 1958, p. 533. *Journals*, July 18, 1959, p. 750.

15

Standing, Special and Joint Committees

15

Standing, Special and Joint Committees

TYPES OF COMMITTEES

§568. (1) There are three types of committees, other than a Committee of the Whole, used in the House of Commons: the standing committee, the special committee and the joint committee.

(2) Standing committees are appointed under the Standing Orders to consider legislation and the Estimates. They may, however, be ordered to conduct such investigations or inquiries as the House may direct. These committees exist throughout a Parliament. Since 1977, some standing committees have been given permanent Orders of References.

(3) Special committees are appointed by the House to inquire into a particular subject. They cease to exist when their final report is presented to the House or upon the prorogation or dissolution of Parliament.

(4) Joint committees may be classified as either standing or special depending upon their method of establishment — by Standing Orders or by motions adopted in each House of Parliament. They are usually of an administrative or investigative nature but have, on occasion, considered legislation. *Journals,* July 15, 1975, p. 711.

GENERAL

§569. (1) Committees are regarded as creatures of the House and are governed for the most part in their proceedings by the same rules which prevail in the House with exception as to seconding of motions, limiting the number of times of speaking and the length of speeches.

(2) Committees receive their authority from the House itself and that authority of the House overrides that of any committee. *Journals,* December 1, 1964, pp. 941-7.

(3) The Speaker has ruled on many occasions that it is not competent for him to exercise procedural control over the committees. Committees are and must remain masters of their own procedure. *Journals,* December 4, 1973, pp. 709-10.

§570.   It is the duty of all committees to give to the matters referred to them due and sufficient consideration.

§571.   Proceedings in the committees are more relaxed in nature than those in the House as the requirements which must be observed in the Chamber are not so strictly enforced when Members sit as committees. *Journals,* March 26, 1971, pp. 453-4.

APPOINTMENT

§572.   The Standing Orders of the House provide for the existence of standing committees; however, a committee cannot consider its Order of Reference until its members have been appointed. *Journals,* December 7, 1953, p. 76. *Journals,* November 5, 1957, p. 82.

§573.   No amendments should be made to the motion for the appointment of a committee that would give the committee greater powers than those set out in the notice. *Journals,* May 10, 1954, p. 599. *Journals,* April 29, 1970, p. 731.

MEMBERSHIP

Striking Committee

§574.   (1) The motion for the appointment of the Striking Committee to prepare the membership lists of the standing committees is made directly after the Speech from the Throne has been reported by the Speaker on the return of the House from the Senate. This Striking Committee meets only at the beginning of a Parliament.

(2) The membership of the committees is allocated by the Striking Committee in generally the same proportion as that of the recognized political parties in the House itself.

Members not appointed

§575.   (1) Members of the House of Commons who have not been appointed members to a committee are entitled to be present at sitting of all committees. But, in accordance with S.O. 65(9), they may not vote, move motions nor be a part of any quorum. They may participate during the committee's examination of witnesses but they do so usually at the discretion of the Chairman and the committee.

(2) On the grounds of established usage and courtesy to the committee, they normally retire when the committee is about to deliberate upon its report. The committee, in case of their refusal to retire, has no power to order them to withdraw as Members cannot be excluded by the authority of the committee. In such circumstances the committee should either adjourn or report the matter to the House.

Record of Membership

§576. (1) The names of the Members present at each sitting of the committee are entered in the *Minutes of Proceedings* by the Clerk of the Committee.

(2) Those Members who have been duly appointed to the committee are listed under the heading "Members of the Committee present", while those who have not been so appointed, but who are present during the debate, are listed under the heading "Other Members present".

Changes in Membership

§577. A committee's membership may be changed at any time in accordance with S.O. 65(4). In practice, however, during committee meetings the Chief Government Whip's representative will initiate a membership change directly in the committee room and then begin the process as stated in the Standing Order. This Member is officially appointed to the committee at the exact time that the Clerk of the Committee receives the advance notification. This advance notification procedure has been accepted with the consent of all parties since 1973.

ORGANIZATION MEETING

§578. Organization meetings are held at the beginning of each Session of Parliament. The first item of business for a committee at the organization meeting is to proceed to the election of a Chairman.

§579. (1) It is generally understood that the power to call a meeting of a committee for the purposes of organization does not rest with every individual member of the committee. *Journals,* December 4, 1969, pp. 157-9.

(2) Organization meetings have always been called upon the instruction of the Chief Government Whip when the House refers or is about to refer matters to the committee. *Debates,* October 28, 1963, p. 4071.

Election of Chairman

§580. (1) The standing committee having met, the members will proceed to elect a Chairman. If a difference of opinion arises as to the choice of a Chairman, the procedure of the House with respect to the election of a Speaker should be followed. Refer to Chapter 4 (A New Parliament: Opening and Closing of a Session), §§179-182.

(2) As in the House, where the Clerk presides over the election of the Speaker, the Clerk of the Committee presides over the election of the Chairman.

§581. When the Chairman is removed from the committee in accordance with S.O. 65(4)(*b*), resigns or becomes unable to perform his duties, the Chair becomes vacant, at which time the committee must then proceed to the election of a new Chairman. The Vice-Chairman has no role in this procedure. Standing Committee on Finance, Trade and Economic Affairs, *Minutes of Proceedings and Evidence,* July 10, 1973, p. 39:4.

§582. (1) A Member may be elected Chairman of the Committee even though he is not present at the meeting. Standing Committee on Indian Affairs and Northern Development, *Minutes of Proceedings and Evidence,* March 7, 1974, p. 1.

(2) If the Chairman is elected in absentia, the Clerk of the Committee proceeds to the election of an Acting Chairman who may either adjourn the meeting or dispose of the routine business. Standing Committee on Indian Affairs and Northern Development, *Minutes of Proceedings and Evidence,* March 7, 1974, p. 1.

§583. When a tie vote occurs during the election of the Chairman, the question remains undecided. If the committee cannot reach a decision, the members disperse. The Clerk of the Committee cannot entertain motions to adjourn. Standing Committee on Miscellaneous Estimates, *Minutes of Proceedings and Evidence,* March 5, 1974, p. 1:4.

§584. When it is known in advance that neither the Chairman nor the Vice-Chairman of the Committee will be present at the next meeting, the Chairman, with the consent of the committee, at a meeting of the committee, may appoint a Member to preside at that next meeting. Standing Committee on Miscellaneous Estimates, *Minutes of Proceedings and Evidence,* April 28, 1977, p. 19:3.

§585. In joint committees, the Clerk of the Committee presides over the election, first of a Joint Chairman from the Senate, and then of a Joint

Chairman from the House of Commons. In both instances all members of the committee, regardless of their House, may vote on each motion.

Election of Vice-Chairman

§586.   Once the committee is properly constituted by virtue of having a membership and a presiding officer, the Chairman follows the usual parliamentary procedure in that only one motion may be before the committee at any time. Therefore, in the process of electing a Vice-Chairman, the Chairman may receive and dispose of only one motion at a time. However, in past practice the rule has been relaxed in this situation to allow other proposed nominations to be presented as notice.

§587.   With the exception of the Standing Joint Committee on Regulations and Statutory Instruments, joint committees do not normally elect a Vice-Chairman, as the Joint Chairmen usually take turns presiding over the meetings of the joint committees.

SPECIAL COMMITTEES

§588.   When the House is considering a motion, of which notice has been given for the appointment of a special committee, a Member cannot move an amendment that the committee be given wider powers than those which were set down in the notice. *Journals,* May 10, 1954, p. 599.

§589.   A special committee has no power to send for any papers or records unless it is duly authorized to do so by Order of the House.

§590.   (1) A special committee cannot, without the leave of the House, divide itself into sub-committees and apportion its functions among such sub-committees, or delegate to a sub-committee any of the authority delegated to it by the House. The committee may, however, avail itself of the services of its members individually or in the form of sub-committees for purposes connected with the business of the committee, such as drafting, which do not involve a delegation of authority.

(2) On giving power to special committees to appoint sub-committees, the House has also ordered that every such sub-committee must report any evidence taken to the special committee.

§591.   A special committee ceases to exist at the moment its final report is presented to the House. The report cannot afterwards be sent back to the committee with instructions to amend it in any particular way unless the House agrees to revive the committee by adding the following words to the motion for recommittal: "and that the Committee for such purposes be revived." *Journals,* December 1, 1964. pp. 941-947.

QUORUM

§592. A quorum is the minimum number of Members required to be in attendance at a sitting in order for the committee to conduct is business. It is a majority of Members appointed to the committee (including the Chairman) unless otherwise ordered by the House.

§593. Until a quorum is present, the committee cannot proceed to its business if that business concerns the making of decisions. It is the duty of the Clerk attending the committee to bring to the attention of the Chairman the fact of the lack of a quorum, whereupon the Chairman must suspend the proceedings until a quorum is again present or adjourn the committee to some future time.

§594. (1) Under the terms of S.O. 65(7), a committee may adopt a motion to reduce its quorum for the purpose of sitting to receive evidence from witnesses and to have that evidence printed.

(2) Under the authority of this motion the Chairman may authorize the printing of appendices to that day's *Minutes of Proceedings and Evidence.*

(3) No motions may be put by the Chairman (although notice may be given of proposed motions) nor divisions taken during committee sittings held under a reduced quorum.

§595. (1) The question of whether a quorum is present in a committee is a matter that should be dealt with in the committee and not in the House. *Journals,* May 28, 1971, p. 586.

(2) In the case of a joint committee, unless the quorum is established by the House and Senate, a joint committee cannot transact business until a quorum of the members appointed by the House and by the Senate to serve on the committee is present.

ADJOURNMENT

§596. Committees should be regularly adjourned from day to day, though the Chairman is frequently allowed to arrange the day and hour of sitting, but this may be done only with the consent of the committee. Sir John Bourinot, Parliamentary Procedure and Practice in the Dominion of Canada (4th ed., 1916), p. 466.

§597. (1) The length of a sitting of a committee is a question for the majority of the members of the committee present to decide. *Journals,* March 26, 1971, p. 453.

(2) A "Block System" was established in 1973 to facilitate the orderly arrangement of committee meetings held during a week. Each committee is given a fixed time allocation in which to sit over a two-week cycle — usually

two sittings in one week and three in the second. Committees usually attempt to stay within this system when scheduling sittings.

SITTINGS BEYOND THE PRECINCTS OF THE HOUSE

§598.   A Committee usually sits in one of the committee rooms of the House, with the necessary arrangements being made by the Clerk of the Committee.

§599.   (1) Committees may be authorized by the House to adjourn from place to place as may be found expedient, or meet at a particular place, but no committee can sit after a prorogation. Bourinot, p. 467.

(2) In recent years, committees have sat and heard evidence outside the precincts of the House. In such cases, unless the committee has been previously authorized to adjourn from place to place, it must obtain the leave of the House for that purpose. *Journals,* October 21, 1976, p. 49. *Journals,* May 6, 1970, p. 752.

(3) A committee has also been given power to travel and hold sittings in a particular place. *Journals*, February 8, 1978, p. 348.

DIVISIONS

§600.   Questions are determined in a committee by a majority show of hands.

§601.   (1) Any member of a committee may ask the Chairman for a recorded division either before the question is put or following a division by a show of hands.

(2) When a recorded division is taken, the names of the members are called out in alphabetical order by the Clerk of the Committee. Each Member, as his name is called, answers "yea" or "nay".

§602.   The decision of the committee is ascertained by the majority of those voting on the question.

§603.   No Member may raise a question of privilege or point of order during the taking of a division.

§604.   (1) A vote may be taken in a committee while the bells are ringing to call Members for a sitting of the House. *Journals,* May 28, 1971, p. 586.

(2) The doors of the committee room are deemed to be locked while a division is being taken, and a Member's vote can be disallowed if he was not in the room when the question was put.

§605.   With the exception of proceedings on private bills, the Chairman of the Committee may vote only when there is an equality of votes. In giving a casting vote the Chairman is guided by the same principles as the Speaker in the House.

ORDER AND DECORUM

§606. (1) Disobedience to the orders of a committee, provided those orders are within the scope of the committee's authority, is a contempt of the House by which the committee was appointed.

(2) The Chairman of the Committee is responsible for order and decorum in the committee.

§607. (1) All decisions of the Chairman may be appealed to the committee.

(2) There is no appeal to the House from the Chairman's ruling except by way of a report from the committee. *Journals,* December 10, 1973, p. 735. *Journals,* May 8, 1974, p. 173.

§608. Procedural difficulties which arise in committees ought to be settled in the committee and not in the House. *Journals,* December 19, 1973, p. 767.

§609. A committee has no authority to punish one of its members or other person for an offence committed against it, as by disorderly words or contemptuous conduct; for example, when a witness refuses to testify, or prevaricates. The committee may only report such offences to the House for its censure.

§610. Reports from committees may be presented with reference to disorderly conduct therein, or to some contempt of the committee's authority, as where a person summoned as a witness refuses to attend or to answer questions, or prevaricates or gives false evidence, or which raise a presumption that a breach of privilege or other contempt of the House has been committed, such as a libel upon the Chairman of the Committee. Sir Erskine May, Treatise on the Law, Privilege, Proceedings and Usage of Parliament (19th ed., 1976), p. 174.

§611. As the committee has no power to censure nor to refer matters to other committees, the Member's motion should state that the matter be referred to the House for its action.

§612. If any information comes before any committee charging any Member of the House, the committee shall only report the information to the House without proceeding further thereupon.

RECORD OF PROCEEDINGS IN COMMITTEES

§613. (1) Standing committees have the power to print from day to day such papers and evidence as may be ordered by them. They print a document entitled *Minutes of Proceedings and Evidence* following each meeting.

(2) The *Minutes of Proceedings* are prepared and signed by the Clerk of the Committee and record the proceedings of the committee.

(3) The *Evidence* is a verbatim record of the debate of the Committee. It is recorded by electronic means from which it is transcribed, translated, printed and distributed to Members.

§614. Minor corrections may be made to the *Evidence* by informing the Clerk of the Committee who causes to have printed an Erratum to the *Minutes of Proceedings and Evidence*. Corrections of an important nature can only be made by the adoption of a motion in the committee.

§615. The Clerk of the Committee is responsible for the safekeeping of all the papers and records of the committee.

SUB-COMMITTEE ON AGENDA AND PROCEDURE

§616. At its organization meeting a committee may establish a Sub-committee on Agenda and Procedure (commonly referred to as the Steering Committee). This sub-committee meets as directed by the committee or at the call of its Chairman, who is also the Chairman of the standing committee. It recommends, by way of a report, how the committee should proceed to study its Order of Reference — advising on such topics as witnesses, times of sittings and various subject matters for each sitting.

§617. The membership is in the same numerical proportion to that of political parties represented in the committee. The names of the Members are put forward to the Chairman by the chief spokesman of each party on the committee after consultation with their Whips.

§618. Although always meeting in camera, the Sub-committee on Agenda and Procedure follows the procedure and practices of committees, albeit in a very informal atmosphere.

§619. The Clerk of the Committee is also the Clerk of the Sub-committee on Agenda and Procedure.

POWERS OF COMMITTEES

§620. Standing committees have the power to examine matters that are referred to them by the House, reporting from time to time and sending for persons, papers and records, sitting while the House is sitting and during the adjournment of the House, printing all necessary papers and evidence, establishing sub-committees as required and delegating all or any of their powers except the power of reporting directly to the House. S.O. 65(8).

§621. (1) A committee can only consider those matters which have been committed to it by the House. *Journals,* June 9, 1928, p. 571.

(2) A committee is bound by, and is not at liberty to depart from, the Order of Reference. Bourinot, p. 469. In the case of a committee upon a bill, the bill committed to it is itself the Order of Reference to the committee, which must report it with or without amendment to the House.

(3) When it has been thought desirable to do so, the House has enlarged the Order of Reference by means of an Instruction. Mandatory Instructions have also been given to committees restricting the limits of their powers, prescribing the course of their proceedings, or directing the committee to make a special report upon certain matters.

(4) At times, a committee may have to obtain leave from the House to make a report when its Order of Reference is limited in scope. Bourinot, p. 471.

Sub-Committees

§622. A sub-committee may not report directly to the House, but only to the committee by which it has been appointed. When the examination of witnesses is delegated to a sub-committee, it is customary for the appointing committee to report the evidence taken by the sub-committee to the House. *Journals,* June 7, 1977, p. 922.

§623. Sub-committees have been given the power to print from day to day their *Minutes of Proceedings and Evidence.* Standing Committee on National Resources and Public Works, *Minutes of Proceedings and Evidence,* May 8, 1973, p. 15:3.

§624. Where committees are empowered to appoint sub-committees they are sometimes authorized to appoint, from outside their own body, additional Members to serve on such sub-committees. *Journals,* May 31, July 5, 1973, pp. 363, 375.

The Power of Committees to Send for Papers

§625. (1) Committees may send for any papers that are relevant to their Orders of Reference. Within this restriction, it appears that the power of the committee to send for papers is unlimited.

(2) The procedure for obtaining papers is for the committee to adopt a motion ordering the required person or organization to produce them. If this Order is not complied with, the committee may report the matter to the House, stating their difficulties in obtaining the requested documents. It is then for the House to decide what action is to be taken.

(3) It cannot, however, be said that this requirement is absolute either in the case of government departments or of public or private bodies, since there are no instances recorded in which obedience to an Order for papers has been insisted on.

§626. (1) A committee cannot require an officer of a department of the Government to produce any paper which, according to the rules and practice of the House, it is not usual for the House itself to insist upon being laid before it. If consideration of public policy can be urged against a motion for papers it is either withdrawn or otherwise dealt with according to the judgment of the House.

(2) The committee can obtain directly from the officers of a department such papers as the House itself may order, but in case the papers can be brought down only by an Address, it is necessary to make a motion on the subject in the House through the Chairman. Bourinot, pp. 470-1.

§627. When a committee requires special information it will report to the House requesting that the necessary papers be referred to it forthwith. *Journals,* March 8, 1875, p. 176.

IN CAMERA SITTINGS

§628. (1) A committee, having the right to exclude strangers at any time, it may be inferred, has the right to sit in private and have its proceedings protected by privilege. The publication of its proceedings in that case would be an offence which the House could deal with upon receiving a report from the committee.

(2) The purpose of in camera sittings is to allow Members to feel free to negotiate, discuss, deliberate and, sometimes, compromise without the glare of publicity, which might add to the difficulties of agreeing to reports when it is desirable that these proceedings be treated in confidence. The final decision of whether to sit in camera, however, rests with the members themselves. *Journals,* June 21, 1955, pp. 781-2.

WITNESSES

§629. Only the committee, by a majority, can make a decision as to which witnesses should be called. *Journals,* January 12, 1971, p. 251.

Protection of Witnesses

§630. Every witness attending before the House or any committee thereof may claim the protection of the House in respect of the evidence he is called upon to give. He may also ask leave to be assisted by counsel. *Journals,* May 30, 1887, p. 188. Bourinot, pp. 73-4. May, p. 694.

§631. The privilege of freedom from arrest and molestation is attached to all witnesses summoned to attend before either House of Parliament, or before parliamentary committees, and to others in personal attendance upon the business of Parliament, in coming, staying and returning. May, p. 110.

Attendance of Witnesses

§632. (1) A witness shall not be summoned to attend before any committee unless a certificate has been filed by a member of the committee stating that the evidence to be obtained from such a witness is material and important. S.O. 66(1). Should the Senate desire the evidence of a Member, it communicates its request to the House by message. The House will then normally give its consent to the Member to appear should he so wish. *Debates,* May 12, 1921, p. 3259. Should a member desire to give evidence before the Senate voluntarily, there is no rule which prevents his appearing, and no application need be made to the House. *Journals,* February 27, 1975, p. 321.

(2) In practice, this procedure is used only when the witness is to be given reasonable travelling and living expenses which would permit him to appear before the committee.

§633. When the committee decides that a certain person should be heard, it may direct the Clerk of the Committee to invite that person to appear, or if necessary, the committee may adopt a motion ordering that person to attend before the committee.

Senators as Witnesses

§634. (1) Whenever it is desired that a Senator should give evidence before a committee, it is customary for the Chairman to request him to come. If he declines the invitation, the Chairman, on behalf of the committee, moves in the House: "That a message be sent to the Senate requesting their Honours give leave to ...., one of their members, to attend and give evidence before the Committee."

(2) A motion that a message be sent to the Senate requesting leave for a Senator to give evidence before a committee of the House of Commons cannot be entertained until a report thereon has been presented by the committee and proper notice given in accordance with the Standing Order. *Journals,* May 17, 1922, p. 243.

Witnesses Sworn

§635. (1) The House of Commons may at any time order witnesses to be examined on Oath before any committee. In addition, any committee of the House may order its witnesses to be examined on Oath.

(2) If a witness to be examined on Oath conscientiously objects to the

taking of the Oath, he may make his solemn affirmation or declaration.

(3) The Oath or Affirmation may be administered by: (a) the Speaker of the House of Commons; (b) the Chairman of the Committee; (c) the Clerk of the Committee if so appointed by the Speaker. Senate and House of Commons Act, R.S.C. 1970, c.S-8, s.32.

(4) The form of the Oath and Affirmation as listed in the Schedule of the Senate and House of Commons Act is as follows:

FORM A

The evidence you shall give on this examination shall be the truth, the whole truth and nothing but the truth. So help you God.

FORM B

I, A.B., do solemnly, sincerely and truly affirm and declare the taking of any oath is according to my religious belief unlawful, and I do also solemnly, sincerely and truly affirm and declare, that the evidence I shall give in this examination shall be the truth, the whole truth and nothing but the truth.

Conduct of Witnesses

§636. A witness must answer all questions directed to him even over his objection that an answer would incriminate him. *Journals,* February 20, 1913, p. 267.

§637. (1) If a witness should refuse to appear, on receiving the order of the Chairman, or if a witness refuses to answer questions, his conduct may be reported to the House and an order immediately made for his attendance at the Bar or before the committee. Standing Committee on Privileges and Elections, *Minutes of Proceedings and Evidence,* May 12, 1976, p. 46:3. If he still refuses to obey, he may be ordered to be sent for in the custody of the Sergeant-at-Arms, or he may be declared guilty of a breach of privilege and ordered to be taken into the custody of the Sergeant-at-Arms.

(2) The conduct of a witness before a committee can be considered by the House only after receiving a report thereon from the committee. *Journals,* May 8, 1974, p. 173.

§638. To tamper with a witness in regard to the evidence to be given before the House or any committee or to endeavour, directly or indirectly, to deter or hinder any person from appearing or giving evidence is a breach of privilege. Corruption or intimidation is not an essential ingredient in this offence. It is equally a breach of privilege to attempt, by persuasion or solicitations of any kind, to induce a witness not to attend, or to withhold evidence or to give false evidence. May, p. 157.

EXPERT ASSISTANCE

§639. Committees may be empowered to appoint persons with expert knowledge for the purposes of their inquiries, either to supply information which is not readily available or to elucidate matters of complexity within the committee's Order of Reference. *Journals,* March 3, 1975, p. 331. Such advisers attend not only meetings of the committee at which evidence is taken, but also meetings at which the committee deliberates. They do not usually examine witnesses; however, they may assist in the preparation of draft reports.

REPORTS TO THE HOUSE

Preparation of Committee Reports

§640. It is the opinion of the committee, as a committee, not that of the individual Members, which is required by the House, and, failing unanimity, the conclusions agreed to by the majority are the conclusions of the committee. Therefore, no signatures may be attached to the report for the purpose of showing any difference of opinion in the committee or the absence thereof; nor may the report be accompanied by any counter-statement, memorandum of dissent, or protest from any dissenting or non-consenting Member or Members; nor may a draft report which has been submitted to the committee, but has not been entertained by it, be printed as an appendix to the report.

§641. (1) If a Member disagrees with certain paragraphs in the report, or with the entire report, he can record his disapproval by dividing the committee against those paragraphs to which he objects, or against the entire report, as the circumstances of the case require; and he can put on record his observations and conclusions, as opposed to those of the majority, by proposing an alternative draft report. May, p. 659.

(2) While the opinions of dissenting Members may be included in a committee report, no separate minority report may be tabled in the House. *Journals,* March 16, 1972, p. 194.

Recommendations in Reports

§642. (1) It is a long-established practice of this House that recommendations coming from a committee and requiring expenditure of money include the traditional words "that the Government give consideration to the advisability of" spending money. *Journals,* April 10, 1973, p. 258.

(2) A committee report cannot directly, or by implication, direct the Government to introduce, or Parliament to enact, legislation. The accepted form of a committee's recommendation dealing with proposed legislation is "that the Government give consideration to the advisability of introducing the necessary legislation". *Journals,* March 31, 1969, pp. 873-4.

(3) The omission of these traditional words does not necessarily require that the report be referred back to the committee for purely formal modification. *Journals,* March 31, 1969, p. 874.

Signing of the Report

§643. The report of the committee is signed by the Chairman, or in his absence, the Vice-Chairman or any other member of the committee. The Chairman signs only by way of authentication on behalf of the committee. He must sign the report even if he dissented from the majority of the committee.

Deliberations Not Completed Before Prorogation

§644. When committees have not completed their enquiries before the end of the session, they may report this fact to the House together with any evidence which may have been taken. In their report, they may recommend that the same subject matter, with the evidence taken in that session, be referred again in the new session.

§645. A committee cannot report the evidence taken before a similar committee in a previous session, except as an appendix, unless it has received authority from the House to consider that evidence.

Report When Committee Cannot Agree

§646. When a committee is unable to agree upon its report, it may make a report to the House to that effect, reporting the *Minutes of Proceedings and Evidence,* or the committee may merely report the *Minutes of Proceedings and Evidence* to the House without any observations or expressions of opinion.

Premature Disclosure of the Report

§647. (1) No act done at any committee should be divulged before it has been reported to the House. Upon this principle the House of Commons of the United Kingdom, on April 21, 1937, resolved "That the evidence taken by any select committee of this House and the documents presented to such committee and which have not been reported to the House, ought not to be published by any member of such committee or by any other person". The publication of proceedings of committees conducted with closed doors or of reports of committees before they are available to Members will, however, constitute a breach of privilege. May, p. 146.

(2) In Canada, when a question of privilege was raised concerning the publication of a committee report before it was presented to the House, the Speaker ruled that the matter could not be resolved as in the British practice because the motion appeared to attack the press for publishing the confidential document but did not attack Members of the House for their

attitude in respect of their own confidential documents, and in missing this point, it missed something most important with respect to the privileges of the House. *Journals,* June 23, 1977, p. 1209.

PRESENTATION OF THE REPORT
TO THE HOUSE

§648. (1) When the Speaker has called for Reports from Committees, during the progress of routine business, the Chairman, or in his absence, a member of the committee, will rise in his place and say he has the honour to present the .... Report of the Committee. He hands the report to the Page, who delivers it to the Table. The report is then printed in the *Votes and Proceedings* of that day. It may also be read by one of the Clerks at the Table if it is to be concurred in later that day.

(2) When a committee presents a report to the House, it also tables a copy of the *Minutes of Proceedings and Evidence* which relates to that report.

§649. A Member may question, in the House, the form of a committee report before a motion has been made to concur in the report. *Journals,* March 27, 1969, p. 854.

CONCURRENCE IN THE REPORT

§650. Motions to concur in any committee report shall be listed, when notice is required, called and disposed of under "Motions" on the *Order Paper. Journals,* January 20, 1970, p. 327.

§651. (1) Any Member may move concurrence in a committee report whether or not he is a member of the committee. *Journals,* January 20, 1970, p. 328.

(2) A motion to move concurrence in a committee report on Estimates may be moved only on an allotted day. *Journals,* December 6, 1973, p. 726.

§652. (1) When a motion is made for concurrence in a committee report, it is competent for the House to adopt it, reject it, or refer it back to the committee. *Journals,* May 22, 1919, pp. 293-4.

(2) A report may be adopted in total or in part.

(3) It is competent for a Member to move an amendment that imposes a condition to the motion for concurrence.

§653. Under S.O. 42, notice must be given for the motion for concurrence in reports of committees, this concurrence being a resolution of the House. If such a motion is brought forward without notice, it can be allowed to proceed only with the unanimous consent of the House.

§654. A motion, with notice, must first be made in the House that the report of a committee presented during a previous session be considered during the current session, and, if such a motion is carried, the House may appoint a day for the consideration of that report.

§655. It is not possible to initiate a debate in the House on the evidence alone of a committee, unless there is before the House a formal report. The report must state the specific question and be brought to the House by means of a specific motion to concur. *Journals,* May 8, 1974, p. 173.

§656. The terms of reference of a committee cannot be altered by amendments to a motion to concur in a committee report. *Journals,* September 17, 1973, p. 559.

§657. When the House is debating the report of a committee, it is not competent for a Member to open the whole subject matter that was originally referred to the committee.

§658. (1) A committee report may be ruled out of order even though it has been received by the House, and a motion to concur therein cannot then be entertained. *Journals,* May 11, 1874, p. 216.

(2) A report from a committee may not be amended in a substantive manner by the House; it must be referred back to the committee. *Journals,* June 24, 1924, p. 439.

§659. (1) Until the report and the *Minutes of Proceedings and Evidence* have been laid upon the Table, it is irregular to refer to them in debate, or to put questions in reference to the proceedings of the committee.

(2) When the report and the *Minutes of Proceedings and Evidence* are before the House, they may be debated at length but Members are not permitted to discuss the conduct or language of members of the committee, except so far as it appears on the tabled report.

(3) If alleged irregular proceedings take place in committee but are not referred to in the report that the committee presented to the House, then it is not competent for the House to go beyond that report to debate this matter. *Journals,* March 31, 1969, p. 874.

Recommittal of the Report With Instructions

§660. (1) When the motion to concur is moved, the House may refer the report back to the committee for further consideration or with instructions to amend it in any respect. It is not competent for a committee to reconsider and reserve its own decision, but if the House resolves that such reconsideration is necessary, the correct procedure is for the House to give the committee instructions which will enable it to consider the whole question again. Bourinot, p. 480.

(2) The procedure for referring a report back to a committee has been to

do so by proposing an amendment to the motion for concurrence. *Journals,* December 1, 1964, p. 941.

§661. It is not in order to amend the motion to concur in the report for the purpose of recommitting the report with instructions that the committee request an extension of its terms of reference. *Journals,* April 17, 1973, pp. 286-7.

§662. An amendment to recommit a report of a committee, with instructions to amend it so as to recommend that at the next session of Parliament the committee be empowered to consider new matters related to the subject-matter referred to the committee, was ruled out on the grounds that the House cannot instruct a committee to take certain matters in consideration at a future session of Parliament, as references made by the House to a committee lapse at prorogation. *Journals,* June 19, 1934, p. 474.

§663. A special committee ceases to exist at the moment its final report is presented to the House. Therefore the report cannot afterwards be sent back to the committee with instructions to amend it in any particular way unless the House agrees to revive the committee by adding the following words to the motion for recommittal: "and that the Committee for such purpose be revived." *Journals,* December 1, 1964, pp. 941-947.

Report Considered Final

§664. The report of a standing committee should be considered final only when it is adopted by the House; because, until then, the House can refer it back to the committee with instruction to amend it in any particular. *Journals,* May 30, 1928, pp. 476-8. *Journals,* April 1, 1969, p. 880.

§665. The House may appoint a day for the consideration of a committee report for a future day by giving forty-eight hours notice. The debate will be taken up when "Motions" are called at the commencement of that sitting.

16

Petitions

16

Petitions

Right to Petition — Form of Petitions — Remonstrances — Signatures — Substance of the Petition — Petitions from Aliens — Presentation of Petitions — Method of Presentation — Irregularity in Petitions — Procedure Following Presentation of the Petition — The Report of the Clerk of Petitions — Petitions of Urgency.

RIGHT TO PETITION

§666. The right of petitioning the Crown and Parliament for redress of grievances is acknowledged as a fundamental principle of the constitution and has been exercised without interruption since 1867.

§667. Although the House of Commons is a representative institution, it only considers questions submitted by its elected Members. Therefore the ordinary citizen has no right to appear personally before the House of Commons. If he has a grievance, he may present a written petition through a Member within the conditions laid down in the Standing Orders of the House.

§668. The practice of addressing petitions to the House of Commons has decreased considerably, now mainly due to the development of Courts of Justice and administrative bodies.

FORM OF PETITIONS

§669. Every petition should commence with the superscription:

"To the Honourable the House of Commons in Parliament assembled.
"The Petition of the undersigned .... humbly sheweth."

Then follows the subject-matter of the petition, in the third person throughout and commencing each paragraph with the word "That". The conclusion should be the "Prayer" tersely and clearly expressing the particular object which the petitioners have in view in coming before Parliament.

The petition should close with the formal words: "and your petitioners, as in duty bound, will ever pray."

Finally, the signatures are affixed to the petition.

§670. Without a Prayer, a document will not be taken as a petition; and a paper, assuming the style of a declaration, an address of thanks, or a remonstrance only, without a proper form of prayer, will not be received.

§671. Petitions not addressed to "The Honourable the House of Commons in Parliament assembled" and containing no prayer cannot be received. *Journals,* June 13, 1917, p. 342.

§672. All petitions must be endorsed by a Member and be dated. *Journals,* July 2, 1964, p. 492.

§673. Petitions may be written, typewritten, or printed; they must be free from erasures or interlineations. Appendices may not be attached thereto, whether in the shape of letters, affidavits, certificates, statistical statements or documents of any character.

Remonstrances

§674. A petition should not be merely a remonstrance or a listing of grievances. *Journals,* June 7, 1972, pp. 361-2.

§675. Remonstrances respectfully worded and concluding with a proper form of prayer may be received.

Signatures

§676. A petition must have original signatures or marks, and not copies from the original nor signatures of agents on behalf of others, except in the case of incapacity by sickness. The signatures must be written upon the petition itself and not pasted upon or otherwise transferred to it. Sir Erskine May, Treatise on the Law, Privileges, Proceedings and Usage of Parliament (19th ed., 1976), pp. 812-13.

§677. (1) A petition was not received because there were not three signatures on the sheet containing the prayer. *Journals,* March 12, 1930, p. 86.

(2) The practice has always been to read the rule concerning the placing of signatures as though it meant that where there are more than three persons petitioning the House, at least three of them must sign the page containing the Prayer. This rule is never interpreted as precluding one or two petitioners from approaching the House. *Journals,* March 4, 1960, p. 236. Sir John Bourinot, Parliamentary Procedure and Practice in the Dominion of Canada (4th ed., 1916), p. 235.

§678. If the Chairman of a public meeting signs a petition on behalf of those so assembled, it is only received "as the petition of the individual", and is so entered in the *Journals,* because the signatures of one party for others cannot be recognized. Bourinot, p. 236.

§679. Petitions of a general character, signed by persons other than those immediately interested and asking for a modification or change of the financial or fiscal policy of the Dominion, on the ground that such change will be beneficial to the country at large, stand precisely in the position of petitions asking for an imposition of taxes for general purposes and may consequently be received by the House. *Journals,* February 16, 1877, p. 37.

§680. Petitions of corporations must be under their common seal.

§681. A petition forwarded by telegraph cannot be received inasmuch as it has no signature attached to it. Bourinot, p. 236.

SUBSTANCE OF THE PETITION

§682. (1) The language of a petition should be respectful, temperate and free from disrespect to the Sovereign or offensive imputation upon the character and conduct of Parliament, the Courts of Justice, or any other tribunal or constituted authority.

(2) A petition should seek the redress of grievances and should refrain from expressing an opinion with regard to the House, the Government or the positions taken by Members of the House. Expressions which would be in order from a Member of the House may not be in order when presented as a petition. *Journals,* December 11, 16, 1974, pp. 187, 212.

(3) A petition should not contain statements which constitute charges of a very strong character against a Minister or senior officials. *Journals,* June 7, 1972, p. 362.

§683. (1) A petition is irregular if it does not set forth a case in which the House has jurisdiction to interfere. *Journals,* February 16, 1956, p. 163. *Journals,* June 7, 1972, p. 362.

(2) A petition cannot be considered if it concerns a matter delegated by Parliament to another body. *Journals,* June 7, 1972, p. 361. *Journals,* October 24, 1973, p. 591.

(3) A petition stating that the election of a Member of the House is void and praying that the petitioner be declared duly elected cannot be received, as Parliament has vested in the courts exclusive jurisdiction over matters relating to the election of its Members. *Journals,* February 15, 1881, pp. 199-200. *Journals,* May 6, 1926, p. 295.

§684. A petition praying the House to take into its favourable consideration the desirability of recommending the ordering of a new trial, in the case of a person convicted of a criminal offence, cannot be received as it reflects improperly on the Courts of Justice. *Journals,* April 5, 1909, p. 234.

§685. (1) A petition praying for an exemption from an import duty is out of order because it involves a burden upon the public revenue which requires the recommendation of the Crown. *Journals,* March 22, 1875, p. 260.

(2) A petition praying for the imposition of an import duty has been ruled out of order because it involved a public charge and could not be received unless recommended by the Crown. *Journals,* March 18, 1875, p. 241.

(3) The House will refuse to receive any petition that directly asks for a grant of money out of the public revenues unless such grant has first been recommended by the Crown. But the House does not reject petitions which ask simply for legislation or for "such measures as the House may think expedient to take" with respect to public works.

(4) A petition involving an expenditure of money cannot be referred to a Special Committee. *Journals,* June 21, 1869, p. 307.

§686. A petition may not allude to debates in either House of Parliament or to intended motions if merely announced, but when notices have been formally given and printed on the *Notice Paper* petitions referring to them are received. May, p. 815.

§687. A petition containing a representation that an existing law which has been under consideration in various ways and which will be looked into by a committee and is to be the subject of further consideration is a matter of general concern and may not be brought into immediate discussion under S.O. 67(8). *Journals,* May 30, 1975, p. 588.

PETITIONS FROM ALIENS

§688. (1) Aliens, not resident in Canada, have no right to petition Parliament. *Journals,* March 20, 1880, p. 165.

(2) Exceptions to this rule were made in 1878 and 1883 in favour of the Connecticut Mutual Life Insurance Company and certain persons of Portland, Maine, U.S.A. Bourinot, p. 236.

PRESENTATION OF PETITIONS

§689. As the Speaker does not take part in debates, and may be called to give decisions on the regularity of petitions, he does not present petitions to the House. When asked by his constituents to do so, he must avail himself of the services of another Member. Bourinot, p. 231. May, p. 817.

§690. A Member may petition the House but his petition should be presented by another Member. May, p. 818.

§691. A Member cannot be compelled to present a petition. In a subsequent action, it was held that there is no right in a person desirous of petitioning the

House to compel any Member to present his petition and that no action will lie against a Member for refusing to do so. May, p. 817.

Method of Presentation

§692. (1) While a Member may, if he desires, present a petition from his place in the House during Routine Proceedings and before the Introduction of Bills, he may also present his petition by filing it with the Clerk of the House.

(2) When a Member presents a petition, he may not make a speech nor present argument in support of the petition. *Debates,* April 13, 1973, p. 3228.

Irregularity in Petitions

§693. It is the duty of Members to read petitions which are sent to them before they are presented and, if they observe any irregularity, to return them to the petitioners. May, p. 818.

PROCEDURE FOLLOWING PRESENTATION OF THE PETITION

§694. (1) While a Member has clearly a right to ask that a petition be read, it is a privilege, like many others, subject to the approval of the House itself. In case of opposition, the Speaker will put the Member's motion, "that the petition be read", formally to the House.

(2) A petition may be received by the House provided it is in the proper form. Before it may be read by the Clerk, it must be free of opinions and expressions casting reflections on positions taken by the Government. *Journals,* December 11, 16, 1974, pp. 187, 212.

§695. A petition having been presented, and being in order as to the form, may, with unanimous consent, be read by the Clerk, and may thereafter, with unanimous consent, be referred to a Committee. *Journals,* October 19, 1962, pp. 123-24. *Journals,* December 11, 1970, p. 195. *Journals,* December 18, 1970, p. 221.

§696. When the particular arguments, facts or general importance require it, a motion is introduced that the petition be ordered printed in the *Journals* for the information of Members.

The Report of the Clerk of Petitions

§697. (1) The Clerk of Petitions, usually a designated Clerk of Committees, reports upon the petition on the next day following its presentation, stating that it does or does not meet the requirements of the Standing Orders as to form.

(2) This Report is given to the Clerk of the House, who lays it upon the Table and, at the same time, the Speaker reports to the House that it has been tabled.

(3) If the Report states that the petition does not meet the requirements of the Standing Orders as to form, the Speaker rules that the petition cannot be received. *Journals,* March 4, 1960, p. 235. *Journals,* July 2, 1964, p. 492.

PETITIONS OF URGENCY

§698.   (1) In case of urgency, a petition may be immediately considered but the grievances must be such as to require speedy and urgent remedy.

(2) Petitions affecting the House will at once be taken into consideration in accordance with parliamentary usage in all cases of privilege.

17

Proceedings on Public Bills

17

Proceedings on Public Bills

Public Bills — Form of a Bill — The Title — The Preamble — The Enacting Clause — The Clauses — The Schedules — Explanatory Notes — Marginal Notes — Stages of a Bill — First Reading — Introduction — Numbering of Public Bills — Appointment for Second Reading — Examination of Bills — Bills with the same Purpose as other Bills of the same Session — Differences in Texts — Time Allocation for Stages of Bill — Second Reading — Amendments at Second reading — Six Months' Hoist Amendment — Reasoned Amendments — Referral of Subject Matter to a Committee — Effect of Reasoned Amendment — Reviving Bills — Bills Dropped — Order Discharged and Bill Withdrawn — Committee Stage — Instructions — Admissible Instructions — Inadmissible Instructions — Function of a Committee on a Bill — Order in which Bill is Considered — Postponement of Preamble and Clause 1 — Debate on the Bill — Amendments to a Bill — Notice of Amendments — Withdrawal of Amendments — Order in Which Amendments are Taken — The Admissibility of Amendments in Committee — Amendments Ruled Out of Order after Discussion Begun — Postponement of Clauses — Division of Clauses — Schedules — Preamble — Title — Reprint of a Bill — Reports to the House — Procedure for Passage of Bill in a Committee of the Whole — Report Stage — Notice of Motions in Amendment — Rules Concerning Motions in Amendment — Grouping and Voting on Motions in Amendment — Deferred Division — Concurrence at Report Stage — Royal Consent — Third Reading Stage — Amendments on Third Reading — Recommittal of a Bill — Communication Between Houses — Consideration of the Bill by the Senate — House consideration of Senate Amendments — Conferences — Royal Assent.

PUBLIC BILLS

§699. This chapter describes the various proceedings by which a public bill must pass through in order to become a law. Unless specified the chapter concerns all public bills whether they are introduced by Ministers of the Crown, private Members or originate in the Senate.

§700. According to Canadian Standing Orders and practice, there are only two kinds of bills — public and private. The British hybrid bill is not recognized in Canadian practice. *Journals,* February 22, 1971, p. 351. A public bill relates to matters of public policy while a private bill relates to matters of a particular interest or benefit to a person or persons. A bill containing provisions which are essentially a feature of a private bill cannot be introduced as a public bill. *Journals,* March 12, 1875, p. 213. A bill designed to exempt one person from the application of the law is a private bill and not a public bill. *Journals,* October 23, 1975, p. 796.

§701. (1) There is nothing in the rules and no precedent to prevent the setting down of more than one bill or motion dealing with the same subject. *Journals,* July 3, 1969, p. 1290.

(2) Two or more interdependent bills may be under consideration in the House at the same time. Should changes be made in one bill so that it ceases to be consonant or consistent with the other, then the problem must be resolved at the Committee of the Whole or report stage of the second bill to reach those stages. *Journals,* February 5, 1973, p. 95.

(3) There is no rule or custom which restrains the presentation of two or more bills relating to the same subject and containing similar provisions. But if a decision of the House has already been taken on one such bill, for example, if the bill has been given or refused a second reading, the other is not proceeded with if it contains substantially the same provisions and such a bill could not have been introduced on a motion for leave. But if a bill is withdrawn, after having made progress, another bill with the same objects may be proceeded with. *Journals,* October 29, 1957, p. 64.

§702. A Special Order to preserve the precedence of a public bill on the *Order Paper,* unless specified to the contrary, is limited in its effect only to the next occasion on which the bill is reached. *Journals,* May 19, 1970, p. 822.

FORM OF A BILL

§703. (1) Although there is no specific set of rules or guidelines governing the content of a bill, there should be a theme of relevancy amongst the contents of a bill. They must be relevant to and subject to the umbrella which is raised by the terminology of the long title of the bill. *Journals,* May 6, 1971, p. 532.

(2) Some of the constituent parts of a bill are essential; some are optional. The title is an essential part; the preamble is not.

The Title

§704. A bill may have two titles, one long and one short. Both the long title and the short title may be amended, if amendments to the bill make it necessary.

(1) *Long Title* — The long title sets out in general terms the purposes of the bill. It should cover everything in the bill.

(2) *Short Title* — The short title, under which the Act is cited amongst the statutes, is set out in the first clause — "This Act may be cited as the ..." Acts to amend Acts do not have short titles. Occasionally the long title at the head of the bill and the title set out in the short title clause are not identical, as in the case of an Appropriation Act.

The Preamble

§705. The purpose of a preamble is to state the reasons and intended effects of the proposed legislation. Though a preamble is not necessary in a public bill, it is sometimes inserted in bills of great importance in order to place on record the intentions of the framers of the bill. For example, the Arctic Waters Pollution Prevention Act, R.S.C. 1970, c.2 (1st Supp.).

The Enacting Clause

§706. (1) The enacting clause is a short paragraph which follows the long title and precedes the clauses of the bill. This clause, which is an essential part of a bill, reads as follows:

> "Her Majesty, by and with the advice and consent of the Senate and House of Commons of Canada, enacts as follows:"

For appropriation Acts, the clause is preceded by words such as the following:

> "MOST GRACIOUS SOVEREIGN,
> "Whereas it appears by message from His Excellency, the Right Honourable ...., Governor General of Canada, and the estimates accompanying the said message, that the sums hereinafter mentioned are required to defray certain expenses of the public service of Canada, not otherwise provided for, for the financial year ending the 31st day of March, 19......; and for other purposes connected with the public service: May it therefore please Your Majesty, that it may be enacted, and be it enacted by the Queen's Most Excellent Majesty, by and with the advice and consent of the Senate and House of Commons of Canada, that:"

(2) The granting or enacting words of bills for granting aids or supplies to the Crown or the enacting words of other bills are part of the framework of the bill and as such are not submitted to the House or its committees for debate or amendment.

The Clauses

§707. (1) A bill is divided into a series of numbered clauses each with a descriptive title printed in the margin (referred to as Marginal Notes). Clauses may be divided into subclauses; subclauses into paragraphs; and paragraphs into sub-paragraphs. Long and complicated bills often have their clauses grouped in "parts" distinguished by Roman numerals and headings in capitals. These Parts may again be broken up into small groups of clauses with a group heading in italics.

(2) The interpretation or definition clause is usually the second clause, following which the order of the bill is usually so arranged that the leading principles are embodied in the opening clauses.

(3) When the bill has passed into law, it becomes an Act and its clauses are known as sections.

The Schedules

§708.   At the end of many bills there is found a set of schedules which contain matters of detail dependent on the provisions of the bill. A schedule is part of the bill and is dependent on one or more of the preceding clauses, by means of which the provisions of the schedule are carried into effect.

Explanatory Notes

§709.   Explanatory notes, though technically not part of the bill, are printed on the page opposite to the relevant clause. A Member may prepare explanatory notes which should be brief and contain nothing of an argumentative character of the contents and objects of his public bill. When the bills are passed into law, the explanatory notes are deleted.

Marginal Notes

§710.   (1) The marginal notes, short titles of clauses and the headings of parts of a bill do not form part of the bill and, therefore, are not open to amendment. *Journals,* May 17, 1956, p. 568.

(2) The Law Clerk and Parliamentary Counsel is responsible for marginal notes and headings. S.O. 84.

STAGES OF A BILL

§711.   (1) A bill must pass through various stages, on separate days, before it receives the approval of the House of Commons. By unanimous consent or in compliance with the Standing Orders, the House may pass legislation through all or any stage in one day.

(2) Although the various stages are treated as interconnected portions of a single process of consideration, each stage is regarded as having its own peculiar function and, to a certain extent, its own more or less limited range of debate.

§712.   The purpose of each stage is as follows:

(1) *First Reading* — The first reading of a bill is a purely formal stage as it is decided without debate or amendment. This stage is coupled with the order to print the bill.

(2) *Second Reading* — The stage of second reading is primarily concerned with the principle of a measure. At this stage, debate is not strictly limited to the contents of a bill as other methods of attaining its proposed objective may be considered. This stage is coupled with an Order to commit the bill.

(3) *In Committee* — In committee the details of a measure are the primary objects of consideration with alterations in its provisions being proposed. Amendments must be compatible with the principle of the bill which the House has affirmed on second reading.

(4) *Report Stage* — This stage, in the House with the Speaker in the Chair, is used to amend, delete, insert or restore specific clauses of a bill.

(5) *Third Reading* — The purpose of the third reading is to review the bill in its final form after the shaping it has received in its earlier stages.

FIRST READING

§713. The first reading of a bill, the order for printing and the appointment of a day for second reading are taken together as one formal stage.

§714. The practice of the House requires that notice for leave to introduce a bill be given; however, it has been dispensed with, in the case of certain bills, on the grounds of urgency.

§715. Every Member who wishes to introduce a bill must give a forty-eight hour notice which appears on the *Notice Paper* and finally under Routine Proceedings on the *Order Paper* on the last day of the notice requirement. S.O. 41.

§716. (1) When the order for the introduction of bills is called, the Member moves formally for "leave to introduce a bill intituled . . ." The Speaker puts the question, "Is it the pleasure of the House that the Honourable Member have leave to introduce his bill?"

(2) The Speaker has refused a motion for leave to introduce a bill on the grounds that its provisions would infringe upon the financial initiative of the Crown. *Journals,* March 27, 1972, p. 223. *Journals,* March 20, 1974, p. 55.

(3) No bill may be introduced either in blank or in an imperfect shape. *Journals,* May 16, 1978, p. 763.

§717. At this stage it is not permissible to argue the bill. Discussion of the bill's merits may take place on the motion for the second reading. The Member is only permitted to explain the provisions of his bill in order that the House will understand its purport. *Debates,* February 13, 1933, p. 2016.

Introduction

§718. (1) The purpose of first reading is to allow any bill to be introduced, printed and distributed so as to give Members an opportunity to study it. There are procedures under which that process can be stopped and can be voted against if necessary. However, the fact that that occurs only in the most extreme and rare circumstances is an indication that regardless of the content of any legislation, no matter how controversial it may be, it is the undoubted right of any Member, whether he be a government Member or a private Member of the House, at least to put in the form of a bill his views and opinions before the House. It is also his right to have the bill printed and distributed in order to ensure that all Members will have an opportunity to examine and study it and therefore discuss it in an intelligent way. That process should not be stopped except on the clearest possible grounds. *Journals,* December 16, 1974, p. 213.

(2) The House has held recorded divisions on the Member's request for leave to introduce a bill. *Journals,* February 13, 1973, p. 115.

§719. At the commencement of a session there are usually a large number of public bills introduced by Members thereby making it impractical or impossible for the Speaker to review the provisions of each of the bills. Therefore, the practice that has been unanimously agreed to, in recent sessions, is that the House proceeds to the introduction and first reading of those bills, so that each may be scrutinized between its introduction and its being called for second reading, in order to allow the Speaker to consider whether there is any defect in the bills in respect of the practice and usages of the House. *Journals,* September 20, 1968, p. 54.

§720. (1) The Speaker, unless he has been informed beforehand, will choose a seconder for the bill. However, that Member chosen is not required to uphold that responsibility. *Debates,* June 29, 1977, p. 7187.

(2) It is the habit of the Chair to indicate a seconder for a bill, and the seconder at first reading always supports the principle of introduction of any bill but is not necessarily in agreement with the subject matter. *Debates,* May 24, 1978, p. 5689.

Numbering of Public Bills

§721. (1) Bills introduced by the Government receive their number as they are introduced, beginning with C-1.

(2) Members usually introduce a large number of public bills in the early days of a new session. Therefore, the Deputy Speaker is called upon to preside over a meeting to establish by draw the precedence of each intended bill beginning with the number C-201. Later in the session as other bills are introduced, they follow the numerical sequence already established.

(3) Bills originating in the Senate (beginning with the number S-1) retain their Senate numbers during their passage through the House.

Appointment for Second Reading

§722. When the House has agreed to the first reading of a bill, the Speaker at once proceeds to ask: "When shall the bill be read a second time?" The answer is generally: "At the next sitting of the House." The bill is placed on the *Order Paper,* in its proper place, for a second reading at a future time. It is purely formal and is proposed with the object of placing the bill on the agenda for a second reading at which time all discussion can more regularly and conveniently take place.

§723. (1) During Private Members' Hour, public bills are called in their numerical sequence.

(2) The practice developed over the last few years has been that the Government takes the necessary steps to schedule, in advance, the business to be considered during Private Members' Hour, having due regard to the priorities established on the *Order Paper* and through consultation. The House should proceed directly to the scheduled item, standing all preceding items by unanimous consent. A Member who feels that the practice has resulted in an injustice on a particular occasion, in that he should have been consulted or given more advance notice, may express his dissatisfaction simply by withholding the required unanimous consent. This obliges the Speaker to call, one by one, all the items preceding the scheduled item. Items not proceeded with when called in this manner will be allowed to stand either at the request of the Government, or by unanimous consent, or be dropped. *Journals,* December 5, 1977, p. 175.

(3) When bills sponsored by Members are called, they are allowed to stand only at the request of the Government and not at the request of the sponsor. *Journals,* April 14, 1961, p. 437.

§724. Government bills are called in whatever order the Government House Leader may so decide.

EXAMINATION OF BILLS

Bills With the Same Purpose as Other Bills of the Same Session

§725. A motion for leave to bring in a bill, the objects of which are substantially the same as those of a bill upon which the House has come to a decision in the current session, is out of order. Sir Erskine May, Treatise on the Law, Privileges, Proceedings and Usage of Parliament (19th ed., 1976), p. 286.

§726. A bill is in order when substantially different from another bill on the same matter previously disposed of during the session. *Journals,* June 4, 1872, p. 213.

§727. An Act which has been passed by both Houses and given Royal Assent may be amended during the same session by the introduction of a new bill; but no amendment can be made to a bill which has passed the Commons or both Houses and has not received Royal Assent. *Journals,* April 12, May 24, 1918, pp. 145, 380. *Journals,* March 31, April 14, 1927, pp. 440, 617.

Differences in Texts

§728. When a variance occurs in either the English or French texts of a bill, it may be treated, with unanimous consent, as an editorial change. *Debates,* March 25, 1976, pp. 12166, 12173.

§729.   The Speaker should not be expected to interpret the language of a measure when one text appears to be at variance with the text in the other official language. *Journals,* January 19, 1970, p. 323.

TIME ALLOCATION FOR STAGES OF BILL

§730.   A motion for the allocation of time may set out in detail some or all of the provisions which are to be made for the further proceedings on the bill.

§731.   The wording "representatives of the parties" in S.O. 75A, S.O. 75B or S.O. 75C does not include independent Members. *Journals,* December 30, 1971, pp. 1013-14.

§732.   Whenever a Minister of the Crown has given notice under S.O. 75C that he will propose a motion for the purpose of allocating a specified number of days or hours for the consideration of a stage of a bill, this notice must be accepted by the Speaker. The type of notice specified in S.O. 75 is not covered by the terms of S.O. 42(1) and therefore does not require forty-eight hours notice. *Journals,* December 1, 1971, p. 948.

§733.   On one occasion, a motion under S.O. 75C contained conditions concerning exact times for each motion at the report stage and for third reading, in addition to setting conditions for speeches. *Journals,* December 30, 1971, p. 1013.

SECOND READING

§734.   The second reading is the most important stage through which the bill is required to pass; for its whole principle is then at issue and is affirmed or denied by a vote of the House. It is not regular on this occasion, however, to discuss in detail the clauses of the bill.

§735.   (1) When a bill comes up for a second reading in its proper course, one of the Clerks at the Table will read the order aloud:

> "Second Reading and reference to the .... Committee on .... of Bill C-......, An Act . . ."

(2) Whereupon the Member in charge of the measure will move its second reading:

> "That the Bill be now read a second time and referred to the .... Committee on . . ."

§736.   The principle of relevancy in an amendment governs every proposed motion which, on the second reading of a bill, must not include in its scope other bills then standing for consideration by the House. Nor may such an amendment deal with the provisions of the bill upon which it is moved, nor anticipate amendments thereto which may be moved in committee, nor attach conditions to the second reading of the bill.

§737.   The resumed debate on the second reading of a bill cannot be set aside by a private Member's substantive motion because, in applying the anticipation rule, bills must be given the right of way and take precedence over motions. *Journals,* February 24, 1936, pp. 67-8.

§738.   An amendment which has been negatived in the Address in Reply to the Speech from the Throne cannot be moved on the second reading of a bill. *Journals,* June 11, 1942, p. 381.

§739.   On the second reading of an amending bill it is the principle of the amending bill, not the principle of the Act, which is the "business under consideration". Debate and proposed amendments must therefore relate exclusively to the principle of the amending bill. *Journals,* November 14, 1949, p. 237. *Journals,* October 15, 1962, p. 77.

AMENDMENTS AT SECOND READING

§740.   There are three types of amendments that may be proposed at the second reading stage of a bill. These are:

1.   the six months' hoist;
2.   the reasoned amendment;
3.   the referral of the subject matter to a committee.

§741.   (1) A reasoned amendment and a six months' hoist cannot be moved in one motion. *Journals,* February 24, 1970, p. 486.

(2) A reasoned amendment cannot oppose the principle of the bill and also refer the subject-matter to a committee; it must do one or the other. *Journals,* March 22, 1972, p. 208. *Debates,* February 23, 1978, pp. 3216-17.

Six Months' Hoist Amendment

§742.   A traditional way of opposing the second reading of a bill is to move an amendment to the question that deletes all the words after the word "That" and substitutes the following:

"Bill C-. . ., An Act . . ., be not now read a second time but that it be read a second time this day six months hence."

§743.   An established form of amendment such as the "six months'" formula, used to obtain the rejection of a bill, is not capable of amendment.

Reasoned Amendments

§744.   It is also competent for a Member, who desires to place on record any special reasons for not agreeing to the second reading of a bill, to move what is known as a "reasoned amendment". This amendment leaves out all the words in the main question after the word "That" to add other words. A reasoned amendment is in the form of a motion and may fall into one of several categories:

(1) It must be declaratory of some principle adverse to, or differing from, the principles, policy or provisions of the bill.

    (a)   It may not propose an alternative scheme. *Journals,* April 14, 1969, p. 895.

    (b)   It may not approve the principle of a bill and at the same time enunciate a declaration of policy. *Journals,* February 13, 1970, p. 431.

    (c)   It may oppose the principle rather than the subject-matter. *Journals,* September 7, 1971, p. 778. *Journals,* October 21, 1968, p. 148.

(2) It may express opinions as to any circumstances connected with the introduction or prosecution of the bill, or otherwise opposed to its progress. It may oppose the principle of the bill but not propose that the bill be withdrawn and a new one introduced. *Journals,* May 14, 1971, p. 554.

§745.   The following rules govern the contents of reasoned amendments:

(1) The principle of relevancy in an amendment governs every such motion. The amendment must "strictly relate to the bill which the House, by its order, has resolved upon considering", and must not include in its scope other bills then standing for consideration by the House. *Journals,* April 24, 1934, p. 272.

(2) The amendment must not be concerned in detail with the provisions of the bill upon which it is moved nor anticipate amendments thereto which may be moved in committee. *Journals,* March 10, 1933, p. 299. *Journals,* March 8, 1934, p. 156. *Journals,* June 11, 1942, p. 380. *Journals,* January 19, 1970, p. 323.

(3) It is not permissible to propose merely the addition of words to the question, "That the bill be now read a second time", as such words must, by implication, attach conditions to the second reading. *Journals,* February 17, 1970, p. 454. *Journals,* April 23, 1971, p. 502.

(4) An amendment which amounts to no more than a direct negation of the principle of the bill is open to objection. *Journals,* January 25, 1973, p. 68.

Referral of Subject Matter to a Committee

§746.   (1) An amendment, urging a committee to consider the subject-matter of a bill, might be moved and carried if the House were adverse to giving the bill itself a second reading and so conceding its principle. But where further information is desired in direct relation to the terms of the bill before the House, the advantage of referring the bill to a committee could be explained in the second reading stage.

(2) The amendment may seek further information in relation to the bill by either committee, the production of papers or other evidence.

§747. (1) The House cannot, under the guise of referring the subject-matter to a committee, refer also certain provisions of the bill itself. This is going beyond a reference of the subject-matter. It is an Instruction to consider certain provisions of the bill, which can only be done after the bill has been read a second time and referred to a Committee.

(2) The House cannot both refuse to give the second reading and refer some provisions of the bill to a committee. It shall have to make its choice. *Journals,* March 22, 1949, p. 233.

§748. (1) On the motion for the second reading of a bill amending the Canada Grain Act and a proposed amendment that the subject matter be referred to the Standing Committee on Agriculture and Colonization, the Speaker ruled the proposed amendment out of order on the grounds that the Committee had not yet been appointed. *Journals,* February 10, 1947, p. 55.

(2) While the subject-matter of a bill may be referred to a standing or special committee, it cannot be referred to a Committee of the Whole. *Journals,* January 20, 1971, p. 270.

(3) An amendment cannot propose the reference of the subject-matter of a bill to a body which is not in existence. *Journals,* January 21, 1971, p. 274.

§749. An amendment to defer second reading of a bill until the subject-matter has been considered by a committee is out of order in that it does not oppose the principle of the bill but merely attaches a condition. *Journals,* October 21, 1968, p. 147. *Journals,* February 17, 1970, p. 454.

Effect of Reasoned Amendment

§750. According to modern practice, after a reasoned amendment has been carried on the second or third reading of a bill, no attempt at further progress is made. It must be borne in mind, however, that the amendment, if agreed to, does not necessarily arrest the progress of the bill, the second reading of which may be moved on another occasion. The technical effect of such an amendment is to supersede the question for now reading the bill a second time; and the bill is left in the same position as if the question for now reading the bill a second time had been simply negatived. The House refuses on that particular day to read the bill a second time, and gives its reasons for such refusal; but the bill is not otherwise disposed of. May, p. 500.

REVIVING BILLS

§751. (1) When the motion that the bill be now read a second time is negatived, it is competent for a Member to move immediately without notice: "That the Bill be read a second time on .... next". On this motion being agreed to, the bill takes its place on the *Order Paper*. The same practice is in effect with respect to the bill at any previous or succeeding stage.

(2) When the order for the second reading of a bill has lapsed owing to the House being counted out, it may be revived on a subsequent day by the House adopting a motion being put without notice. *Journals,* July 3, 1917, p. 403.

BILLS DROPPED

§752. When the Order of the Day for Private Members' Public Bills is read and no motion is made for the second reading or other stage of a bill or for its postponement, it becomes a dropped order and does not appear again upon the *Order Paper,* unless it is reinstated on the *Notice Paper.*

ORDER DISCHARGED AND BILL WITHDRAWN

§753. When the order for the second reading has been read, a Member may move, if he should not wish to proceed with the bill, that the order be discharged and the bill withdrawn. Or if the motion has been actually made for the second reading, it must first, with leave of the House, be withdrawn. It is irregular to go into the merits of a bill on a motion that the order for a second reading be postponed or discharged. Sir John Bourinot, Parliamentary Procedure and Practice in the Dominion of Canada (4th ed., 1916), pp. 510-11.

COMMITTEE STAGE

§754. (1) Every public bill, when it is read a second time, is referred to a committee before any amendments may be made to it. S.O. 74(1).

(2) To "commit" a bill means to refer it to a committee, where it is to be considered and reported.

(3) It is perfectly regular to refer a number of bills at the same time to a Committee of the Whole, which may consider them all on the one day without the Chairman leaving the Chair on each separate bill. *Journals,* March 9, 1978, p. 468.

§755. (1) All bills based upon Supply or Ways and Means resolutions are committed to a Committee of the Whole; although exceptions have been made to this practice. *Journals,* November 17, 1975, p. 864.

(2) Unless otherwise ordered, in giving a bill a second reading it shall be referred to a standing committee but it may, however, be referred to a special or joint committee or to a Committee of the Whole. S.O. 74(2).

(3) Unanimous consent is required to redirect a bill to a different

standing committee to that originally proposed. *Debates,* April 4, 1978, p. 4119.

(4) Bills may be withdrawn from one committee and referred to another committee. *Journals,* June 9, 1977, p. 1109.

INSTRUCTIONS

§756. (1) An Instruction is a motion empowering a committee to do something which it could not otherwise do, or to direct it to do something which it might otherwise not do. It directs the order and course of the committee's proceedings and extends or restricts the order of reference according to the discretion of the House. Committees, in case of doubt, may ask instructions from the House as to the course they should take with reference to the matters under their consideration. *Journals,* September 17, 1973, p. 558.

(2) The purpose of the Instruction must be supplementary and ancillary to the purpose of the bill, and must fall within the general scope and framework of the bill. It is irregular to introduce into a bill, by an Instruction to the committee, a subject which should properly form the substance of a distinct measure, having regard to usage and the general practice of enacting distinct statutes for distinct branches of law.

(3) There are two types of Instructions — permissive and mandatory.

§757. (1) The object of a permissive Instruction, which is the more ordinary form, is to confer on the committee authority to do something which, without the Instruction, it would have no power to do. Instructions of this kind merely empower the committee to take the course of action specified, leaving it to the discretion of the committee whether or not they will exercise the power.

(2) A permissive Instruction is one which is generally made concerning a referred bill and customarily states explicitly in the motion that the committee have the power to make the provision required. The intention is to give a committee power to do a certain thing if it thinks proper not to command them to do it. The committee is not bound to obey the permissive Instructions. *Journals,* April 3, 1882, p. 248.

§758. The object of mandatory Instructions is to define the course of action which the committee must follow.

§759. (1) The time for moving an Instruction is immediately after the committal of the bill, or, subsequently, as an independent motion. The Instruction should not be given while the bill is still in the possession of the House, but rather after it has come into the possession of the committee. If the bill has been partly considered in committee, it is not competent to propose an Instruction.

(2) A Member cannot, under the guise of an Instruction, interfere with the work of a committee which has not yet reported.

§760. (1) Instructions may be given to a Committee of the Whole or to any committee of the House. Any number of Instructions may be moved successively to a committee on the same bill; each question for an Instruction is separate and independent of every other. An Instruction cannot be moved to make any provision which imposes a tax or charge upon the people.

(2) A mandatory Instruction can be given to a joint committee only with the concurrence of both Houses. If either House gives a mandatory Instruction to a joint committee, but no corresponding Instruction is given by the other House, then the Instruction, though binding upon the members appointed to serve on the joint committee by the first House, is not binding on the joint committee, as a committee.

Admissible Instructions

§761. (1) *Extension of objects* — An Instruction is necessary to authorize the introduction into a bill of amendments, which extend its provisions to objects not strictly covered by the subject-matter of the bill as agreed to on the second reading, provided that these objects are cognate to its general purposes.

(2) *Division of bill* — An Instruction is required to enable a committee to divide a bill into two or more bills, but such an Instruction is in order only if the bill is drafted into two or more distinct parts or else comprising more than one subject matter, which lends itself to such division into parts. *Journals,* January 26, 1971, pp. 283-5.

(3) *Consolidation of bills* — An Instruction is required to empower a committee to consolidate two bills into one bill.

(4) *Priority to portion of bill* — An Instruction is required if the House desires that a committee give priority to the consideration and reporting separately of a portion of a bill.

(5) *Power to hire staff* — Instructions have been given to committees to hire additional staff to assist it in its inquiries. *Journals,* March 3, 1975, p. 331.

(6) *Power to adjourn from place to place* — Instructions have been given to committees to adjourn from place to place both within and outside Canada for the purposes of receiving evidence. *Journals,* October 21, 1976, p. 49.

Inadmissible Instructions

§762. No Instruction is permissible which is irrelevant, foreign, contradictory or superfluous to the contents of the bill.

FUNCTION OF A COMMITTEE ON A BILL

§763. The function of a committee on a bill is to go through the text of the bill clause by clause and, if necessary, word by word, with a view to making such amendments in it as may seem likely to render it more generally acceptable. May, p. 506.

§764. (1) A committee is bound by the decision of the House, given on second reading, in favour of the principle of the bill, and should not, therefore, amend the bill in a manner destructive of this principle.

(2) The committee may so change the provisions of the bill that when it is reported to the House it is in substance a bill other than that which was referred. A committee may negative every clause and substitute new clauses, if relevant to the bill as read a second time.

(3) The objects (also referred to as the principle or scope) of a bill are stated in its long title, which should cover everything contained in the bill as it was introduced. Amendments, however, are not necessarily limited by the title of the bill.

(4) An amendment which is outside the scope of the bill is out of order and cannot be entertained, unless a special Instruction has been given by the House to the committee.

ORDER IN WHICH BILL IS CONSIDERED

§765.   Unless the committee otherwise orders, the text of a bill is considered in the following order:

    (1) Clauses;
    (2) New Clauses;
    (3) Schedules;
    (4) New Schedules;
    (5) Preamble (if any);
    (6) Title.

§766.   (1) The clauses of a bill in committee must be considered in their proper order; that is, beginning with Clause 1 then taking up Clause 2 and so on, to the end of the bill. The Chairman usually calls out the number of each clause and reads the marginal note; he may read the clause at length if it is demanded by the committee. Each clause is a distinct question and must be separately discussed. When a clause has been agreed to, it is irregular to discuss it again on the consideration of another clause.

(2) All the clauses of the bill should be considered before any new clauses are introduced. However, this practice is not rigorously followed as the committee is generally guided by what is most convenient in each particular case.

Postponement of Preamble and Clause 1

§767.   By S.O. 75, the title, preamble and Clause 1 (if it contains only the short title) stand postponed until the consideration of all the clauses and schedules is completed. It is the business of the committee to settle the clauses first and then to consider the preamble (if there is one) and title in reference to the adopted clauses.

Debate on the Bill

§768. (1) Before beginning its clause by clause study, the committee will usually call the sponsor of the bill and such witnesses, as it deems necessary, to give evidence upon the merits of the bill.

(2) This debate on Clause 1 (if it is not the short title) is normally wide ranging, covering all the principles and details of the bill.

AMENDMENTS TO A BILL

§769. Amendments may be made in every part of a bill, whether in the title, preamble, clauses or schedules; clauses may be omitted; new clauses and schedules may be added.

Notice of Amendments

§770. (1) When a Member intends to move an amendment in committee on a bill, he is not required to give notice of his amendment. It has been found expedient, however, in some cases to give notice where the Member desires to call special attention to his proposal.

(2) The practice has been that Members proposing to introduce amendments have given them to the Chairman and to the Clerk of the Committee who ensures that they are translated, compiled and circulated for the information of the members of the committee.

Withdrawal of Amendments

§771. After the question on the amendment has been proposed from the Chair, the amendment can be withdrawn only with unanimous consent at the request of the Member who moved it.

Order in Which Amendments Are Taken

§772. (1) When several amendments are offered at the same place in a clause, an amendment to leave out words in order to insert other words takes precedence over an amendment merely to leave out words. Subject to this qualification, the Chairman normally calls amendments in the order in which they would appear in the bill. It is also within his discretion to decide that an amendment is being offered at a wrong place or that it should be moved as a new clause.

(2) Amendments should be proposed in the order of the lines of a clause. If the latter part of a clause is amended, it is not competent for a Member to move to amend an earlier or antecedent part of the same clause. If an amendment to the latter part of a clause is negatived or withdrawn, it is competent to propose one to an earlier part.

(3) An amendment should relate to a specific clause in a bill and not to two or more clauses. *Journals,* June 20, 1969, p. 1218.

(4) For the convenience of the committee, the Chairman frequently permits debate to range over several amendments which raise different aspects of the proposal in the actual amendment under consideration.

The Admissibility of Amendments in Committee

§773.   An amendment which is out of order on any of the following grounds cannot be put from the chair:

(1) An amendment is out of order if it is irrelevant to the bill, beyond its scope or governed by or dependent upon amendments already negatived.

(2) An amendment must not be inconsistent with, or contradictory to, the bill as so far agreed to by the committee, nor must it be inconsistent with a decision which the committee has given upon a former amendment.

(3) An amendment is out of order if it is offered at the wrong place in the bill, if it is tendered to the committee in a spirit of mockery or if it is vague or trifling.

(4) (a) An amendment is inadmissible if it refers to, or is not intelligible without, subsequent amendments or schedules, or if it is otherwise incomplete. (b) An amendment may not make the clause which it is proposed to amend unintelligible or ungrammatical. *Journals,* March 28, 1969, p. 862.

(5) An amendment which is equivalent to a negative of the bill, or which would reverse the principle of the bill as agreed to at the second reading stage is not admissible.

(6) An amendment to delete a clause is not in order, as the proper course is to vote against the clause standing part of the bill. *Journals,* June 23, 1920, p. 435.

(7) An amendment is out of order if it imposes a charge upon the Public Treasury, if it extends the objects and purposes, or relaxes the conditions and qualifications as expressed in the Royal Recommendation. *Journals,* June 17, 1969, p. 1172.

(8) (a) An amendment may not amend a statute which is not before the committee. *Journals,* March 28, 1969, p. 862. *Journals,* June 11, 1970, p. 993. (b) An amendment may not amend sections from the original Act unless they are specifically being amended in a clause of the bill before the committee. *Debates,* December 15, 1977, p. 1909.

(9) An amendment may not be proposed to insert words at the commencement of a clause with a view to proposing an alternative scheme to that contained in the clause or to leave out from the first word to the end of the clause in order to substitute other words or to effect a redrafting of the clause, such amendments being in the nature of a new clause. Bourinot, p. 522.

(10) A substantive amendment may not be introduced by way of a modification to the interpretation clause of a bill. *Journals,* May 21, 1970, p. 835.

(11) An amendment to include in a bill a statute which has already ceased to have effect is out of order, but an amendment may be moved to

continue the Act which is still in force but would cease to have effect if steps were not taken to continue its existence.

Amendments Ruled Out of Order After Discussion Begun

§774.   If it appears during the course of discussion that an amendment or new clause which has been moved is out of order, then the Chairman directs the committee's attention to this fact and withdraws the amendment or clause from further consideration by the committee. May, p. 525. As examples, the discussion of an amendment or clause brings forward the fact:

(1)   that the question raised thereby had already been decided by the committee;

(2)   that the amendment was inconsistent with the previous decision of the committee or referred to a part of the clause prior to the part last amended;

(3)   that it would have no effect or was unnecessary;

(4)   that it was beyond the scope of the bill or would constitute, if agreed to, a negative of the bill.

POSTPONEMENT OF CLAUSES

§775.   (1) A clause may be postponed, upon motion, provided that no amendment has been made thereto and that no proposed amendment has been negatived. In either of these cases the postponement of a clause is irregular. If, however, an amendment has been proposed and withdrawn the clause may be postponed. A part of a bill or a consecutive group of clauses en bloc may also be postponed.

(2) A proposal to postpone the only effective clause of a bill until the subordinate clauses have been considered or to postpone part of a clause is out of order.

(3) Postponed clauses, unless provisions to the contrary are made in the motion, are considered after the other clauses of the bill have been disposed of but before any new clauses are introduced.

DIVISION OF CLAUSES

§776.   A committee has the power to divide a clause or to decide that the first part of a clause shall be considered as an entire clause. A motion to divide a clause must be taken before the clause is adopted.

SCHEDULES

§777.   Schedules to a bill are treated in the same manner as the clauses. They are considered, as a rule, after new clauses are disposed of. If a schedule is disagreed to, another cannot be offered to replace it, until the remaining schedules have been disposed of.

§778. When a bill is introduced to give effect to an Agreement and the Agreement is scheduled to the bill as a completed document, amendments cannot be made to the schedule. An amendment to the clauses of the bill for the purpose of withholding legislative effect from the document contained in the schedule is in order; also as are amendments to those clauses which deal with matters not determined by the document contained in the schedule. *May,* p. 523.

PREAMBLE

§779. (1) When all the clauses and schedules have been agreed to, the preamble is considered; amendments may be moved thereto if rendered necessary by amendments made to the bill. The Chairman puts the question "Shall the preamble of the bill carry?"

(2) Substantive amendments to the preamble are inadmissible unless the modification is proposed for purposes of clarification or uniformity. *Journals,* January 19, 1970, p. 323.

(3) Where the bill, as introduced, does not contain a preamble, it is not competent for the committee to introduce one.

TITLE

§780. (1) The title may be amended if the bill has been so altered as to necessitate such an amendment. *Journals,* February 13, 1970, pp. 433-4.

(2) When a committee has found it advisable to alter the title of the bill, they have reported that fact to the House. The title will be changed on the adoption of the motion for concurrence at the report stage. *Journals,* February 20, 1970, p. 477.

REPRINT OF A BILL

§781. A bill which has been amended in committee is normally ordered reprinted for use of the Members at the report stage. *Debates,* April 6, 1970, p. 5520.

REPORTS TO THE HOUSE

§782. The House is not supposed to be informed of the proceedings of a committee on a bill until the bill has been reported; discussion of the clauses, with the Speaker in the Chair, when the bill is still before the committee, is consequently irregular.

§783. There is no authority that a committee of the House, when considering a bill, should report anything to the House except the bill itself. *Journals,* December 20, 1973, p. 774.

PROCEDURE FOR PASSAGE OF BILL IN A COMMITTEE OF THE WHOLE

§784. The proceedings on a public bill in a Committee of the Whole are similar to those proceedings in the Standing Committee.

(1) If the Committee of the Whole cannot go through the whole bill at one sitting it directs the Chairman to report progress and ask leave to sit again. When the committee is about to rise, the Chairman says: "Shall I report progress and ask leave to sit again?" and, if there are no dissenting voices, the Chairman reports to the Speaker, who has resumed his Chair: "Mr. Speaker, the Committee of the Whole are considering Bill C-. . . . and have instructed me to report progress and ask leave to sit again at the next sitting of the House" or if the committee is likely to take up the bill again on that day, he says: "Later this day".

(2) A motion to report progress having been negatived cannot be repeated during the pendency of the same question, being subject to the same rule as that observed in the House itself, which will not permit a motion for the adjournment of the debate to be repeated without some intermediate proceeding.

(3) The proceedings of a Committee of the Whole on a bill may be brought abruptly to a close by an order: "That the Chairman do now leave the Chair" or by a proof that a quorum is not present. The Chairman, in such cases, being without instruction from the Committee, makes no report to the House. A bill disposed of in this manner disappears from the *Order Paper,* though it may be revived by an order of the House.

(4) When a Committee of the Whole on a bill is revived, its proceedings are resumed at the point at which they were interrupted, having been valid and duly recorded in the *Minutes* until the Chairman was directed to leave the Chair.

§785. When the bill has been fully considered, the Chairman puts the question: "Shall I report the bill, with (or without) amendment?" which, being agreed to, he leaves the Chair without question put, and the Speaker resumes his Chair; upon which the Chairman reports from the Committee of the Whole that it has considered Bill C-. . ., an Act . . ., and instructed him to report the same with (or without) amendment.

§786. When a bill or other matter has been partly considered in a Committee of the Whole and the Chairman has reported progress and asked leave to sit again, the House may give leave to the Committee to sit again on a particular day. On that day when the order for the Committee of the Whole has been read, the Speaker shall forthwith leave the Chair without putting any question and the House shall thereupon resolve itself into a Committee of the Whole.

REPORT STAGE

§787. In general, the report stage of a public bill is one of reconsideration of events that have taken place in committee. The consideration of a bill is now a more formal repetition of the committee stage with the applicable rules of debate which are proper when the Speaker is in the Chair. Although amendments which were rejected in committee and amendments attempting to restore the original text of the bill may be proposed, the Speaker's power of selection of motions in amendment is a check upon the excessive repetition of debates which have already taken place in committee. S.O. 75(10). *Journals,* April 23, 25, 1975, pp. 468, 487.

§788. It is only when there is a motion in amendment proposed and debated at the report stage that there cannot be two stages on the same day. When there are no further amendments proposed at the report stage there may be a debate on third reading in that same sitting. Because the report stage is not a reading stage, the House can have the adoption of the report stage and third reading on the same day. *Journals,* February 24, 1969, p. 738.

§789. Debate on report stage begins when the Order of the Day is called as follows:

> "Consideration of the report stage of Bill C-..., An Act ..., as reported (with or without amendment) from the .... Committee on ...."

Notice of Motions in Amendment

§790. Notice of motions in amendment at the report stage may be filed only until the bill is first considered at that stage. Once report stage is entered on, no further motions, except those of a clerical or consequential nature, can be accepted. *Journals,* June 2, 1970, p. 908.

Rules Concerning Motions in Amendment

§791. Motions in amendment at the report stage are moved to the bill and not to a particular clause.

§792. The moving of motions in amendment to a public bill at the report stage is governed by the practice or tradition which has developed whereby only the same class of amendments which were moved at the committee stage may be moved at the report stage. Consequently, the rules concerning the admissibility of amendments at the committee stage detailed earlier are applicable to motions in amendment moved at the report stage of the bill.

§793. (1) In committee, an amendment to delete a clause is an expanded negative and is out of order. At report stage, a motion to delete a clause stands by itself. *Journals,* February 13, 1969, pp. 698-9. *Journals,* June 29, 1976, p. 1385.

(2) A motion to delete a clause in a one-clause bill is not different from a

similar motion moved on a bill with two or more clauses. *Journals,* February 13, 1969, p. 699.

(3) A reasoned amendment may not be moved at the report stage. *Journals,* April 16, 1969, pp. 906-7.

§794.   The title may be amended at the report stage to make it conform with the contents of the bill.

Grouping and Voting on Motions in Amendment

§795.   (1) At the commencement of the report stage of a bill, the Speaker by virtue of S.O. 75(10) may select or combine motions in amendment for debate as he may think fit. At this time, he may also give notice of those motions which are of procedural concern and ask for guidance on their procedural acceptability.

(2) By practice, the Speaker will also decide whether the motions will be voted separately or in groups.

Deferred Division

§796.   When a division has been demanded by at least five Members rising in their places, the Speaker may defer the calling of the recorded division until any or all the motions in amendment for that bill have been debated.

Concurrence at Report Stage

§797.   (1) After the disposal of all motions attempting to amend the bill, the Member in charge of the bill will move:

"That the Bill, as amended, be concurred in at the report stage."

(2) If motions in amendment were agreed to by the House at the report stage the Member in charge of the bill will move:

"That the Bill, as amended, be concurred in at the report stage with further amendments."

(3) The motion for concurrence is disposed of without debate.

ROYAL CONSENT

§798.   (1) The consent of the Sovereign (to be distinguished from the Royal Assent to Bills) is given by a Minister of the Crown to bills (and occasionally amendments) affecting the prerogative, hereditary revenues, personal property or interest of the Crown. *Journals,* April 26, 1978, p. 696.

(2) The Royal Consent is generally given at the earliest stage of debate and its omission, when it is required, renders the proceedings on the passage of a bill null and void. May, p. 594.

§799.   (1) The consent of the Crown is always necessary in matters involving the prerogatives of the Crown. This consent may be given at any stage of a bill before final passage; though in the House it is generally signified on the motion for second reading. This consent may be given by a special message or by a verbal statement by a Minister of the Crown, the latter being the usual procedure in such cases. It will also be seen that a bill may be permitted to proceed to the very last stage without receiving the consent of the Crown but if it is not given at the last stage, the Speaker will refuse to put the question. It is also stated that if the consent be withheld, the Speaker has no alternative open to him except to withdraw the measure. *Journals,* April 25, 1966, p. 434.

(2) The procedure with respect to signifying the consent is different from that in giving the recommendation of the Crown. The recommendation precedes every grant of money, the consent may be given at any stage before final passage, and is always necessary in matters involving the rights of the Crown, its patronage, its property or its prerogatives. Bourinot, p. 413.

§800.   In any case where a private Member wishes to obtain the consent of the Crown, he may ask the House to agree to an Address for leave to proceed thereon before the introduction of the bill. Bourinot, p. 413.

§801.   The Royal Consent to a bill is not required unless it affects the personal property of the Sovereign as distinguished from property the Sovereign may hold for his Subjects. *Journals,* December 14, 1970, p. 201.

THIRD READING STAGE

§802.   (1) When an Order of the Day for the third reading of a bill is called, the same type of amendments which are permissible at the second reading stage are permissible at the third reading stage with the restriction that they cannot deal with any matter which is not contained in the bill.

(2) The question for the third reading may be negatived, but as previously stated (in reference to the second reading) such a vote is not fatal to the bill.

(3) Debate on the third reading of a bill begins after the Order of the Day is called and the Member in charge of the bill moves:

"That the Bill be now read a third time and do pass."

§803.   It is only when there is a motion in amendment proposed and debated at the report stage that there cannot be two stages on the same day. When there are no further amendments proposed at the report stage there may be a debate on third reading in that same sitting. Because the report stage is not a reading stage, the House can have the adoption of the report stage and third reading on the same day. *Journals,* February 24, 1969, p. 738.

AMENDMENTS ON THIRD READING

§804.   There are limitations on the type of amendments that can be moved on third reading. They must be relevant to the bill which they seek to amend. They should not seek to give a mandatory Instruction to a committee. They should not contradict the principle of the bill as adopted on second reading. *Journals,* August 3, 1940, p. 332. *Journals,* January 27, 1967, p. 1238.

§805. An amendment may not be moved expressing opinions as to any circumstances connected with its introduction or prosecution, or seeking further information in relation to the bill by committee or commissioners, the production of papers or other evidence, or the opinion of judges. The third reading stage of a bill is not directly connected with any provision of the bill.

§806. An amendment may not be a reasoned amendment and at the same time attempt to recommit the bill. *Journals,* June 9, 1977, pp. 1108-9.

§807. An amendment which would instruct a committee to request a further financial recommendation is out of order. *Journals,* June 4, 1970, p. 935.

Recommital of a Bill

§808. (1) A bill may be recommitted to a Committee of the Whole or to a committee by a Member moving an amendment to the third reading motion.
   (2) Any Member may move to recommit a bill for one of the following purposes:

   (a) to enable a new clause to be added to the bill when the House, on report, has passed the stage at which new clauses are taken;
   (b) to enable the committee to reconsider amendments they had previously made.

§809. Only that part of the bill as is specified in the order for recommittal is considered in the committee. If a bill is recommitted in respect of specified amendment to a clause, only those amendments and amendments that are relevant to them may be moved. When the amendments have been disposed of in respect of any clause, the question that the clause be adopted must be then put.

§810. A bill may be recommitted a number of times with or without limitations. It may be recommitted, amended in committee, reported back to the House, considered at the report stage and read a third time at the one sitting of the House by a Special Order adopted by the House.

COMMUNICATION BETWEEN HOUSES

§811. When a bill has passed all its stages, the House communicates the bill to the Senate by message, acquainting the Senate that the bill has passed in the Commons.

CONSIDERATION OF THE BILL BY THE SENATE

§812. (1) The Senate proceeds to pass the bill in all its stages. If the Senate amends the bill in any form, they communicate a message to the House in order that the House be advised and decide upon concurrence in the amendments.

(2) Should the Senate desire the evidence of a Member, it communicates its request to the House by message. The House will then normally give its consent to the Member to appear should he so wish. *Debates,* May 21, 1921, p. 3259. Should a Member desire to give evidence before the Senate voluntarily, there is no rule which prevents his appearing, and no application need be made to the House. *Journals,* February 27, 1975, p. 321.

(3) The Speaker reads the messages from the Senate announcing that bills passed by the Commons have been amended. These amendments are then printed in that day's *Votes and Proceedings* with the bill being placed on the *Order Paper.*

HOUSE CONSIDERATION OF SENATE AMENDMENTS

§813. (1) When the consideration of Senate amendments to the bill has been put down as an Order of the Day, the House proceeds to consider them under a motion moved by the sponsor of the bill: "That the amendments made by the Senate be read a second time and concurred in." The debate on this motion must be confined to the amendments under consideration and may not extend to other amendments or to the general merits of the bill. *Debates,* January 31, 1978, p. 2395.

(2) If the Senate amendments are agreed to by the Commons, a message is sent acquainting the Senate accordingly and the bill is returned to the Senate to await Royal Assent.

(3) The House may concur in amendments proposed by the Senate in whole or in part. Objections to Senate amendments have been stated directly in the motion for disposing of these amendments. *Journals,* September 2, 1958, p. 533. *Journals,* July 18, 1959, p. 750.

§814. When the House of Commons does not agree to the Senate amendments, it adopts a motion which states reasons for its disagreement. This is communicated to the Senate. If the Senators persist in their amendments, they send a message informing the House of this fact. Upon this, the House either accepts the amendments or adopts a motion requesting a conference to which each House appoints Members; and a date is fixed for their meeting. Should they again disagree, the House may accept the amendments or the Senate may withdraw them, but when neither of these courses is followed, no further action is taken on the bill.

Conferences

§815. (1) Either House may demand a conference upon the following matters: to communicate Resolutions or Addresses to which the concurrence of the other House is desired; concerning the privileges of Parliament; to acquire or to communicate statements of facts on which bills have been passed by either House; to offer reasons for disagreeing to, or insisting on, amendments; or any other subjects allowed to be proper for such a proceeding. Bourinot, pp. 274-280.

(2) While a bill or other matter is pending, it is irregular to demand a conference upon it.

§816. (1) The rules and practice of the House recognize two forms of meeting between representatives of the Senate and House of Commons to settle difficulties over amendments; the conference and the free conference.

(2) The conference, which has fallen into disuse, is a meeting of managers from both Houses at which a written message is delivered, traditionally without the exchange of a single word.

(3) The free conference is a meeting of managers attempting, by discussion, to effect an agreement between the two Houses.

§817. According to British practice, the number of managers appointed by the Commons is double that of the House of Lords. In Canada there has been no consistency, although equal numbers are commonly appointed.

§818. It is the right of the Senate to appoint both the time and place of meeting, regardless of which House has requested the conference.

§819. (1) When the time comes for the conference, the names of the managers for the House are called over and they leave for the meeting. While the conference is meeting, the sittings of both Houses are suspended.

(2) The managers for the House of Commons come first to the conference and stand uncovered at the table. The Senate managers remain sitting and covered during the conference except when receiving the message from the Commons or while speaking during a free conference. Sir Erskine May, Treatise on The Law, Privileges, Proceedings and Usage of Parliament (10th ed., 1893), pp. 413-16.

ROYAL ASSENT

§820. When bills, either public or private, have been finally agreed to by both the Senate and the House of Commons, they await only the Royal Assent to be declared to Parliament to give them the complement and perfection of law. May, pp. 561-2.

§821. (1) When the bills are ready for the Royal Assent, the Speaker receives a message from Government House, which he communicates to the House, stating that the Governor General or his deputy will proceed to the Senate Chamber for the purpose of giving Royal Assent to certain bills later this day.

(2) At the appointed time, the Gentleman Usher of the Black Rod arrives in the House to inform the Speaker that the Governor General desires the immediate attendance of the House. Accordingly the Speaker and the Members go to the Senate Chamber.

(3) Upon returning to the House, the Speaker reports that the Governor General was pleased to give, in Her Majesty's name, the Royal Assent to certain bills, a list of which is recorded in the *Journals*. *Journals,* April 20, 1978, p. 667.

§822. (1) The Royal Assent is rarely given by the Governor General in person. This role is usually performed by a Justice of the Supreme Court of Canada acting on behalf of the Governor General.

(2) The Clerk of the Parliaments (the Clerk of the Senate) endorses on every Act, immediately after the title thereof, the day, month and year when the Act was assented to in Her Majesty's name; such endorsement is taken to be a part of the Act, and the date of such assent is the date of the commencement of the Act, if no other date of commencement is therein provided. Interpretation Act, R.S.C. 1970, c.I-23, s.5.

§823. (1) If a bill should receive the Royal Assent and be afterwards discovered not to have passed its proper stages in both Houses or be otherwise not in conformity with the constitutional procedure, it is in such cases so much waste paper.

(2) If the Clerk of either House forgets to sign a bill as passed, that fact does not invalidate a bill which has passed all its constitutional stages; he may rectify the error later. It is the fact that the *Journals* show that the bill has passed which should govern.

18

Offer of Money to Members:
Bribery in Elections

18

Offer of Money to Members: Bribery in Elections

Offer of Bribe — Acceptance of Bribe or Fees — Corrupt Electoral Practices.

OFFER OF BRIBE

§824.   Standing Order 76 is founded upon a resolution passed by Parliament in England on May 2, 1695. In the spirit of this resolution, the offer of a bribe in order to influence a Member in any of the proceedings of the House, or of a committee, has been treated as a breach of privilege, being an insult not only to the Member himself but also to the House. Sir Erskine May, Treatise on the Law, Privileges, Proceedings and Usage of Parliament (19th ed., 1976), p. 149.

ACCEPTANCE OF BRIBE OR FEES

§825.   (1) The acceptance of a bribe by a Member is an offence under s.108 of the Criminal Code, R.S.C. 1970, c.C-34.

(2) The acceptance of fees by Members for professional services connected with any proceedings or measures of Parliament, is also forbidden under the spirit of this rule, nor is it consistent with parliamentary or professional usage for a Member to advise as a paid counsel upon any private bill before Parliament. Sir John Bourinot, Parliamentary Procedure and Practice in the Dominion of Canada (4th ed., 1916), pp. 57-8.

CORRUPT ELECTORAL PRACTICES

§826.   Matters concerning corrupt practices during elections are the subject of ss.65 to 90 of the Canada Elections Act, R.S.C. 1970, c. 14, (1st Supp.).

19

Internal Economy

19

Internal Economy

Commissioners of Internal Economy — Standing Committee on Management and Members' Services.

COMMISSIONERS OF INTERNAL ECONOMY

§827. (1) The Governor in Council appoints four members of the Queen's Privy Council for Canada who are also Members of the House to be, with the Speaker, Commissioners of Internal Economy. These names are communicated by message to the House from the Governor General within the first week of each session of Parliament.

(2) In the event of the Speaker's death, disability or absence from Canada, or during any dissolution or prorogation of Parliament, any three of the Commissioners may carry out the provisions of the House of Commons Act. House of Commons Act, R.S.C. 1970, c.H-9, s.16(4).

(3) The Clerk of the House of Commons is the Secretary to the Commissioners of Internal Economy.

§828. (1) The powers of the Speaker for the purposes of administration under the terms of the House of Commons Act are extended to last until the election of his successor by the next Parliament. House of Commons Act, s.15.

(2) The provisions of the Act state that the Clerk of the House and Sergeant-at-Arms shall make Estimates of the sums required for the service of the House and shall submit the same to the Speaker who approves them before transmitting them to the Minister of Finance. These Estimates are subsequently laid before the House with the other proposed budgetary Estimates for the coming fiscal year.

§829. All sums of money to be spent from that amount voted by Parliament shall be subject to the order of the Commissioners, or any three of them, of whom the Speaker shall be one. House of Commons Act, s.16(3).

STANDING COMMITTEE ON MANAGEMENT AND MEMBERS' SERVICES

§830. (1) In 1975, the Standing Committee on Management and Members' Services was established to advise the Speaker and the Commissioners of Internal Economy on the administration of the House and the provision of services and facilities to Members.

(2) The Committee was established as a result of a recommendation of the Standing Committee on Procedure and Organization that it was essential to provide a system whereby Members, other than Ministers, could participate in the development of management and administrative decisions. *Journals,* July 18, 1975, p. 726.

§831. All matters relating to the administration of the House and concerning services and facilities to Members are deemed to be referred to the Committee on the first day of each session. S.O. 65(13).

§832. (1) The Chairman of the Committee has been chosen from the membership of the Official Opposition.

(2) The Committee, which usually meets in camera, delegates its work to numerous subcommittees.

(3) The Committee does not normally report to the House but authorizes its Chairman to communicate its recommendations directly to the Speaker.

20

Effect of Prorogation on Orders for Returns

20

Effect of Prorogation on Orders for Returns

EFFECT OF PROROGATION ON ORDERS FOR RETURNS

§833. (1) Returns are completed by the Departments of the Government but, as often happens, a large number cannot be prepared in time to be laid before the House during the session in which they are ordered. In such event, they are simply tabled in the next session. *Journals,* February 27, 1974, p. 6.

(2) When a session is prorogued before a Return is presented it is not the modern practice to renew the Address or Order in the following session, as the Order is held to have force from one session to another until it is complied with.

§834. Returns have sometimes been brought down several years after having been ordered. *Journals,* April 17, 1877, p. 284.

EFFECT OF DISSOLUTION ON ORDERS FOR RETURNS

§835. A dissolution of the House immediately puts an end to all outstanding orders for Returns.

21

Private Bills

21

Private Bills

Private Legislation — Determining whether certain Bills should be Public or Private — Presentation of Petition and Printed Copy of proposed Bill — Form of a Private Bill — Compliance with the Standing Orders — Publication of Notices — Petitions for Private Bills which do not meet the requirements of the Standing Orders — Committee proceedings concerning the publication of Notices — Committee proceedings concerning the presentation of late Petitions — Presentation of the Committee Report — First reading of a Private Bill — Private Bills from the Senate — Numbering of a Private Bill — Fees Payable — Refund Fees — Proceedings on the Order for Private Members' Business — Second reading of a Private Bill — Amendments — Committee Stage of a Private Bill — Hearing of Witnesses — Hearing of Counsel — Divisions in Committee — Amendments in Committee — Proceedings on the Preamble — Preamble not Proven — Procedure when Preamble not proven — Reprint of a Private Bill — Report to the House — Report Stage of a Private Bill — Third Reading of a Private Bill — Amendments by the Senate — Parliamentary Agents — Sponsors of Private Bills — Records of Private Bills.

PRIVATE LEGISLATION

§836.   Private legislation is legislation of a special kind for conferring particular powers or benefits on any person or body of persons, including individuals and private corporations, in excess of or in conflict with the general law. Sir Erskine May, Treatise on the Law, Privileges, Proceedings and Usage of Parliament (19th ed., 1976), p. 857.

§837.   (1) A private bill is solicited by the parties who are interested in promoting it and is founded upon a petition which must be duly deposited in accordance with the Standing Orders of the House.

(2) Private bills are read as many times and similar questions are put and, in general, the same rules of debate and procedure are maintained throughout as for public bills.

Determining Whether Certain Bills Should Be Public Or Private

§838.   There are four principles which have been followed in determining whether a private bill should not be allowed to proceed as such, but should be introduced as a public bill. May, p. 863. These are as follows:

(1) That public policy is affected.

(2) That the bill proposes to amend or repeal public acts. In these cases, the nature and degree of the proposed repeal or amendment have to be considered and provisions of this kind in private bills demand peculiar vigilance, lest public laws be lightly set aside for the benefit of particular persons or places.

(3) The magnitude of the area and the multiplicity of the interests involved.

(4) The fact that the bill though partly of a private nature has as its main object a public matter. In this case the fact that Standing Orders have to be complied with is often an important factor in deciding whether a bill should be a private bill.

PRESENTATION OF PETITION AND PRINTED COPY OF PROPOSED BILL

§839. (1) The Clerk of the House of Commons causes to have published in the *Canada Gazette* all the Standing Orders applicable to the presentation of private bills. In addition he sets out the final date for the receiving of petitions which, according to S.O. 90, is six weeks from the opening of a session.

(2) The computation of days from the opening of Parliament after which petitions for private bills are to be presented, begins on the day on which the Speech from the Throne is delivered. *Journals,* March 24, 1873, p. 58.

§840. (1) For every private bill, a petition, signed by the parties who are promoters for the bill, must be presented to the House of Commons by the Member sponsoring the bill. The Member must deposit with the Clerk of the House, not later than the first day of each session, a printed copy of the proposed bill.

(2) This bill is studied by the Examiner of Private Bills (the Chief of the Committees and Private Legislation Branch) to ensure uniformity and strict conformity with Standing Order of the House.

(3) Promoters may obtain model bills from the Clerk of the House.

§841. The rules that govern petitions apply to those for private bills, and it is therefore important that every applicant for private legislation carefully observe those rules, as an informality may jeopardize the measure he is applying for. Sir John Bourinot, Parliamentary Procedure and Practice in the Dominion of Canada (4th ed., 1916), p. 583.

§842. The signature of a petitioner must appear on the sheet containing the whole or part of the prayer; it must be in the hand-writing of the party interested. An agent cannot sign for another person except in case of illness.

§843. A clear day must elapse between the days of presentation and reception of a petition.

§844. (1) It is a recognized principle in Parliament, that Ministers of the Crown should not initiate or promote private bill legislation.

(2) No notice is required for a motion to change the promoter of a public or private bill after its introduction. *Journals,* March 14, 1884, p. 238.

FORM OF A PRIVATE BILL

§845. The form of a private bill is similar to that of a public bill with the exception that it must have a preamble which is generally written in the following terms:

> "Whereas (the person/corporation named), has by its petition prayed that it be enacted as hereinafter set forth and it is expedient to grant the prayer of the said petition: Therefore Her Majesty, by and with the advice and consent of the Senate and House of Commons, enacts as follows:"

COMPLIANCE WITH THE STANDING ORDERS

§846. The Clerk of Petitions reports whether the petition meets the requirements of the Standing Orders as to form. His Report is given to the Clerk of the House who lays it upon the Table.

PUBLICATION OF NOTICES

§847. (1) All applications to Parliament for private bills shall be advertised by a notice published in the *Canada Gazette* and in some leading newspapers.

(2) The promoters, through their Parliamentary Agent, must present to the Clerk of the House a statutory declaration establishing proof of compliance with the requirements of notice.

(3) Following the tabling of the petition for a private bill in the House it is examined by the Examiner of Petitions for Private Bills (the Chief of the Committees and Private Legislation Branch) who reports to the House whether the petition has complied with the requirements of S.O. 93 in relation to the publication of notices in the *Canada Gazette* and leading newspapers.

PETITIONS FOR PRIVATE BILLS WHICH DO NOT MEET THE REQUIREMENTS OF THE STANDING ORDERS

§848. When petitions for private bills do not meet the requirements of the Standing Orders, the Chairman of the Standing Committee on Miscellaneous Private Bills and Standing Orders moves in the House that the petition together with the Report of the Clerk of Petitions or the Report of the Examiner of Petitions for Private Bills, as the case may be, be referred to the

Standing Committee on Miscellaneous Private Bills and Standing Orders to make such recommendations as it deems advisable.

§849. (1) The Standing Committee on Miscellaneous Private Bills and Standing Orders does not consider petitions which the Examiner of Petitions for Private Bills has found to comply with the Standing Orders in all particulars. If the Examiner finds any irregularity in the petition or in the notices required, the committee takes the matter into consideration and may recommend to the House a waiver or suspension of a Standing Order if deemed advisable. Bourinot, p. 584.

(2) The Committee determines and reports to the House whether the Standing Orders not complied with should or should not be dispensed with and whether, in their opinion, the parties should be permitted to proceed with their bill, or any portion of it, and upon what terms and conditions.

(3) The Committee may recommend the suspension of a Standing Order and that a charge be levied under the terms of S.O. 91(3).

Committee Proceedings Concerning the Publication of Notices

§850. (1) There are many instances where the Committee has felt justified in dispensing with a notice altogether when it was fully aware that all parties interested had been sufficiently notified or that no interests were affected except those of the petitioners.

(2) When, in any case, the notice, upon examination, proves to be insufficient, it is so reported to the House, and (unless accompanied by a recommendation to suspend the Standing Order) all further action in the matter is dropped; the decision of the Committee is rarely overruled by the House.

§851. In judging as to the sufficiency of a notice submitted for its examination, the Committee compares its terms with those of the petition. Any important variance or omission in the former is fatal either to the whole measure or to a particular provision therein. In some instances the notice (though published in the prescribed manner in other respects) has been unfavourably reported on because it did not sufficiently indicate the objects sought to be attained.

§852. If the notice is found to be too general in its terms, or if no mention is made of certain matters included in the petition which require a specific notice, these facts are reported, with the bill being restricted within the terms of the notice. If the matters so omitted are allowed to be inserted in the bill, due provision is made therein for the protection of all parties whose rights might be affected by the want of a specific notice.

§853. A private bill containing provisions not contemplated in the notice should be referred to the Standing Committee on Miscellaneous Private Bills and Standing Orders to report whether the powers to be conferred are in excess of the notice given or whether they are substantially included in it. *Journals,* March 28, 1870, p. 116.

Committee Proceedings Concerning the Presentation of Late Petitions

§854. When the usual time for receiving petitions for private bills has expired, the parties interested in a private bill may present a petition praying to be permitted to lay before the House a petition for the passing of a necessary bill. It is usual to allow such a petition and to refer it to the Standing Committee on Miscellaneous Private Bills and Standing Orders. Bourinot, p. 587.

§855. After an unfavourable report from the Committee, the House has referred petitions back to the Committee, with an Instruction to consider and report as to the expediency of suspending a Standing Order.

§856. It has occasionally happened that after certain petitions have been unfavourably reported on, further evidence has been produced, sufficient to satisfy the Committee. In such cases it has made a further report, representing either that the notice has since been continued so as to complete the full time required or that it has been amended so as to meet the requirements of the Standing Order, or that the evidence subsequently adduced proved that the notice was sufficient for all parties concerned.

Presentation of the Committee Report

§857. The Chairman of the Standing Committee on Miscellaneous Private Bills and Standing Orders presents the Committee's Report to the House and moves its concurrence at the earliest opportunity.

FIRST READING OF A PRIVATE BILL

§858. When the Examiner of Petitions for Private Bills reports favourably upon the petition, the Clerk of the House lays upon the Table the private bill which is read a first time, printed and ordered for second reading at the next sitting of the House in accordance with S.O. 100(1).

Private Bills From the Senate

§859. When the House receives a message from the Senate desiring it to concur in a private bill, that bill is then deemed to read a first time and ordered for second reading at the next sitting of the House pursuant to S.O. 100(2).

Numbering of a Private Bill

§860. Private bills originating in the House of Commons are numbered in consecutive sequence beginning with C-1001. Those private bills originating in the Senate retain their Senate number during their passage through the House.

FEES PAYABLE

§861.   The fees payable for the introduction of private bills are set forth in S.O. 91.

Refunds of Fees

§862.   (1) A motion may be introduced in the House to refund fees paid in relation to a private bill; however, this motion can only be moved after the committee stage has been finalized. *Journals,* December 9, 1974, pp. 179-181.

(2) The motion may be proposed in the following words:

> "That, pursuant to Standing Order 99 the Standing Committee on Miscellaneous Private Bills and Standing Orders be authorized to consider and make recommendations upon the fees paid by .... in relation to ...."

(3) When there is a case for reimbursement a report is made by the Committee to the House and, if it is concurred in, a copy of the House's decision is forwarded to the Receiver General of Canada who may pay the refund out of the Consolidated Revenue Fund. Financial Administration Act, R.S.C. 1970, c.F-10, s.16.

§863.   (1) When it is not intended to proceed with a bill, the regular course is to move, at the same time, for leave to withdraw it and to refund the fees. Bourinot, p. 604.

(2) It is usual to refund the fees upon a notice to that effect being made on the recommendation of a committee when:

(a)   the promoters have asked leave to withdraw the bill;

(b)   the bill has been rejected by the committee;

(c)   its provisions have been amalgamated with another;

(d)   the powers applied for have been materially diminished;

(e)   the bill has been withdrawn in the House after having been favourably reported by the committee;

(f)   the necessity for the passage of the bill arose from no fault of the promoters but from circumstances beyond their control;

(g)   the bill is a mere amendment to a previous Act;

(h)   the project provided for in the bill is of great public benefit;

(i)   the bill is of a purely humanitarian, charitable, philanthropic or religious character affecting no commercial interest;

(j)   the committee makes no report on the bill;

(k)   the bill, if passed, never comes into force; or

(l)   a bill from the Commons has been rejected by the Senate. Bourinot, pp. 603-4.

(3) The fees paid on a bill that has not become law may be refunded in a subsequent session. *Journals,* July 2, 1892, p. 417. *Journals,* May 26, 1976, p. 1313.

PROCEEDING ON THE ORDER FOR PRIVATE MEMBERS' BUSINESS

§864. The practice developed over the last few years is that the Government takes the necessary steps to schedule, in advance, the business to be considered during Private Members' Hour, having due regard to the priorities established on the *Order Paper* and through consultation. The House should proceed directly to the scheduled item, standing all preceding items by unanimous consent. A Member who feels that the practice has resulted in an injustice on a particular occasion, in that he should have been consulted or given more advance notice, may express his dissatisfaction simply by withholding the required unanimous consent. This obliges the Speaker to call one by one, all the items preceding the scheduled item. Items not proceeded with when called in this manner will be allowed to stand either at the request of the Government or by unanimous consent or be dropped. *Journals,* December 5, 1977, p. 173.

§865. In practice, an order for resuming the adjourned debate on the second reading of a private Members' bill is proceeded with only at the request of the sponsor of the bill or a Member authorized to act on his behalf. The practice is to allow a bill to stand when the Member who has sponsored it is not present, though he may not have authorized another Member to act on his behalf. In other words, the absent Member is deemed to have asked that the bill stand until the next sitting day. *Journals,* June 23, 1950, p. 570.

SECOND READING OF A PRIVATE BILL

§866. (1) The second reading stage of a private bill corresponds to the second reading stage of public bills. In agreeing to the bill the House affirms the general principle, or expediency, of the measure. The expediency of a private bill is mainly founded upon allegations of fact which have not yet been proved. The House affirms the principle of the bill, conditionally subject to the proof of such allegations before a committee. Where, irrespective of such facts, the principle is objectionable, the House will consent to the second reading; but otherwise the expediency of the measure is usually left for the consideration of a committee. This is the first occasion on which the bill is before the House and if its principle is opposed this is the proper time for attempting its defeat.

(2) Debate at the second reading stage concerns only the principle of the bill and not any evidence that may be involved. *Journals,* December 4, 1962, p. 355.

§867. (1) Second reading of private bills is debated at various times on Tuesdays, Thursdays and Fridays during Private Members' Hour in accordance with S.O. 15 and S.O. 20.

(2) Private bills when read a second time stand referred to one of the following Standing Committees:

(a) Standing Committee on Finance, Trade and Economic Affairs;
(b) Standing Committee on Transport and Communications; or
(c) Standing Committee on Miscellaneous Private Bills and Standing Orders.

Amendments

§868. The rules and types of amendments that may be proposed at the second reading stage of public bills applies equally to those for private bills. A Member cannot, on an amendment to the motion for the second reading of a private bill, propose an alleged improvement in public laws. *Journals,* April 30, 1948, p. 407.

§869. If the second reading is deferred for six months or if the bill is rejected, no new bill for the same object can be offered until the next session.

COMMITTEE STAGE OF A PRIVATE BILL

§870. (1) The committee cannot consider a private bill until after one week's notice has been affixed in the lobby; nor in the case of any such bill originating in the Senate, until after twenty-four hours like notice. S.O. 103(1).

(2) At each sitting, a list of the bills which are ready for consideration is laid before the committee, in the order of their reference. They are usually taken up in that order, unless it may be otherwise agreed upon for the convenience of parties in attendance. Where no such arrangement is made, the bill is taken up in its order.

§871. When the committee is about to proceed to the consideration of a private bill, the parties are called in, and the preamble is read. Instances may arise in which the committee may feel it desirable that they should reserve their judgement upon the preamble until certain details of the bill have been settled. In such cases, they postpone the preamble until after the consideration of the clauses.

§872. If the promoters inform the committee that they do not desire to proceed further with the bill, this fact is reported to the House and the bill will be ordered to be withdrawn. If any other parties before the committee, either as petitioners or opponents of the bill, desire to proceed with it, the committee may permit them to do so.

Hearing of Witnesses

§873. (1) Any contest as to the locus standi (right to appear) of the petitioners opposed to the bill is settled by the committee.

(2) In practice, those persons who are opposed to the bill communicate with the committee asking to be heard. The committee will decide if and when the persons will be heard and whether or not they may be represented by counsel. The procedure followed is identical to that of a committee on a public bill.

Hearing of Counsel

§874. The promoters of the bill or witnesses opposed to the bill may be represented by counsel. No Member may act as counsel before any committee nor may any Member of either House act as counsel before the other House without special permission. When such permission is given it is understood that the Member who receives it will not be permitted to vote on the bill, if it should be received by the House of which he is a Member.

Divisions in Committee

§875. All questions before committees on private bills are decided by a majority of voices. Whenever the voices are equal, including the voice of the Chairman, the Chairman has a second or casting vote. S.O. 104.

Amendments in Committee

§876. (1) A committee on a private bill is precluded from making amendments which are beyond the scope of the bill as defined by the clauses and schedules of the bill. It is within their competence, however, to make amendments in the bill which are within those purposes, though such amendments, necessarily, must not enlarge the powers sought by the bill.

(2) The admissibility of amendments made at the committee stage of a private bill is governed by the same principles as those for public bills.

§877. The committee has no authority to make any amendments which may involve an infraction of the Standing Orders or which may affect the interests of the parties interested, without due notice having been given to the same. The committee has made, with the consent of the parties, very material alterations in a bill and in such cases, they reported that fact to the House. *Journals,* April 21, 1868, p. 212.

§878. The committee has no power to entertain questions in reference to the compliance with the Standing Orders (which pertains solely to the Standing Committee on Miscellaneous Private Bills and Standing Orders) unless by Special Order from the House. This Order is given only when the House, on the report of that Committee, allows parties to proceed with their bill on complying with certain Standing Orders which they had previously neglected. *Journals,* December 9, 1974, p. 179.

PROCEEDINGS ON THE PREAMBLE

§879. The preamble of a private bill is usually considered first unless the bill is for a variety of purposes. In such cases consideration of the preamble or the parts not relevant is normally postponed until after the consideration of the various clauses.

§880. It is within the power of the committee to make alterations in the preamble, either by striking out or modifying such allegations as may not have been substantiated to their satisfaction, or by expunging such parts as the promoters may wish to have withdrawn. No new allegations or provisions ought to be inserted, either in the preamble or the bill, except such as are covered by the Petition and the Notice. Every material alteration, with reasons, made to the preamble must be reported to the House.

Preamble Not Proven

§881. It has been ruled in the House of Commons of the United Kingdom that when a committee has resolved that the preamble has not been proven it is not competent for the committee to reconsider and reverse its decision. Consequently, it is for the House to give the committee instructions which will enable it to re-consider the whole question again.

§882. Committees have reported against bills on the following grounds:

(1) insufficient evidence offered in favour of the preamble; antagonistic evidence;
(2) no proof of the consent of the parties interested;
(3) the petitions against the measure being as numerous as, or even more numerous than, those in its favour;
(4) a great difference of opinion in the locality affected as to the expediency of the measure;
(5) legislative interference not being desirable or necessary;
(6) the bill would interfere with lawsuits pending or with existing rights;
(7) the power sought would not advance the interest of the locality;
(8) the bill asking for an extension of the powers of a certain company to purposes entirely foreign to its original charter;
(9) most unusual provisions; or
(10) the provisions of a general Act affording sufficient facilities to the promoters to obtain the powers asked for.

Procedure When Preamble Not Proven

§883. When a committee reports that the preamble of a private bill is not proven, the Member sponsoring the bill should move a motion under Routine Proceedings in order to place the bill upon the *Order Paper*. When the Order for Private Bills is called, other motions to refer the bill back to the committee may be considered. *Journals,* July 18, 1963, pp. 225-6.

REPRINT OF A PRIVATE BILL

§884. If necessary, the committee may order, at the expense of the promoters, that the bill be reprinted, as amended.

REPORT TO THE HOUSE

§885. (1) It is the duty of every committee to report to the House a bill that has been committed to them and not, through long adjournments, to withhold from the House the result of their proceedings.

(2) If a committee does not report back a bill, the House should take cognizance of the matter. Bourinot, p. 614.

§886. If the committee is of the opinion that the bill falls under that class which requires the consent of the Crown before its passage, it will report this fact to the House; and the consent, if received, will be signified by a Minister of the Crown at a future stage of the proceedings.

§887. A Report from a committee on a private bill prior to its passage which recommends that the fees payable under the Standing Orders be held in abeyance goes beyond the order of reference of that committee. *Journals,* December 9, 1974, p. 179.

REPORT STAGE OF A PRIVATE BILL

§888. Under S.O. 116, the provision of a report stage for public bills applies equally to private bills. *Journals,* February 26, 1976, p. 1070.

THIRD READING OF A PRIVATE BILL

§889. (1) The same rules for the third reading stage apply for private bills as for public bills. Bills may be recommitted to a committee for reconsideration. When this occurs, any Instruction which the House deems necessary may be given to the committee.

(2) If the Member who has given notice of an amendment to a private bill is not in his seat when the bill is called for third reading, no other Member may move the amendment on his behalf. *Debates,* May 25, 1928, p. 3379.

AMENDMENTS BY THE SENATE

§890. When a private bill is returned from the Senate with amendments, these amendments are referred to the committee which originally studied the bill.

§891. (1) If the committee reports concurrence in the Senate amendments, they will be read immediately in the House a second time and, if agreed to, will be returned to the Senate with the usual message.

(2) If the committee reports that the amendments should be disagreed to for certain reasons, the House may consider the amendments forthwith, and having read them a second time may disagree with those on which the committee has reported unfavourably for the reasons set forth in the committee Report. The House will then "insist" or "not insist" on its amendments if the message is received that the other House disagrees to them.

(3) The committee may recommend that certain amendments be made to the Senate amendments. *Journals,* May 12, 1886, p. 255.

PARLIAMENTARY AGENTS

§892. (1) The persons by whom the promotion of private bills and the conduct of proceedings upon petitions against such bills are carried out are called parliamentary agents.

(2) Members may not be agents. No officer or clerk of the House is allowed to transact private business before the House, for his emolument or advantage, either directly or indirectly. Bourinot, p. 582.

SPONSORS OF PRIVATE BILLS

§893. It is the practice in the House of Commons for Members to take charge of private bills and to sponsor their progress through the House and its committees, but it is contrary to the law and usage of Parliament that any Member of the House should be permitted to engage, either by himself or any partner, in the management of private bills before this or the other House of Parliament for pecuniary reward. Bourinot, p. 581.

RECORDS OF PRIVATE BILLS

§894. (1) A register containing the particulars of parliamentary agents is kept in the Committees and Private Legislation Branch.

(2) A record is made of all matters pertaining to private bills. S.O. 112.

Appendix 1

Forms and Formulae

Appendix 1

Forms and Formulae

Motions — Speaker's Formulae — Deputy Speaker's Formulae.

MOTIONS

No. 1

Election of the Speaker

That .... Member for the Electoral District of ...., do take the Chair of this House as Speaker.

No. 2

Election of the Chairman of Committee of the Whole, Deputy Chairman and Assistant Deputy Chairman of Committees of the Whole

That .... Member for the Electoral District of ...., be elected Chairman (*or* be appointed Deputy Chairman *or* Assistant Deputy Chairman) of Committees of the Whole House.

No. 3

Address in Reply to the Speech from the Throne

N.B. The following varies when the Speech is read by the Sovereign or the Administrator.

That the following Address be presented to His Excellency the Governor General of Canada:

To His Excellency the Right Honourable Chancellor and Principal Companion of the Order of Canada, Chancellor and Commander of the Order of Military Merit, Governor General and Commander-in-Chief of Canada:

MAY IT PLEASE YOUR EXCELLENCY:

We, Her Majesty's most loyal and dutiful subjects, the House of

Commons of Canada, in Parliament assembled, beg leave to offer our humble thanks to Your Excellency for the gracious Speech which Your Excellency has addressed to both Houses of Parliament.

No. 4

Amendment to Address in Reply to Speech from Throne

That the following be added to the Address: ....

No. 5

Engrossing and Presenting the Address

N.B. Immediately after the Address in Reply to the Speech from the Throne has been adopted, the following motion is made:

That the Address be engrossed and presented to His Excellency the Governor-General by the Speaker.

No. 6

Designation of a Continuing Order of Supply under S.O. 58

That this House at its next sitting consider the Business of Supply.

No. 7

Appointment of the Selection Committee

That a Committee be appointed to prepare and report, in accordance with S.O. 65, lists of Members to compose the Standing and Standing Joint Committees of this House; that the Committee be composed of ....; and that the provisions of S.O. 65(1) be suspended in relation to the number of Members on the said Committee.

No. 8

Concurrence in the Report of the Selection Committee

That the Report of the .... Committee appointed to prepare and report lists of Members to compose the Standing Committees of this House presented .... (*this day*) be concurred in.

No. 9

Appointment of a Special Committee or a Special Joint Committee

N.B. Not all of the following paragraphs are required in each case.

That a Special (Joint) Committee (of the Senate and) of the House of Commons be appointed to consider ....;

That (*number*) Members of the House of Commons, to be designated at a later date, be members on the part of this House on the Special Joint Committee;

That the Committee have power to appoint from among its Members such subcommittees as may be deemed advisable and necessary and to delegate to such sub-committees all or any of their powers except the power to report directly to the House;

That the Committee have poqer to sit during sittings and adjournments of the House of Commons;

That the Committee have power to report from time to time, to send for persons, papers and records, and to examine witnesses and to print such papers and evidence from day to day as may be ordered by the Committee;

That the Committee have power to adjourn from place to place within Canada;

That the Committee be empowered to retain the services of advisers to assist in its work; and that it also be empowered to retain the professional, clerical and stenographic help as may be required;

That the papers and evidence received and taken on the subject in the .... Session(s) of the .... Parliament be referred to the Committee;

That the Committee submit its report not later than ....;

That the quorum of the Committee be .... Members, whenever a vote, resolution or other decision is taken, so long as both Houses are represented and that the Joint Chairmen be authorized to hold meetings, to receive evidence and authorize the printing thereof, when .... Members are present so long as both Houses are represented; and

That a Message be sent to the Senate requesting that the House do unite with this House for the above purpose, and to select, if the Senate deems it to be advisable, Members to act on the proposed Special Joint Committee.

No. 10

Concurrence in Appointment of a Joint Committee

That the House of Commons do unite with the Senate in the appointment of a Joint Committee of both Houses of Parliament to (here follows the purpose and powers of the Committee);

That the Members to serve on the part of this House be ....; and

That a Message be sent to the Senate to inform that House accordingly.

No. 11

Instruction to a Committee

That it be an Instruction to the .... Committee on
.... that they have power to ....

No. 12

Concurrence in a Report from a Committee

That the .... Report of the .... Committee on
........................, presented to the House on ...., be concurred
in.

No. 13

Recommittal of Committee Report

That the .... Report be not now concurred in but that it be
recommitted to the .... Committee on .... with
instruction that they have power to amend the same so as to recommend that
....

No. 14

Referring the Estimates to Committees

That the Estimates of sums required for service of Canada for the fiscal
year ending March 31, 19. ., be referred to the several Standing Committees of
the House, as follows:
To the Standing Committee on Agriculture:
Agriculture Votes 1, 5, 10, 15, 20, L30, 35 and 40 etc.

No. 15

Reporting Progress in Committee of the Whole

"I move, Mr. Chairman, that you do now rise and report progress."

No. 16

For the Chairman to leave the Chair in Committee of the Whole

"I move, Mr. Chairman, that you do now leave the Chair."

No. 17

Voting supplies in Committee

N.B. By the Chairman.

"Shall Vote .... under (*name of Department*) carry?"

No. 18

Notice of Opposition to an Item in the Estimates

Notice is hereby given of opposition to Vote (*number*) under (*name of Department*) in the Supplementary Estimates) for the fiscal year ending March 31, 19...

No. 19

Concurrence in Opposed Items

That Vote (*number*) under (*name of Department*) (in the Supplementary Estimates) for the fiscal year ending March 31, 19... be concurred in.

No. 20

Concurrence in the Estimates

That the Main (Supplementary) Estimates for the year ending March 31, 19..., except the item(s) disposed of earlier this day, and less the amounts voted in Interim Supply, be concurred in.

No. 21

Extended Adjournment of the House

That when the House adjourns on (*day and date*), it shall stand adjourned until (*day and date*), provided that any any time prior to that date, if it appears to the satisfaction of the Speaker, after consultation with the Government, that the public interest requires that the House should meet at an earlier time during the adjournment, the Speaker may give notice that he is so satisfied, and thereupon the House shall meet at the time stated in such notice, and shall transact its business as if it had been duly adjourned to that time; and

That, in the event of the Speaker's being unable to act owing to illness or other cause, the Deputy Speaker or the Deputy Chairman of Committees shall act in his stead for all purposes of this order.

No. 22

Extending a sitting of the House under S.O. 6(5)(*a*)

N.B. The motion must be proposed in the hour preceding an interruption, such as Private Members' Hour, dinner hour or daily adjournment time.

That the House continue to sit (beyond the ordinary hour of daily adjournment *or* through the lunch hour *or* through the dinner hour) for the purpose of continuing consideration of (*here Member states the business to be continued which must be under consideration at that time by the House*).

No. 23

Sitting on Saturday

That the House shall sit on Saturday, (*date*); and
That, for the purpose of S.O. 2, 6, and 15, the sitting shall be deemed to be a Friday, except that Private Members' Business shall not be taken up.

No. 24

Adjournment of the House
for the Purposes of Discussing a Motion under S.O. 26

A Member says: "Mr. Speaker, I ask leave to move the adjournment of the House, under S.O. 26, for the purpose of discussing a specific and important matter requiring consideration, namely (*here describe the question to be debated, notice of which must be supplied to the Speaker at least two hours prior to the opening of the sitting or as soon as practicable but before the opening of the sitting*)."
The Speaker shall decide whether the matter is proper to be discussed. If leave is granted by the House, The Speaker sets down the time the matter will be discussed according to the Standing Order.
At this time the Member moves the following: That this House do now adjourn.

No. 25

Suspension of a Sitting

That the sitting be suspended (until .... o'clock p.m. this day *or* until .... o'clock a.m. this day *or* to the call of the Chair *or* until the ringing of the Bells).

No. 26

Adjournment of the House

That this House do now adjourn.

No. 27

Adjournment of Debate

That the debate be now adjourned.

No. 28

The Previous Question

That the Question be now put.

No. 29

Reading the Orders of the Day

N.B. Either may be used.

(a) That the Orders of the Day be now read.
(b) That the House do now proceed to the Orders of the Day.

No. 30

Proceeding to Another Order

That the House do now proceed to Order No. (*here specify the Order*).

No. 31

Discharging an Order of the Day

That Order No. .... under (*here state where the item is listed on the Order Paper and describe the item*) be discharged.

No. 32

Reverting to an Order of Business

That the House do not revert to Routine Proceedings (*or to a particular item under Routine Proceedings or to Government Orders.*).

No. 33

Member to be now heard

That the honourable Member for (*name of constituency*) be now heard.

No. 34

Leave to Introduce a Bill

I ask the leave of the House to introduce a Bill respecting
....

No. 35

First Reading of a Bill

That the Bill be now read a first time and be printed.

No. 36

First Reading of a Senate Bill

That Bill S-............, An Act ...., be now read a first time.

No. 37

Second Reading of a Bill

That Bill C-............, An Act .... be now read a second time
and referred to the Standing Committee on ....

No. 38

Amendments to the Order for Second Reading — Reasoned Amendments

That all the words after the word "That" be deleted and the following
substituted therefor: this House declines to give second reading to Bill C-
............, An Act ...., (*here state reasons*) ....

No. 39

The Six Months' Hoist

That the motion be amended by deleting all the words after the word
"That" and substituting the following therefor:
"Bill C-............, An Act ...., be not now read a second time
but that it be read a second time this day six months hence."

No. 40

Bill Withdrawn at Second Reading Stage and Subject-Matter Referred to Committee

(a)   That the motion be amended by deleting all the words after the word

"That" and substituting the following therefor:

"Bill C-............, An Act ...., be not now read a second time but that the Order for Second Reading be discharged, the Bill withdrawn and the subject-matter thereof referred to the .... Committee on ...."

(b) *N.B. The following is used when the main motion has not been moved:*

"That Bill C-............, An Act ...., be withdrawn, the Order for Second Reading discharged and the subject-matter thereof referred to the .... Committee on ...."

No. 41

Motions to amend a Bill at the Report Stage

(1) That Bill C-............, An Act ...., be amended by deleting Clause ....

(2) That Bill C-............, An Act ...., be amended in Clause .... by

(a) striking out lines .... to .... at page .... and substituting the following therefor:

....

(b) adding immediately after line .... at page .... the following new subsection:

....

(3) That Bill C-............, An Act ...., be amended by adding immediately after line .... at page .... the following new Clause:

.... and by renumbering the subsequent Clauses accordingly.

No. 42

Concurrence at the Conclusion of the Report Stage

That Bill C-............, An Act .... (as amended) be concurred in.

No. 43

Third Reading of a Bill

That Bill C-............, An Act .... be now read a third time and do pass.

No. 44

Amendments to the Order for Third Reading — Recommittal of a Bill

That the motion be amended by deleting all the words after the word "That" and substituting the following therefor:

"Bill C-............, An Act ...., be not now read a third time but be referred back to the (Committee of the Whole House *or* Standing Committee on ....) for the purpose of reconsidering Clause(s) ...."

No. 45

Concurrence in Senate Amendments

That the amendments made by the Senate to Bill C-............, An Act ...., be now read a second time and concurred in.

No. 46

Disagreement to Senate Amendments

That a Message be sent to the Senate to acquaint Their Honours that this House disagrees with the amendment made by the Senate to Bill C-............, An Act ...., for the following reasons:

No. 47

Agreeing with Senate Amendments to Money Bills

That the amendments made to Bill C-............, An Act to .... be now read a second time and concurred in; but that this House, while disapproving of any infraction of its privileges or rights by the other House, in this case waives its claims to insist upon such rights and privileges, but the waiver of said rights and privileges is not to be drawn into a precedent.

And that a Message be sent to the Senate to acquaint Their Honours therewith.

No. 48

Amendments to Senate Amendments

That the amendments made by the Senate to Bill C-............, An Act ...., be concurred in with the exception of the (*number of the amendment*) amendment to which this House proposes the following amendment:

(*Here mention amendment*)

And that a Message be sent to the Senate to acquaint Their Honours therewith.

No. 49

Conference with the Senate when the Senate (House) insists on its Amendments

That a Message be sent to the Senate (House) respectfully requesting a free conference with Their Honours to consider the reasons advanced by the Senate (House) for insisting upon its amendments to Bill C-............., An Act ...., and any amendments which at such conference it may be considered desirable to make to the Bill or amendments thereto.

No. 50

Appointing the Managers of the Conference

N.B. Upon reception of Senate's Message acceding to the request for the Conference.

That .... be appointed Managers on behalf of this House of the free conference with the Senate with respect to the amendments made to Bill C-............., An Act ....; and

That a Message be sent to the Senate to acquaint Their Honours therewith:

No. 51

Report of Managers

Your Managers beg to report that they duly hold a conference with the Managers appointed by the Senate with respect to the amendments made by the Senate to Bill C-............., An Act ...., and that the Managers of the Senate have agreed to recommend that Senate amendments numbered ...., be amended to read as follows: ....

No. 52

Production of Papers

That an Order of the House do issue for a copy of ....

No. 53

Address for the Production of Papers

That a humble address be presented to His Excellency praying that he will cause to be laid before this House a copy of all ....

No. 54

Correcting Entries in the Votes and Proceedings or Journals

That the *Votes and Proceedings* (*or* the *Journals*) of the sitting of .... be corrected by striking out the words .... in line .... in the left (right) column, page ...., or by inserting the words .... between the words .... and .... in line .... in the left (right) column, page .... and substituting therefore the words ....

No. 55

Cancelling Entries in the Votes and Proceedings or Journals

That the Entries in the *Votes and Proceedings* (*or Journals*) of the sitting of .... in connection with .... be expunged.

No. 56

Rescinding Resolutions

That the resolution (*or* Order) adopted by the House on .... as follows ...., be rescinded.

No. 57

Taking Down Unparliamentary Words

That the words .... which have just been used by ...., Member for ...., be taken down by the Clerk.

No. 58

Deciding Whether the Words Taken Down have been used

That the House is of the opinion that the words which have been taken down and read by the Clerk were used by ...., Member for ....

No. 59

Clearing the Galleries

N.B. Either may be used.

(a) Shall strangers be ordered to withdraw.
(b) That strangers be ordered to withdraw.

No. 60

Suspension of a Member after being named by the Speaker

That the honourable Member for (*name of constituency*) be suspended from the service of the House for the remainder of today's sitting (*or longer*).

No. 61

Directing the Sergeant-at-Arms to take a Member into Custody

That ...., Member for ...., be taken into custody by the Sergeant-at-Arms.

No. 62

Directing a Member to attend in his Place to Answer for His Conduct

That ...., Member for ...., having refused to comply with an order given to him by the House on .... do attend in his place tomorrow to answer for his conduct.

No. 63

Censuring and Temporarily suspending a Member

That the House do censure ...., Member for ...., and exclude him from the Chamber for fifteen days (*or for the rest of the sitting, or any other period, as the case may be*).

No. 64

Having an Admonition or Reprimand entered in the Journals

That the admonition (*or* reprimand) delivered by the Speaker against the .... Members for .... be entered in the *Journals*.

No. 65

Relieving from Punishment

That ...., Member for ...., be relieved from the suspension pronounced upon him.

No. 66

Directing the Speaker to Admonish or Reprimand

That .... be admonished (*or* reprimanded) by the Speaker for (*here describe the breach committed*).

No. 67

Notice of Closure

N.B. By the Minister of the Crown.

"I give notice that at the next sitting of the House, immediately before the Order of the Day is called for resuming debate on the motion ...., and on any amendments proposed thereto, I will move that the debate shall not be further adjourned."

No. 68

For Applying Closure

That the debate on the motion for .... and on any amendments proposed thereto, shall not be further adjourned.

No. 69

Time Allocation under S.O. 75A

N.B. By a Minister of the Crown, without notice.

"Under the provisions of Standing Order 75A, I wish to state that the representatives of all parties have reached an agreement with regard to a proposed allotment of time for the disposition of (*here one or more stages may be mentioned*) of Bill C-.............., An Act ...."

The Minister then moves

"That, in relation to Bill C-.............., an Act ...., (*time allocation*) shall be allotted to the (stage *or* stages) of the Bill; and .... (*here set forth the terms of any agreed allocations*)."

No. 70

Time Allocation under S.O. 75B

N.B. By a Minister of the Crown, without notice.

"Under the provisions of S.O. 75B, I wish to state that a majority of the representatives of all parties have reached an agreement with regard to a proposed allotment of time for the (*here one stage is mentioned or the report stage and third reading stage may be mentioned or the report stage and third reading stage may be mentioned if in conformity with S.O. 75(13)*) of Bill C-............., an Act ...."

N.B. The Minister then moves:

"That, in relation to Bill C-............., An Act ...., (*time allocation*) shall be allotted to the consideration of the (stage *or* stages) of the Bill; .... (*here set forth the terms of any agreed allocations*)."

No. 71

Notice of Motion for Time Allocation under S.O. 75C

N.B. By a Minister of the Crown from his place in the House.

"That an agreement could not be reached under the provisions of Standing Order 75A or 75B with respect to an allocation of time to the (*stage of Bill*) of Bill C-............., An Act ...., and, under the provisions of Standing Order 75C, I give notice of my intention to move a time allocation motion at the next sitting of the House for the purpose of allotting a specified number of days or hours for the consideration and disposal of proceedings at that stage of the Bill."

No. 72

Motion for Time Allocation under S.O. 75C

That, in relation to Bill C-............., An Act ...., not more than (*time allocation*) shall be allotted to the further consideration of the (*stage of Bill*); and .... (*here set forth the terms of any time allocations*).

No. 73

For Hearing the Evidence of a Senator before a Committee

That a Message be sent to the Senate requesting that Their Honours will give leave to the Honourable ...., one of their Members, to attend and give evidence before the Standing (*or* Special) Committee of this House on ....

No. 74

For Amending the British North America Act in some respects

That a humble Address be presented to Her Majesty the Queen in the following words:

To the Queen's most Excellent Majesty:

Most Gracious Sovereign:

We Your Majesty's most dutiful and loyal subjects, the Senate and the Commons of Canada in Parliament assembled, humbly approach Your Majesty, praying that You may graciously be pleased to cause a measure to be laid before the Parliament of the United Kingdom to be expressed as follows:

An Act to amend the British North America Act, 1867.

Whereas the Senate and House of Commons of Canada in Parliament assembled have submitted an Address to Her Majesty praying that Her Majesty may graciously be pleased to cause a measure to be laid before the Parliament of the United Kingdom for the enactment of the provisions hereinafter set forth;

Be it therefore enacted by the Queen's most Excellent Majesty, by and with the advice and consent of the Lords Spiritual and Temporal, and Commons, in this present Parliament assembled, and by the authority of the same, as follows: ....

No. 75

Designation of a Day for Consideration of Ways and Means Motions

N.B. By a Minister of the Crown.

"Pursuant to S.O. 60(2), I request that an Order of the Day be designated for the consideration of a Ways and Means motion .... notice of which was laid upon the Table on (*day and date*)."

No. 76

Concurrence in a Ways and Means Motion

That a Ways and Means motion to amend the .... Act laid upon the Table on .... be concurred in.

No. 77

Designation of a Day for Consideration of Ways and Means Motion (Budget)

N.B. By a Minister of the Crown.

"Pursuant to S.O. 60(2), I request that an Order of the Day be designated for (*day and date*) at 8:00 o'clock p.m., in order to permit a budget presentation by the Minister of Finance."

No. 78

Ways and Means Motion (Budget)

That this House approves in general the budgetary policy of the Government.

No. 79

Petition to the House of Commons

To the Honourable the House of Commons of Canada, in Parliament assembled:

The Petition of the undersigned .... of the .... of ....

That (*here state the object desired by the petitioner*).

Wherefore your petitioner humbly prays that Your Honourable House may be pleased to ....

And as in duty bound your petitioner will ever pray.

(*Signature*)

(*Seal in case of an existing Corporation*) (*Date*)

No. 80

Vacancy in the House, Notification to the Speaker by Two Members

ELECTORAL DISTRICT
OF ....
HOUSE OF COMMONS

To the Honourable the Speaker of the House of Commons:

We, the undersigned, hereby give notice, in pursuance of s. 10 of the House of Commons Act, that a vacancy has occurred in the representation of the House of Commons, for the Electoral District of (*here state Electoral District*), in the Province of ...., by reason of (*cause of vacancy and name of Member vacating seat*), the Member therefor.

Given under our Hands and Seals, at ...., this .... day of ....

(*Signatures*)

Member for the Electoral District of .... (*Seal*).
Member for the Electoral District of .... (*Seal*).

No. 81

Resignation of a Member

ELECTORAL DISTRICT
OF ....
HOUSE OF COMMONS

To the Honourable the Speaker of the House of Commons:

I, ..., Member of the House of Commons, for the Electoral District of ...., in the Province of ...., do hereby resign my seat in the House of Commons for the constituency aforesaid, effective midnight .... (*day*) ....

Given under my Hand and Seal this .... day of .... 19.... .

(*Signature*)   (*Seal*)

Witness:

Witness:

N.B. Two witnesses required

No. 82

Resignation of a Member in absence of the Speaker, Notification to any Two Members

ELECTORAL DISTRICT
OF ....
HOUSE OF COMMONS

To ...., Member of the House of Commons for .... (*Electoral District*)

and

........................, Member of the House of Commons for .... (*Electoral District*)

I, ..., Member of the House of Commons, for the Electoral District of ...., in the Province of ...., do hereby resign my seat in the House of Commons for the constituency aforesaid, effective midnight .... (*day*) ....

Given under my Hand and Seal this .... day of .... 19.... .

(*Signature*)   (*Seal*)

Witness:

Witness:

N.B. Two witnesses required

No. 83

Vacancy, Absence of the Speaker, Notification by Two Members to the Chief Electoral Officer

ELECTORAL DISTRICT
OF ....
HOUSE OF COMMONS

To the Chief Electoral Officer for Canada:

We, the undersigned, hereby give notice, in pursuance of s. 11 of the House of Commons Act, the Speaker being absent from Canada, that a vacancy has occurred in the representation in the House of Commons, for the Electoral District of ...., in the Province of ...., by reason of (*cause of vacancy and name of Member*), the Member therefor, and you are hereby authorized to issue a new Writ for the election of a Member to fill such a vacancy.

Given under our Hands and Seals at .... this .... day of .... 19.... .

(*Signatures*)

Member for the Electoral District of .... (*Seal*).
Member for the Electoral District of .... (*Seal*).

No. 84

Introduction of Member

"Mr. Speaker, I have the honour to present to you ...., Member for the Electoral District of ...., who has taken the Oath, signed the roll and now claims the right to take his seat."

SPEAKER'S FORMULAE

No. 85

On being elected

N.B. The newly-elected Speaker may make any remarks he thinks proper, but in doing so, he must also say:

"I beg to return my humble acknowledgements to the House for the great honour you have been pleased to confer on me by choosing me to be your Speaker."

No. 86

On Arriving at the Senate Chamber following his Election

"May it please Your Excellency:

"The House of Commons have elected me their Speaker, though I am but little able to fulfil the important duties thus assigned to me.

"If, in the performance of those duties, I should at any time fall into error, I pray that the fault may be imputed to me, and not to the Commons, whose servant I am, and who through me, the better to enable them to discharge their duty to their Queen and Country, humbly claim all their undoubted rights and privileges, especially that they may have freedom of speech in their debates, access to Your Excellency's person at all reasonable times, and that their proceedings may receive from Your Excellency the most favourable construction."

No. 87

On Returning from the Reading of the Speech from the Throne

"I have the honour to inform the House that when the House did attend His Excellency, the Governor General this day in the Senate Chamber, His Excellency was pleased to make a speech to both Houses of Parliament, of which I have, to prevent mistakes, obtained a copy, which is as follows:"

No. 88

Introduction of a Bill

"........................, seconded by ...., moves for leave to introduce a bill intituled: An Act ....

"It is the pleasure of the House that the Honourable Member shall have leave to introduce the Bill?

"Carried.

"........................, seconded by ...., moves, That the Bill be now read a first time and be printed.

"Is it the pleasure of the House to adopt the motion?

"Carried.

Clerk Assistant: "First Reading of this Bill.

"When shall the Bill be read a second time?

"Next sitting of the House?

"Agreed."

No. 89

Second Reading of a Bill

"........................, seconded by ...., moves, That Bill C-

............, An Act ...., be now read a second time and referred to the Standing Committee on ....

"Is it the pleasure of the House to adopt the motion?

"Carried.

Clerk Assistant: "Second Reading of this Bill.

"Accordingly, the Bill stands referred to the .... Committee on ...."

No. 90

Concurrence at the Report Stage of a Bill

"........................, seconded by ...., moves, That Bill C-............, An Act ...., (as amended), be concurred in.

"Is it the pleasure of the House to adopt the motion?

"Carried.

"When shall the Bill be read a third time?

"Now?

"Now." (*or* "Next sitting of the House").

No. 91

Leaving the Chair for House to go into Committee of the Whole

"Pursuant to S.O. 54, I do now leave the Chair for the House to go into Committee of the Whole."

No. 92

On Receiving a Report from the Chairman of a Committee of the Whole

"........................, from the Committee of the Whole, reports that they have considered Bill C-............, An Act ...., and have directed him to report the same (with *or* without) amendment(s).

"When shall the Report be received?

"Now?

"Now.

"........................, seconded by ...., moves, That Bill C-............, An Act ...., (as amended), be concurred in.

"Is it the pleasure of the House to adopt the motion?

"Carried.

"When shall the Bill be read a third time?

"Now?

"Now.

"........................, seconded by ...., moves, That Bill C-

.............., An Act ...., be now read a third time and do pass.
"Is it the pleasure of the House to adopt the motion?
"Carried.
Clerk Assistant: "Third Reading of this Bill."

No. 93

Receiving a Report from the Chairman of a Committee of the Whole Reporting Progress on a Bill

".........................., from the Committee of the Whole, reports that they have considered Bill C-.............., An Act ...., made progress thereon and requests leave to consider the Bill again (at the next sitting of the House *or* later this day).
"When shall the report be received?
"Now?
"Now.
"When shall the Committee have leave to sit again?
"Next sitting of the House (*or* later this day)?
"Agreed."

No. 94

Putting a question to the House

"Is the House ready for the question?
"The question is as follows:

N.B. Speaker reads motion

"Is it the pleasure of the House to adopt the motion?
"Carried."

N.B. If several Members call 'No', the Speaker says:

"All those in favour of the motion will please say 'Yea'.
"All those opposed will please say 'Nay'.
"In my opinion, the 'Yeas' (*or* 'Nays') have it.
"I declare the motion 'carried' (*or* 'lost')."

N.B. If five or more Members rise, the Speaker says:

"Call in the Members"

N.B. When the Members are in, the Speaker reads the motion again, and says:

"All those in favour of the motion will please rise."

N.B. After these have been recorded

"All those opposed to the motion will please rise."

N.B. After the Clerk has announced the result

"I declare the motion carried (*or* lost)."

No. 95

Naming a Member

"Mr. ...., with regret I have to name you for disregarding the authority of the Chair."

No. 96

Adjourning the House

"It being (*time*) o'clock p.m. (a.m.) this House stands adjourned until tomorrow (later this day) at 2:00 o'clock p.m. (11:00 o'clock a.m.) pursuant to S.O. 2(1)."

No. 97

In the Senate, for Royal Assent to an Appropriation Bill

Mr. Speaker says:
"MAY IT PLEASE YOUR HONOUR:
"The Commons of Canada have voted Supplies required to enable the Government to defray certain expenses of the public service.
"In the name of the Commons I present to Your Honour the following bill:
"An Act for granting to Her Majesty certain sums of money for the public service, for the financial year ending the 31st March 19..... .
"To which Bill I humbly request Your Honour's assent."

No. 98

On Returning from the Senate following Royal Assent

"I have the honour to inform the House that when the House did attend his Honour the Deputy to His Excellency the Governor General in the Senate Chamber, His Honour was pleased to give, in Her Majesty's name, the Royal Assent to certain Bills (*or* to a certain Bill).

DEPUTY SPEAKER'S FORMULAE

No. 99

Reporting a Bill With or Without Amendment from a Committee of the Whole

"Mr. Speaker, the Committee of the Whole have considered Bill C-.............., An Act ...., and have directed me to report the same (with *or* without) amendment(s)."

No. 100

Reporting Progress on a Bill

"Mr. Speaker, the Committee of the Whole have considered Bill C-.............., An Act ...., and have directed me to report progress thereon and request leave to consider the Bill again later this day (*or* at the next sitting of the House)."

No. 101

Report to the Speaker of an Appeal of Chairman's Decision

"Mr. Speaker, the question is an appeal to the Speaker of a decision of the Chairman of the Committee of the Whole under the provisions of S.O. 55(4), as follows:

"When Clause .... of Bill C-............. was being considered in Committee of the Whole .... (*here state a short resume of facts and the Chairman's decision*)

"Whereupon the honourable Member for .... appealed to the Speaker from the decision of the Chair."

Appendix 2

Standing Orders of the
House of Commons

Appendix 2

Standing Orders of the
House of Commons

PUBLIC BUSINESS

Procedure in unprovided cases

1. In all cases not provided for hereafter or by sessional or other orders, the usages and customs of the House of Commons of the United Kingdom of Great Britain and Northern Ireland as in force at the time shall be followed so far as they may be applicable to this House.

CHAPTER I

SITTINGS OF THE HOUSE

Times and days of sittings

2. (1) The House shall meet on Mondays, Tuesdays, Wednesdays and Thursdays at 2.00 o'clock p.m. and on Fridays at 11 o'clock a.m. unless otherwise provided by standing or special order of this House.

Morning sittings during debate on Address to His Excellency

(2) The House shall meet at 11.00 o'clock a.m. on any day or days appointed for the consideration of the order for resuming debate on the motion for an Address in Reply to His Excellency's Speech and on any amendment proposed thereto, except Wednesdays and the first day so appointed when the House shall meet at 2.00 o'clock p.m.

House not to sit

(3) The House shall not meet on New Year's Day, Good Friday, the day fixed for the celebration of the birthday of the Sovereign, St. John the Baptist Day, Dominion Day, Labour Day, Thanksgiving Day, Remembrance Day and Christmas Day. When the 24th day of June and the 1st day of July fall on a Tuesday, the House shall not meet on the 23rd day and the 30th day of June.

Quorum of twenty

3. (1) The presence of at least twenty members of the House, including Mr. Speaker, shall be necessary to constitute a meeting of the House for the exercise of its powers.

Lack of quorum

(2) If at the time of meeting there be not a quorum, Mr. Speaker may take the Chair and adjourn the House until the next sitting day.

House adjourns where want of quorum

(3) Whenever Mr. Speaker adjourns the House for want of a quorum, the time of the adjournment, and the names of the Members then present, shall be inserted in the Journal.

Mr. Speaker to receive Black Rod

4. When the Sergeant-at-Arms announces that the Gentleman Usher of the Black Rod is at the door, Mr. Speaker shall take the Chair, whether there be a quorum present or not.

Attendance required

5. Every Member is bound to attend the service of the House, unless leave of absence has been given him by the House.

Evening interruptions

6. (1) At 6:00 o'clock p.m. on Mondays, Tuesdays and Thursdays, Mr. Speaker shall leave the Chair until 8:00 o'clock p.m.

Mid-day interruption

(2) At 1:00 o'clock p.m. on any day on which a morning sitting is held, Mr. Speaker shall leave the Chair until 2:00 o'clock p.m.

Daily adjournment

(3) At 10:00 o'clock on Mondays, Tuesdays and Thursdays, at 6:00 o'clock p.m. on Wednesdays and at 5:00 o'clock p.m. on Fridays, Mr. Speaker shall adjourn the House until the next sitting day.

When motion to adjourn required

(4) When it is provided in any standing or special order of this House that any business specified by such order shall be continued, forthwith disposed of, or concluded in any sitting, the House shall not be adjourned before such proceedings have been completed except pursuant to a motion to adjourn proposed by a Minister of the Crown.

Motion to continue or extend sitting

(5) (*a*) When Mr. Speaker is in the Chair, a Member may propose a motion, without notice, to continue a sitting through a lunch or dinner hour or beyond the ordinary hour of daily adjournment for the purpose of considering a specified item of business or a stage or stages thereof subject to the following conditions:

Motion to relate to business

(i) The motion must relate to the business then being considered provided that proceedings in any Committee of the Whole may be temporarily interrupted for the purpose of proposing a motion under the provisions of this Standing Order.

When motion to be made

(ii) The motion must be proposed in the hour preceding the time at which the business under consideration should be interrupted by a lunch or dinner hour, Private Members' Hour or the ordinary time of daily adjournment.

No debate

(iii) The motion shall not be subject to debate or amendment.

When objection taken

(*b*) When Mr. Speaker puts the question on such motion, he shall ask those Members who object to rise in their places. If ten or more Members then rise, the motion shall be deemed to have been withdrawn, otherwise, the motion shall have been adopted.

Business interrupted

7. At the ordinary time of adjournment of the House, unless otherwise provided, the proceedings shall be interrupted and the business under consideration at the termination of the sitting shall stand over until the next sitting day when it will be taken up at the same stage where its progress was interrupted.

No debate preparatory to a division

8. When Members have been called in, preparatory to a division, no further debate is to be permitted.

When vote recorded

9. (1) Upon a division, the "yeas" and "nays" shall not be entered upon the minutes, unless demanded by five members.

When time limited for division bells

(2) When, under the provisions of any Standing Order or other order of this House, Mr. Speaker has interrupted any proceeding for the purpose of putting forthwith the question on any business then before the House, the bells to call in the Members shall be sounded for not more than fifteen minutes.

Speaker mute in debate — When Speaker to vote

10. Mr. Speaker shall not take part in any debate before the House. In case of an equality of voices, Mr. Speaker gives a casting vote, and any reasons stated by him are entered in the Journal.

Pecuniary interest

11. No Member is entitled to vote upon any question in which he has a direct pecuniary interest, and the vote of any Member so interested will be disallowed.

Decorum in the House — No appeal

12. (1) Mr. Speaker shall preserve order and decorum, and shall decide questions of order. In deciding a point of order or practice, he shall state the Standing Order or other authority applicable to the case. No debate shall be permitted on any such decision, and no such decision shall be subject to an appeal to the House.

Decorum when question put

(2) When Mr. Speaker is putting a question, no Member shall enter, walk out of or across the House, or make any noise or disturbance.

Decorum when Member speaking

(3) When a Member is speaking, no Member shall pass between him and the Chair, nor interrupt him, except to raise a point of order.

(4) No Member may pass between the Chair and the Table, nor between the Chair and the Mace when the Mace has been taken off the Table by the Sergeant-at-Arms.

At adjournment

(5) When the House adjourns, Members shall keep their seats until Mr. Speaker has left the Chair.

Notice of strangers

Question that strangers withdraw — Speaker or Chairman decides

13. If any Member takes notice that strangers are present, Mr. Speaker or the Chairman (as the case may be), shall forthwith put the question that strangers be ordered to withdraw, without permitting any debate or amendment; provided that Mr. Speaker, or the Chairman, may, whenever he thinks proper, order the withdrawal of strangers.

Conduct of strangers

14. Any stranger admitted into any part of the House or gallery who misconducts himself, or does not withdraw when strangers are directed to withdraw, while the House or any Committee of the Whole House is sitting, shall be taken into custody by the Sergeant-at-Arms; and no person so taken into custody shall be discharged without the special order of the House.

CHAPTER II

BUSINESS OF THE HOUSE

Prayers

15. (1) Mr. Speaker shall read prayers every day at the meeting of the House before any business is entered upon.

Routine business

(2) Not more than two minutes after the reading of prayers, the business of the House shall commence. Members, other than Ministers of the Crown, may propose motions pursuant to Standing Order 43 at this time. Not later than 2:15 p.m., or 11:15 a.m., as the case may be, oral questions shall be taken up. At 3:00 p.m., or 12:00 noon, as the case may be, the House shall proceed to the ordinary daily routine of business, which shall be as follows:

Presenting Reports from Standing or Special Committees.
Tabling of Documents (Pursuant to Standing Order 41(2)).
Statements by Ministers.
Introduction of Bills.
First Reading of Senate Public Bills.
Government Notices of Motions.
Motions (except those permitted before oral questions).

Statements by Ministers

(3) On Statements by Ministers, as listed in section (2) of this Standing Order, a Minister of the Crown may make a short factual announcement or statement of government policy. A spokesman for each of the parties in opposition to the government may comment briefly thereon and Members may be permitted to address questions thereon to the Minister. Mr. Speaker shall limit the time for such proceedings as he deems fit.

Day by day order of business

(4) Except as otherwise provided in these Standing Orders, the order of business for the consideration of the House, day by day, after the daily routine shall be as follows:

(Monday)

Questions on Order Paper.
Government Orders.
(From five to six o'clock p.m. — Private Members' Business)
Notices of Motions.
Public bills.

(Tuesday)

Questions on Order Paper.
Government Orders.
(From five to six o'clock p.m. — Private Members' Business)
Public Bills.
Private Bills.
Notices of Motions.

(Wednesday)

Questions on Order Paper.
Notices of Motions for the Production of Papers.
Government Orders.

(Thursday)

Questions on Order Paper.
Government Orders.
(From five to six o'clock p.m. — Private Members' Business)
A.   On the first and each alternate Thursday thereafter:
      Notices of Motions (Papers).
      Private Bills.
      Public Bills.
B.   On the second and each alternate Thursday thereafter:
      Private Bills.
      Notices of Motions (Papers).
      Public Bills.

(Friday)

Questions on Order Paper.
Government Orders.
(From four to five o'clock p.m. — Private Members' Business)

A. On the first and each alternate Friday thereafter:
Notices of Motions.
Public Bills.
Private Bills.

B. On the second and each alternate Friday thereafter:
Public Bills.
Notices of Motions.
Private Bills.

Supply, Address and Budget suspends Private Members' Business

(5) On any day designated for the consideration of the business of supply or for resuming the Address or the Budget debates, the consideration of Private Members' Business, if provided for in such sitting, shall be suspended.

Lapse of Private Members' hours

(6) After the order for Private Members' Business on Mondays and Tuesdays has been reached for a total of forty times in a session, the provisions in section (4) of this Standing Order which provide for such business of those days shall lapse.

Private Members' Business suspended

16. The proceedings on Private Members' Business shall not be suspended except as provided for in Standing Orders 15(5), 26(12) and 44 or when otherwise specified by any special order of this House.

Question of privilege

17. (1) Whenever any matter of privilege arises, it shall be taken into consideration immediately or at a time appointed by Mr. Speaker.

Notice required

(2) Unless notice of motion has been given under Standing Order 42, any Member proposing to raise a question of privilege other than one arising out of proceedings in the Chamber during the course of a sitting shall give to the Speaker a written statement of the question at least one hour prior to the opening of a sitting.

Precedence on Order Paper

18. (1) All items standing on the Orders of the Day, except Government Orders, shall be taken up according to the precedence assigned to each on the *Order Paper*.

Calling of government business

(2) Government Orders shall be called and considered in such sequence as the Government determines.

Questions and Orders not taken up

19. (1) Questions put by Members and notices of motions, not taken up when called may (upon the request of the government) be allowed to stand and retain their precedence; otherwise they will disappear from the Order Paper. They may, however, be renewed.

When orders may be stood or dropped

(2) Orders not proceeded with when called, upon the like request, may be allowed to stand retaining their precedence; otherwise they shall be dropped and be placed on the Order Paper for the next sitting after those of the same class at a similar stage.

Orders postponed

(3) All orders not disposed of at the adjournment of the House shall be postponed until the next sitting day, without a motion to that effect.

Precedence to Private Members' Business

20. (1) The day to day precedence on the Order Paper of Private Members' Business, except as otherwise provided, shall be as follows:

(*a*) Third reading and passage of bills;

(*b*) Consideration at the Report Stage of any bill reported from a Standing or Special Committee or a Committee of the Whole House;

(*c*) Bills ordered by the House for reference to a Committee of the Whole House;

(*d*) Senate amendments to bills;

(*e*) Second reading and reference of bills to a committee;

(*f*) Other orders according to the date thereof.

On adjournment or interruption

(2) After any bill or other order in the name of a private Member has been considered in the House or in any committee of the whole and any proceeding thereon has been adjourned or interrupted, the said bill or order shall be placed on the Order Paper for the next sitting at the foot of the list under the respective heading for such bills or orders.

Government notices of motion — when no debate

21. (1) Government notices of motions for the House to go into a committee of the whole at the next sitting of the House when put from the Chair shall be decided without debate or amendment.

When government notice of motion transferred to Government Orders

(2) When any other government notice of motion is called from the Chair, it shall be deemed to have been forthwith transferred to and ordered for consideration under Government Orders in the same or at the next sitting of the House.

When Senate and House disagree

22. (1) In cases in which the Senate disagree to any amendments made by the House of Commons, or to which the House of Commons has disagreed, the House of Commons is willing to receive the reasons of the Senate for their disagreeing or insisting (as the case may be) by message, without a conference, unless at any time the Senate should desire to communicate the same at a conference.

Conference

(2) Any conference between the two Houses may be a free conference.

Reasons for conference

(3) When the House requests a conference with the Senate, the reasons to be given by this House at the same shall be prepared and agreed to by the House before a message be sent therewith.

Messages to and from the Senate

23. A Clerk of this House may be the bearer of messages from this House to the Senate. Messages from the Senate may be received at the bar by a Clerk of this House, as soon as announced by the Sergeant-at-Arms, at any time while the House is sitting, or in committee, without interrupting the business then proceeding.

Motion to read orders takes precedence

24. A motion for reading the Orders of the Day shall have preference to any motion before the House.

Motion to adjourn

25. A motion to adjourn, unless otherwise prohibited in these Standing Orders, shall always be in order, but no second motion to the same effect shall be made until some intermediate proceeding has taken place.

Important matter — discussion of

26. (1) Leave to make a motion for the adjournment of the House for the purpose of discussing a specific and important matter requiring urgent consideration must be asked immediately before the calling of Government Orders.

Written statement two hours prior to opening

(2) A Member wishing to move, "That this House do now adjourn", under the provisions of this Standing Order shall give to Mr. Speaker, at least two hours prior to the opening of a sitting, a written statement of the matter proposed to be discussed. If the urgent matter is not then known, the Member shall give his written statement to Mr. Speaker as soon as practicable but before the opening of the sitting.

Making statement

(3) When requesting leave to propose such a motion, the Member shall rise in his place and present without argument the statement referred to in section (2) of this Order.

Speaker's prerogative

(4) Mr. Speaker shall decide, without any debate, whether or not the matter is proper to be discussed.

Speaker to take into account

(5) In determining whether a matter should have urgent consideration, Mr. Speaker shall have regard to the extent to which it concerns the administrative responsibilities of the government or could come within the scope of ministerial action and he also shall have regard to the probability of the matter being brought before the House within reasonable time by other means.

Reserving decision

(6) If Mr. Speaker so desires, he may defer his decision upon whether the matter is proper to be discussed until later in the sitting, when he may interrupt the proceedings of the House for the purpose of announcing his decision.

Speaker not bound to give reasons

(7) In stating whether or not he is satisfied that the matter is proper to be discussed, Mr. Speaker is not bound to give reasons for his decision.

When question put

(8) If Mr. Speaker is satisfied that the matter is proper to be discussed, the Member shall either obtain the leave of the House, or, if such leave be refused, the assent of not less than twenty Members who shall thereupon rise in their places to support the request; but, if fewer than twenty Members and not less than five shall thereupon rise in their places, the House shall, on division, upon question put forthwith, determine whether such motion shall be made.

Motion to stand over

(9) If it is determined that the Member may proceed, the motion shall stand over until 8.00 o'clock p.m. on that day, provided that Mr. Speaker, at his discretion, may direct that the motion shall be set down for consideration on the following sitting day at an hour specified by him.

When moved on Wednesday

(10) When a request to make such a motion has been made on any Wednesday, and Mr. Speaker directs that it be considered the same day, the House shall rise at 6.00 o'clock p.m. and resume at 8.00 o'clock p.m.

When moved on Friday

(11) When a request to make such a motion has been made on any Friday, and Mr. Speaker directs that it be considered the same day, it shall stand over until 3.00 o'clock p.m.

Debate not to be suspended by Private Members' business

(12) Debate on any such motion shall not be interrupted by "Private Members' Business".

Time limit on debate

(13) Proceedings on any such motion may continue beyond the ordinary hour of daily adjournment but, when debate thereon is concluded prior to that hour in any sitting, the motion shall be deemed to have been withdrawn. In any other case, Mr. Speaker, when he is satisfied that debate has been concluded, shall declare the motion carried and forthwith adjourn the House until the next sitting day.

Time limit on speeches

(14) No Member shall speak longer than twenty minutes during debate on any such motion.

Debate to take precedence. Exception

(15) The provisions of this Standing Order shall not be suspended by the operation of any other Standing Order relating to the hours of sitting or in respect of the consideration of any other business; provided that, in cases of conflict, Mr. Speaker shall determine when such other business shall be considered or disposed of and he shall make any consequential interpretation of any Standing Order that may be necessary in relation thereto.

Conditions

(16) The right to move the adjournment of the House for the above purposes is subject to the following conditions:
  (a) The matter proposed for discussion must relate to a genuine emergency, calling for immediate and urgent consideration;
  (b) not more than one such motion can be made at the same sitting;
  (c) not more than one matter can be discussed on the same motion;
  (d) the motion must not revive discussion on a matter which has been discussed in the same session pursuant to the provisions of this standing order;
  (e) the motion must not raise a question of privilege;
  (f) the discussion under the motion must not raise any question which, according to the Standing Orders of the House, can only be debated on a distinct motion under notice.

Certified copy of Journals for Governor General

27.   A copy of the Journals of this House, certified by the Clerk, shall be delivered each day to His Excellency the Governor General.

CHAPTER III

RULES OF DEBATE

Member speaking

28.   Every Member desiring to speak is to rise in his place, uncovered, and address himself to Mr. Speaker.

Members rising simultaneously

29.   When two or more Members rise to speak, Mr. Speaker calls upon the Member who first rose in his place; but a motion may be made that any Member who has risen "be now heard", or "do now speak", which motion shall be forthwith put without debate.

When a Member shall withdraw

30.   If anything shall come in question touching the conduct of any

Member, or his election, or his right to hold his seat, he may make a statement and shall withdraw during the time the matter is in debate.

Time limit on speeches when Speaker in Chair

31. (1) Unless otherwise provided in these Standing Orders, when Mr. Speaker is in the Chair, no Member, except the Prime Minister and the Leader of the Opposition, or a Minister moving a government order and the Member speaking in reply immediately after such Minister, or a Member making a motion of "no-confidence" in the government and a Minister replying thereto, shall speak for more than forty minutes at a time in any debate.

During Private Members' hour

(2) When the business of Private Members is being considered, no Member shall speak for more than twenty minutes at a time.

Debatable motions

32. (1) The following motions are debatable:
Every motion:

(*a*) standing on the order of proceedings for the day, except as otherwise provided in these Standing Orders;

(*b*) for the concurrence in a report of a standing or special committee;

(*c*) for the previous question;

(*d*) for the second reading and reference of a bill to a standing or special committee or to a committee of the whole House;

(*e*) for the consideration of any amendment to be proposed at the report stage of any bill reported from any standing or special committee;

(*f*) for the third reading and passage of a bill;

(*g*) for the consideration of Senate amendments to House of Commons bills;

(*h*) for a conference with the Senate;

(*i*) for the adjournment of the House when made for the purpose of discussing a specific and important matter requiring urgent consideration;

(*j*) for the consideration of a ways and means order (Budget);

(*k*) for the consideration of any motion under the order for the consideration of the business of supply;

(*l*) for the adoption in committee of the whole of the motion, clause, section, preamble or title under consideration;

(*m*) for the appointment of a committee;

(*n*) for reference to a committee of any report or return laid on the Table of the House;

(*o*) for the suspension of any Standing Order unless otherwise provided; and

Routine motions debatable

(*p*) such other motion, made upon Routine Proceedings, as may be required for the observance of the proprieties of the House, the maintenance of its authority, the appointment or conduct of its officers, the management of its business, the arrangement of its proceedings, the correctness of its records, the fixing of its sitting days or the times of its meeting or adjournment.

Motions not debatable

(2) All other motions, unless otherwise provided in these Standing Orders, shall be decided without debate or amendment.

Closure — Notice required — Time limit on speeches

All questions put at 1 a.m.

33. Immediately before the order of the day for resuming an adjourned debate is called, or if the House be in committee of the whole, any Minister of the Crown who, standing in his place, shall have given notice at a previous sitting of his intention so to do may move that the debate shall not be further adjourned, or that the further consideration of any resolution or resolutions, clause or clauses, section or sections, preamble or preambles, title or titles, shall be the first business of the committee, and shall not further be postponed; and in either case such question shall be decided without debate or amendment; and if the same shall be resolved in the affirmative, no Member shall thereafter speak more than once, or longer than twenty minutes in any such adjourned debate; or, if in committee, on any such resolution, clause, section, preamble or title; and if such adjourned debate or postponed consideration shall not have been resumed or concluded before one o'clock in the morning, no Member shall rise to speak after that hour, but all such questions as must be decided in order to conclude such adjourned debate or postponed consideration, shall be decided forthwith.

Procedure when called to order or a point of order

Speaker may allow a debate

34. (1) Any Member addressing the House, if called to order either by Mr. Speaker or on a point raised by another member, shall sit down while the point is being stated, after which he may explain. Mr. Speaker may permit debate on the point of order before giving his decision, but such debate must be strictly relevant to the point of order taken.

Irrelevance or repetition — Naming a Member

(2) Mr. Speaker or the Chairman, after having called the attention of the House, or of the committee, to the conduct of a Member who persists in

irrelevance, or repetition, may direct him to discontinue his speech, and if then the Member still continues to speak, Mr. Speaker shall name him or, if in committee, the Chairman shall report him to the House.

Disrespectful or offensive language — Reflection on a vote

35. No Member shall speak disrespectfully of Her Majesty, nor of any of the Royal Family, nor of His Excellency or the person administering the Government of Canada; nor use offensive words against either House, or against any Member thereof. No Member may reflect upon any vote of the House, except for the purpose of moving that such vote be rescinded.

Reading the question where not printed

36. When the question under discussion does not appear on the Order Paper or has not been printed and distributed, any Member may require it to be read at any time of the debate, but not so as to interrupt a Member while speaking.

No Member to speak twice — Exception

37. (1) No Member may speak twice to a question except in explanation of a material part of his speech which may have been misquoted or misunderstood, but then he is not to introduce any new matter, and no debate shall be allowed upon such explanation.

Right of reply

(2) A reply shall be allowed to a Member who has moved a substantive motion, but not to the mover of an amendment, the previous question or an instruction to a committee.

Reply closes debate

(3) In all cases Mr. Speaker shall inform the House that the reply of the mover of the original motion closes the debate.

CHAPTER IV

ADDRESS IN REPLY TO HIS EXCELLENCY'S SPEECH

Address debate eight days

38. (1) The proceedings on the order of the day for resuming debate on the motion for an Address in Reply to His Excellency's Speech and on any amendments proposed thereto shall not exceed eight sitting days.

Appointed days to be announced — Precedence

(2) Any day or days to be appointed for the consideration of the said order shall be announced from time to time by a Minister of the Crown and on any such day or days this order shall have precedence of all other business except the ordinary daily routine of business.

Subamendment disposed of on second day

(3) On the second of the said days, if a subamendment be under consideration at fifteen minutes before the ordinary time of daily adjournment, Mr. Speaker shall interrupt the proceedings and forthwith put the question on the said subamendment.

Amendments disposed of on fourth and sixth days

(4) On the fourth and sixth of the said days, if any amendment be under consideration at thirty minutes before the ordinary time of daily adjournment, Mr. Speaker shall interrupt the proceedings and forthwith put the question on any amendment or amendments then before the House.

Main motion disposed of on eighth day

(5) On the eighth of the said days, at fifteen minutes before the ordinary time of daily adjournment, unless the said debate be previously concluded, Mr. Speaker shall interrupt the proceedings and forthwith put every question necessary to dispose of the main motion.

When amendments precluded

(6) The motion for an Address in Reply shall not be subject to amendment on or after the seventh day of the said debate.

Time limits on speeches

(7) No Member, except the Prime Minister and the Leader of the Opposition, shall speak for more than thirty minutes at a time in the said debate; provided that forty minutes shall be allowed to the mover of either an amendment or of a subamendment.

CHAPTER V

QUESTIONS, RETURNS AND REPORTS

Written questions

39. (1) Questions may be placed on the Order Paper seeking information from Ministers of the Crown relating to public affairs; and from other Members, relating to any bill, motion, or other public matter connected with the business of the House, in which such Members may be concerned; but in putting any such question or in replying to the same no argument or opinion is to be offered, nor any facts stated, except so far as may be necessary to explain the same; and in answering any such question the matter to which the same refers shall not be debated.

Starred questions — Limit of three

(2) (*a*) Any Member who requires an oral answer to his question may distinguish it by an asterisk, but no Member shall have more than three such questions at a time on the daily Order Paper.

Reply printed in Hansard

(*b*) If a Member does not distinguish his question by an asterisk, the Minister to whom the question is addressed hands the answer to the Clerk of the House who causes it to be printed in the official reports of the debates.

Transfer of question to Notices of Motion

(3) If, in the opinion of Mr. Speaker, a question on the Order Paper put to a Minister of the Crown is of such a nature as to require a lengthy reply, he may, upon the request of the government, direct the same to stand as a notice of motion, and to be transferred to its proper place as such upon the Order Paper, the Clerk of the House being authorized to amend the same as to matters of form.

Question made order for return

(4) If a question is of such a nature that, in the opinion of the Minister who is to furnish the reply, such reply should be in the form of a return, and the Minister states that he has no objection to laying such return upon the Table of the House, his statement shall, unless otherwise ordered by the House, be deemed an order of the House to that effect and the same shall be entered in the *Votes and Proceedings* as such.

Daily question period

Speaker decides urgency — Time limit

(5) Before the Orders of the Day are proceeded with, questions on matters of urgency may be addressed orally to Ministers of the Crown, provided however that, if in the opinion of Mr. Speaker a question is not urgent, he may direct that it be placed on the Order Paper, provided also that the time allowed for a question period prior to the calling of the Orders of the Day shall not exceed forty minutes.

Notice of question for adjournment proceedings

(6) A Member who is not satisfied with the response to a question asked on any day at this stage, or a Member who has been told by Mr. Speaker that his question is not urgent, may give notice that he intends to raise the subject-matter of his question on the adjournment of the House. The notice referred to herein, whether or not it is given orally during the question period before the Orders of the Day, must be given in writing to Mr. Speaker not later than 4.00 o'clock p.m. the same day.

Adjournment proceedings

40. (1) At 10.00 o'clock p.m. on any Monday, Tuesday or Thursday, Mr. Speaker may, notwithstanding the provisions of Standing Orders 6(3) and 32(2), deem that a motion to adjourn the House has been made and seconded, whereupon such motion shall be debatable for not more than thirty minutes.

Notice required and time limit on speeches

(2) No matter shal be debated during the thirty minutes herein provided, unless notice thereof has been given by a Member as provided in Standing Order 39(6). No debate on any one matter raised during this period shall last for more than ten minutes.

Question time seven minutes — Answer time three minutes

(3) The Member raising the matter may speak for not more than seven minutes. A Minister of the Crown, or a Parliamentary Secretary speaking on behalf of a Minister, if he wishes to do so, may speak for not more than three minutes. When debate has lasted for a total of thirty minutes, or when the debate on the matter or matters raised has ended, whichever comes first, Mr. Speaker shall deem the motion to adjourn to have been carried and he shall adjourn the House until the next sitting day.

Time in announcing future business not to count

(4) The time required for any questions and answers concerning the future business of the House, whether this item takes place before or after the thirty minute period herein provided, shall not be counted as part of the said thirty minutes.

Selection of matters to be raised

(5) When several Members have given notices of intention to raise matters on the adjournment of the House, Mr. Speaker shall decide the order in which such matters are to be raised. In doing so, he shall have regard to the order in which notices were given, to the urgency of the matters raised,

and to the apportioning of the opportunities to debate such matters among the members of the various parties in the House. Mr. Speaker may, at his discretion, consult with representatives of the parties concerning such order and be guided by their advice.

Questions to be announced

(6) By not later than 5.00 o'clock p.m. on any Monday, Tuesday or Thursday, Mr. Speaker shall indicate to the House the matter or matters to be raised at the time of adjournment that day.

Suspension of adjournment proceedings

(7) When it is provided in any standing or special order of this House that any specified business shall be continued beyond the ordinary time of daily adjournment or that any such business shall be forthwith disposed of or concluded in any sitting, the adjournment proceedings in that sitting shall be suspended.

Returns, reports deposited pursuant to statutory or other authority

41. (1) Any return, report or other paper required to be laid before the House in accordance with any Act of Parliament or in pursuance of any resolution or standing order of this House may be deposited with the Clerk of the House on any sitting day, and such return, report or other paper shall be deemed for all purposes to have been presented to or laid before the House.

Report or paper deposited by Minister or Parliamentary Secretary

(2) A Minister of the Crown, or a Parliamentary Secretary acting on behalf of a Minister, may, in his place in the House, state that he proposes to lay upon the Table of the House, any report or other paper dealing with a matter coming within the administrative responsibilities of the government, and, thereupon, the same shall be deemed for all purposes to have been laid before the House.

Recorded in Votes and Proceedings

(3) In either case, a record of any such paper shall be entered in the *Votes and Proceedings* of the same day.

CHAPTER VI

NOTICES

When notice required

42. (1) Forty-eight hours' notice shall be given of a motion for leave to present a bill, resolution or address, for the appointment of any committee, or for placing a question on the Order Paper; but this rule shall not apply to bills after their introduction, or to private bills, or to the times of meeting or adjournment of the House. Such notice shall be laid on the Table before six o'clock p.m., or before five o'clock p.m. on a Friday, and be printed in the *Votes and Proceedings* of that day.

Notice of business during prorogation or adjournment — Special Order Paper

(2) In the period prior to the first session of a Parliament, during a prorogation or when the House stands adjourned, and the government has represented to Mr. Speaker that any government measure or measures should have immediate consideration by the House, Mr. Speaker shall cause a notice of any such measure or measures to be published on a special Order Paper and the same shall be circulated prior to the opening or the resumption of such session. The publication and circulation of such notice shall meet the requirements of section (1) of this Standing Order.

When Speaker unable to act

(3) In the event of Mr. Speaker being unable to act owing to illness or other cause, the Deputy Speaker shall act in his stead for the purposes of this order. In the unavoidable absence of Mr. Speaker and Mr. Deputy Speaker or when the Office of Speaker is vacant, the Clerk of the House shall have the authority to act for the purposes of this Standing Order.

Notice waived by unanimous consent

43. A motion may, in case of urgent and pressing necessity previously explained by the mover, be made by unanimous consent of the House without notice having been given under Standing Order 42.

Motion by Minister regarding matter of urgent nature

44. (1) In relation to any matter that the government considers to be of an urgent nature, a Minister of the Crown may, at any time when Mr. Speaker is in the Chair, propose a motion to suspend any standing or other order of this House relating to the need for notice and to the hours and days of sitting.

Question proposed after reasons stated by Minister

(2) After the Minister has stated reasons for the urgency of such a motion, Mr. Speaker shall propose the question to the House.

Proceedings on urgent motion

(3) Proceedings on any such motion shall be subject to the following conditions:

(a) Mr. Speaker may permit debate thereon for a period not exceeding one hour;

(b) the motion shall not be subject to amendment except by a Minister of the Crown;

(c) no Member may speak more than once nor longer than ten minutes;

(d) proceedings on any such motion shall not be interrupted or adjourned by any other proceeding or by the operation of any other order of this House.

Objection by 10 or more Members

(4) When Mr. Speaker puts the question on any such motion, he shall ask those who object to rise in their places. If ten or more Members then rise, the motion shall be deemed to have been withdrawn, otherwise, the motion shall have been adopted.

Restricted application

(5) The operation of any order made under the provisions of this Standing Order shall not extend to any proceeding not therein specified.

CHAPTER VII

MOTIONS; AMENDMENTS; NOTICES OF MOTIONS; THE PREVIOUS QUESTION

In writing and seconded — Read in both languages

45. (1) All motions shall be in writing, and seconded, before being debated or put from the Chair. When a motion is seconded, it shall be read in English and in French by Mr. Speaker, if he be familiar with both languages; if not, Mr. Speaker shall read the motion in one language and direct the Clerk at the Table to read it in the other, before debate.

When transferred to Government Orders

(2) When a debate on any motion made prior to the reading of the Orders of the Day is adjourned or interrupted, the order for resumption of the same shall be transferred to and considered under Government Orders.

Privileged motions

46. When a question is under debate, no motion is received unless to amend it; to postpone it to a day certain; for the previous question; for reading the Orders of the Day; for proceeding to another order; to adjourn the debate; to continue or extend a sitting of the House; or for the adjournment of the House.

When amendment precluded

47. A motion to refer a bill, resolution or any question to a Committee of the Whole, or any Standing or Special Committee, shall preclude all amendment of the main question.

Production of papers — When debate desired

48. (1) Notices of motions for the production of papers shall be placed on the Order Paper under the heading "Notices of Motions for the Production of Papers". All such notices, when called, shall be forthwith disposed of; but if on any such motion a debate be desired by the Member proposing it or by a Minister of the Crown, the motion will be transferred by the Clerk to the order of "Notices of Motions (Papers)".

Limits on speeches and debate

(2) When debate on a motion for the production of papers, under the order "Notices of Motions (Papers)", has taken place for a total time of one hour and thirty minutes, Mr. Speaker shall at that point interrupt the debate, whereupon a Minister of the Crown, whether or not such Minister has already spoken, may speak for not more than five minutes, following which the mover of the motion may close the debate by speaking for not more than five minutes. Unless the motion is withdrawn, as provided by Standing Order 50, Mr. Speaker shall forthwith put the question.

Private Member's Notice of Motion — When not proceeded with

49. (1) When a Private Member's Notice of Motion shall have been twice called from the Chair and not proceeded with, it shall be dropped, provided that it may be placed at the foot of the list on the Order Paper upon motion made after due notice.

To be withdrawn

(2) If the notice of motion thus restored is again called from the Chair and not proceeded with, it shall be withdrawn from the Order Paper.

One notice of motion limit

(3) No Member shall have more than one notice of motion at a time on the Order Paper.

No application to notices of motions for production of papers

(4) This standing order shall not apply to notices of motions for the production of papers.

Unanimous consent required to withdraw motion

50.   A Member who has made a motion may withdraw the same only by the unanimous consent of the House.

When motion is contrary to rules and privileges of Parliament

51.   Whenever Mr. Speaker is of the opinion that a motion offered to the House is contrary to the rules and privileges of Parliament, he shall apprise the House thereof immediately, before putting the question thereon, and quote the Standing Order or authority applicable to the case.

The previous question

52.   (1) The previous question, until it is decided, shall preclude all amendment of the main question, and shall be in the following words, "That this question be now put".

(2) If the previous question be resolved in the affirmative, the original question is to be put forthwith without any amendment or debate.

CHAPTER VIII

COMMITTEES OF THE WHOLE HOUSE

Chairman of Committees of Whole

53.   (1) A Chairman of Committees who shall also be Deputy Speaker of the House shall be elected at the commencement of every Parliament; and the Member so elected shall, if in his place in the House, take the Chair of all committees of the whole.

Language knowledge

(2) The Member elected to serve as Deputy Speaker and Chairman of Committees shall be required to possess the full and practical knowledge of the official language which is not that of Mr. Speaker for the time being.

Term of office — Vacancy

(3) The Member so elected as Deputy Speaker and Chairman of Committees shall continue to act in that capacity until the end of the Parliament for which he is elected, and in the case of a vacancy by death, resignation or otherwise, the House shall proceed forthwith to elect a successor.

Ad hoc appointment

(4) In the absence of the Deputy Speaker and Chairman of Committees

of the House, Mr. Speaker may, in forming a Committee of the Whole House, before leaving the Chair, appoint any Member chairman of the committee.

Deputy Chairman and Assistant Deputy Chairman

(5) At the commencement of every session, or from time to time as necessity may arise, the House may appoint a Deputy Chairman of Committees and also an Assistant Deputy Chairman of Committees, either of whom shall, whenever the Chairman of Committees is absent, be entitled to exercise all the powers vested in the Chairman of Committees including his powers as Deputy Speaker during Mr. Speaker's unavoidable absence.

Order for House in Committee of the Whole

54. When an Order of the Day is read for the House to go into a committee of the whole or when it is ordered that a bill or any item or items in the main or supplementary estimates be considered in a committee of the whole, Mr. Speaker shall leave the Chair without question put.

Application of Standing Orders

55. (1) The Standing Orders of the House shall be observed in committees of the whole House so far as may be applicable, except the Standing Orders as to the seconding of motions, limiting the number of times of speaking and the length of speeches.

Relevancy

(2) Speeches in committees of the whole House must be strictly relevant to the item or clause under consideration.

Time limit on speeches

(3) No Member, except the Prime Minister and the Leader of the Opposition, shall speak for more than twenty minutes at a time in any committee of the whole House.

Decorum in Committee

(4) The Chairman shall maintain order in committees of the whole House; deciding all questions of order subject to an appeal to Mr. Speaker; but disorder in a committee can only be censured by the House, on receiving a report thereof. No debate shall be permitted on any decision.

Motion to leave the Chair

56. (1) A motion that the Chairman leave the chair is always in order, shall take precedence of any other motion, and shall not be debatable.

Intermediate proceeding

(2) Such motion, if rejected, cannot be renewed unless some intermediate proceeding has taken place.

Resolutions concurred in forthwith

57. Whenever a resolution is reported from any Committee of the Whole, a motion to concur in the same shall be forthwith put and decided without debate or amendment.

CHAPTER IX

BUSINESS OF SUPPLY AND WAYS AND MEANS

Order for Supply

58. (1) At the commencement of each session, the House shall designate, by motion, a continuing Order of the Day for the consideration of the business of supply.

Business of supply defined

(2) For the purposes of this Standing Order, the business of supply shall consist of consideration in a committee of the whole of any item or items in the main or supplementary estimates; motions, to concur in interim supply, main or supplementary estimates; motions to restore or reinstate any item in the estimates; motions to introduce or pass at all stages any bill or bills based thereon; and opposition motions that under this Standing Order may be considered on allotted days.

Opposition motions — May include estimates

(3) Opposition motions on allotted days may be moved only by Members in opposition to the government and may relate to any matter within the jurisdiction of the Parliament of Canada and also may be used for the purpose of considering reports from standing committees relating to the consideration of estimates or subject-matter thereof or for considering any item or items in main or supplementary estimates in a committee of the whole.

Notice for government motion — Notice for opposition motion or for consideration in Committee of the Whole

(4) (*a*) Forty-eight hours' written notice shall be given of motions to concur in interim supply, main or supplementary estimates, to restore or reinstate any item in the estimates. Twenty-four hours' written notice shall be given of an opposition motion on an allotted day, or of a notice to oppose any item in the

estimates, or for the purpose of setting down any item or items in the main or supplementary estimates for consideration in a committee of the whole.

Speaker's power of selection

(*b*) When notice has been given of two or more motions by Members in opposition to the government for consideration on an allotted day, Mr. Speaker shall have power to select which of the proposed motions shall have precedence in that sitting.

Supply periods — Allotted days

(5) For the period ending not later than December 10, five sitting days shall be allotted to the business of supply. Seven additional days shall be allotted to the business of supply in the period ending not later than March 26. Thirteen additional days shall be allotted to the business of supply in the period ending not later than June 30. These twenty-five days are to be designated as allotted days.

Unused days added to allotted days

(6) When any day or days allotted to the Address Debate or to the Budget Debate are not used for those debates, such day or days may be added to the number of allotted days in the period in which they occur.

Final supplementary estimates after close of fiscal year

(7) When concurrence in any final supplementary estimates relating to the fiscal year that ended on March 31 is sought in the period ending not later than June 30, three days for the consideration of the motion that the House concur in those estimates and for the passage at all stages of any bill to be based thereon shall be added to the days for the business of supply in that period.

Opposition motions have precedence on allotted days

(8) Opposition motions shall have precedence over all government supply motions on allotted days and shall be disposed of as provided in sections (9), (10) and (11) of this Standing Order.

Two votable motions in any supply period — Duration of proceedings

(9) (*a*) In each of the periods described in section (5) of this Standing Order, not more than two opposition motions shall be motions that shall come to a vote. The duration of proceedings on any such motion or on an order setting down any item or items in the main or supplementary estimates for consideration in a committee of the whole shall be stated in the notice relating to

the appointing of an allotted day or days for those proceedings. On the last day appointed for proceedings on a motion that shall come to a vote or on an item or items in the main or supplementary estimates being considered by a committee of the whole, at fifteen minutes before the ordinary time of daily adjournment the Speaker, or the Chairman of the committee of the whole, as the case may be, shall interrupt the proceedings then before the House or the committee of the whole and forthwith put, without further amendment or debate, every question necessary to dispose of the said proceeding and, when required, to report the same to the House.

Notice of proposed amendment in Committee of the Whole — Chairman's power of selection

(*b*) When the House goes into a committee of the whole on an item or items in any set of main or supplementary estimates a Member may give notice to the committee of a proposed amendment to any item or items set down for consideration by the committee; such notice shall be in writing and must be laid upon the Table not later than one hour before the time at which it is required to be disposed of. When notice is given of two or more proposed amendments touching on the same item in the estimates, the Chairman shall have power to select or combine and decide which of the said proposals shall be submitted to the committee. If a proposed amendment is found to be in order, it shall stand as one of the questions to be disposed of pursuant to section (9) (*a*) of this Standing Order.

Motion to concur in report of Committee of the Whole

(*c*) Upon report to the House from a committee of the whole of any resolution or resolutions covering any item or items in the main or supplementary estimates, a motion to concur in the same shall be decided without amendment or debate.

When question put in each period — Ordinary adjournment suspended if necessary

(10) On the last allotted day in each period, but, in any case, not later than the last sitting day in each period, at fifteen minutes before the ordinary time of daily adjournment or when a report has been received from a committee of the whole, the Speaker shall interrupt the proceedings then in progress and, put forthwith successively, without amendment or debate, every question as may be required by section (9) of this Order and such other question or questions as may be necessary to dispose of any item of business relating to interim supply, main or supplementary estimates, the restoration

or reinstatement of any item in the estimates or any opposed item in the estimates, and notwithstanding the provisions of Standing Order 72, for the passage at all stages of any bill or bills based thereon. The Standing Order relating to the ordinary time of daily adjournment shall remain suspended until all such questions have been decided.

Expiration of proceedings

(11) Proceedings on a motion which is not a motion that shall come to a vote shall expire when debate thereon has been concluded or when interrupted pursuant to the provisions of this Standing Order or at the ordinary hour of daily adjournment, as the case may be.

Business of supply takes precedence of government business

(12) On any day or days appointed for the consideration of any business under the provisions of this Standing Order, that order of business shall have precedence over all other government business in such sitting or sittings.

Limits on speeches

(13) During proceedings on any item of business under the provisions of this Standing Order except when the House is in a committee of the whole, no Member may speak more than once or longer than twenty minutes, except that both the mover of a debatable motion and the Member speaking immediately in reply thereto may speak for thirty minutes.

Main estimates referred to and reported by standing committees

(14) In every session the main estimates to cover the incoming fiscal year for every department of government shall be referred to standing committees on or before March 1 of the then expiring fiscal year. Each such committee shall consider and shall report, or shall be deemed to have reported, the same back to the House not later than May 31 in the then current fiscal year.

Supplementary estimates referred to and reported by standing committees

(15) Supplementary estimates shall be referred to a standing committee or committees immediately they are presented in the House. Each such committee shall consider and shall report, or shall be deemed to have reported, the same back to the House not later than three sitting days before the final sitting or the last allotted day in the current period.

Standing committee deemed to be empowered to consider subject-matter of estimates

(15A) When any item or items in the main or supplementary estimates have been withdrawn from a standing committee for the purpose of considering the same in a committee of the whole, the said standing committee or committees shall be deemed to have been empowered to continue the consideration of the subject-matter of any such estimate or estimates for any time remaining for such work under the provisions of sections (14) and (15) of this Standing Order.

When debate on motion to concur permitted

(16) There shall be no debate on any motion to concur in a report of any standing committee on estimates or the subject-matter thereof, as the case may be, which have been referred to it except on an allotted day.

Unopposed items

(17) The adoption of all unopposed items in any set of estimates may be proposed in one or more motions.

Where urgency arises

(18) In the event of urgency in relation to any estimate or estimates, the proceedings of the House on a motion to concur therein and on the subsequent bill are to be taken under Government Orders and not on days allotted in this Order.

Effect of concurrence in estimates

(19) The concurrence in any estimate or estimates or interim supply shall be an Order of the House to bring in a bill or bills based thereon.

Motion to refer estimates to standing committees

59. (1) A motion, to be decided without amendment or debate, may be moved during Routine Proceedings by a Minister of the Crown to refer any item or items in the main or supplementary estimates to any standing committee or committees and, upon report from any such committees, the same shall lie upon the Table of the House.

Estimates deemed withdrawn from standing committee and referred to Committee of the Whole

(2) If a notice is given for setting down any item or items in main or supplementary estimates for consideration in a committee of the whole and if any such item stands referred to a Standing Committee, when the Order of the Day for consideration of the business of supply is read and if Mr. Speaker, in accordance with section 4(*b*) of Standing Order 58, designates the said notice as being the business for consideration, the said item or items shall be deemed to have been withdrawn from any standing committee and shall stand referred to a committee of the whole.

Consideration of estimates not before a standing committee

(3) When notice is given for the purpose of considering any item or items in the main or supplementary estimates which are not then before a standing committee, such item or items shall thereupon stand referred to a committee of the whole.

Notice of Ways and Means

60. (1) A notice of a Ways and Means motion may be laid upon the Table of the House at any time during a sitting by a Minister of the Crown, but such a motion may not be proposed in the same sitting.

Ways and Means designated

(2) An Order of the Day for the consideration of a Ways and Means motion or motions shall be designated at the request of a Minister rising in his place in the House.

Form of motion — budget

(3) When such an order is designated for the purpose of enabling a Minister of the Crown to make a budget presentation, a motion "That this House approves in general the budgetary policy of the Government" shall be proposed.

Budget debate six days

(4) The proceedings on the Order of the Day for resuming debate on such budget motion and on any amendments proposed thereto shall not exceed six sitting days.

First order

(5) When the Order of the Day for resuming the said Budget Debate is called, it must stand as the first order of the day and, unless it be disposed of, no other Government Order shall be considered in the same sitting.

When question put on subamendment

(6) On the second of the said days, if a subamendment be under consideration at fifteen minutes before the expiry of the time provided for government business in such sitting, Mr. Speaker shall interrupt the proceedings and forthwith put the question on the said subamendment.

When question put on amendment

(7) On the fourth of the said days, if an amendment be under consideration at fifteen minutes before the expiry of the time provided for

government business in such sitting, Mr. Speaker shall interrupt the proceedings and forthwith put the question on the said amendment.

When question put on main motion

(8) On the sixth of the said days, at fifteen minutes before the expiry of the time provided for government business in such sitting, unless the debate be previously concluded, Mr. Speaker shall interrupt the proceedings and forthwith put the question on the main motion.

Time limits on speeches

(9) No Member, except the Minister of Finance, the Member speaking first on behalf of the Opposition, the Prime Minister and the Leader of the Opposition, shall speak for more than thirty minutes at a time in the Budget Debate; provided that forty minutes shall be allowed to the mover of a subamendment.

Motion to concur in Ways and Means motion other than budget

(10) When an Order of the Day is read for the consideration of any motion of which notice has been given in accordance with section (1) of this Standing Order, a motion to concur in the same shall be forthwith decided without debate or amendment, but no such motion may be proposed during the Budget Debate.

Effect of motion being adopted

(11) The adoption of any Ways and Means motion shall be an order to bring in a bill or bills based on the provisions of any such motion.

Amendments on Budget Debate and Supply on allotted days

61.   Only one amendment and one subamendment may be made to a motion proposed in the Budget Debate or to a motion proposed under an Order of the Day for the consideration of the business of supply on an allotted day.

CHAPTER X

FINANCIAL PROVISIONS

Recommendation of Governor General

62.   (1) This House shall not adopt or pass any vote, resolution, address or bill for the appropriation of any part of the public revenue, or of any tax or impost, to any purpose that has not been first recommended to the House by a message from the Governor General in the session in which such vote, resolution, address or bill is proposed.

Notice of recommendation

(2) The message and recommendation of the Governor General in relation to any bill for the appropriation of any part of the public revenue or of any tax or impost shall be printed on the Notice Paper and in the *Votes and Proceedings* when any such measure is to be introduced and the text of such recommendation shall be printed with or annexed to every such bill.

Estimates

(3) When estimates are brought in, the message from the Governor General shall be presented to and read by Mr. Speaker in the House.

Commons alone grant aids and supplies

63. All aids and supplies granted to Her Majesty by the Parliament of Canada are the sole gift of the House of Commons, and all bills for granting such aids and supplies ought to begin with the House, as it is the undoubted right of the House to direct, limit, and appoint in all such bills, the ends, purposes, considerations, conditions, limitations and qualifications of such grants, which are not alterable by the Senate.

Pecuniary penalties in Senate bills

64. In order to expedite the business of Parliament, the House will not insist on the privilege claimed and exercised by them of laying aside bills sent from the Senate because they impose pecuniary penalties nor of laying aside amendments made by the Senate because they introduce into or alter pecuniary penalties in bills sent to them by this House; provided that all such penalties thereby imposed are only to punish or prevent crimes and offences, and do not tend to lay a burden on the subject, either as aid or supply to Her Majesty, or for any general or special purposes, by rates, tolls, assessments or otherwise.

CHAPTER XI

STANDING, SPECIAL AND JOINT COMMITTEES; WITNESSES

Striking Committee of seven to report within ten days

65. (1) At the commencement of the first session of each Parliament, a Striking Committee, consisting of seven Members, shall be appointed, whose duty it shall be to prepare and report, within the first ten sitting days after its appointment, lists of Members to compose the following standing committees of the House:

Committees listed

(a) Agriculture, to consist of not more than 30 members;

(b) Broadcasting, Films and Assistance to the Arts, to consist of not more than 20 members;

(c) External Affairs and National Defence, to consist of not more than 30 members;

(d) Finance, Trade and Economic Affairs, to consist of not more than 20 members;

(e) Fisheries and Forestry, to consist of not more than 20 members;

(f) Health, Welfare and Social Affairs, to consist of not more than 20 members;

(g) Indian Affairs and Northern Development, to consist of not more than 20 members;

(h) National Resources and Public Works, to consist of not more than 20 members;

(i) Justice and Legal Affairs, to consist of not more than 20 members;

(j) Labour, Manpower and Immigration, to consist of not more than 20 members;

(k) Regional Development, to consist of not more than 20 members;

(l) Transport and Communications, to consist of not more than 20 members;

(m) Veterans Affairs, to consist of not more than 20 members;

(n) Miscellaneous Estimates, to consist of not more than 20 members;

(o) Miscellaneous Private Bills and Standing Orders, to consist of not more than 20 members;

(p) Privileges and Elections, to consist of not more than 20 members;

(q) Public Accounts, to consist of not more than 20 members to which the Public Accounts and all Reports of the Auditor General shall be deemed to have been permanently referred, immediately the said documents are tabled.

(r) Procedure and Organization, to consist of not more than 12 members; and

(s) On Management and Members' Services which is empowered to advise Mr. Speaker as well as the Commissioners of Internal Economy on the administration of the House and the provisions of services and facilities to Members, to consist of not more than 12 members,

(t) Northern pipelines, to consist of not more than 15 members, to which shall stand permanently referred all reports, orders, agreements, regulations, directions and approvals mentioned in sections 12, 13, 14, 15 and 22 of the Northern Pipeline Act; provided that the said committee shall report thereon at least three times in every session.

Provided that this subsection shall be deleted from the Standing Orders on the day on which the Northern Pipeline Agency ceases to exist.

Election of Chairman and Vice-Chairman

(2) Each of the said committees shall elect a chairman and a vice-chairman at the commencement of every session and, if necessary, during the course of a session.

Joint Committees

(3) The Striking Committee shall also prepare and report lists of Members to compose the following standing joint committees:

(*a*) On Printing, to act as members on the part of this House on the Joint Committee of both Houses on the subject of the printing of Parliament, to consist of 23 members;

(*b*) On the Library of Parliament, so far as the interests of this House are concerned, and to act as members of the Joint Committee of both Houses, to consist of 21 members;

(*c*) On Regulations and other Statutory Instruments, to act as members on the part of this House on the Joint Committee of both Houses established for the purpose of reviewing and scrutinizing statutory instruments standing permanently referred thereto by section 26 of the Statutory Instruments Act, to consist of 12 members;

Provided that a sufficient number of Members of the said joint committees shall be appointed so as to keep the same proportion in such committees as between the memberships of both Houses.

Membership subject to change

(4) (*a*) The membership of standing and joint committees shall be as set out in the report of the Striking Committee, when concurred in by the House, and shall continue from session to session within a Parliament, but shall be subject to such changes as may be effected from time to time.

Membership changes

(*b*) Changes in the membership of any standing, joint or special committee may be effected by a notification thereof, signed by the Member acting as the Chief Government Whip, being filed with the Clerk of the House who shall cause the same to be printed in the *Votes and Proceedings* of the House of that sitting, or of the next sitting thereafter, as the case may be.

Special Committees

(5) A special committee shall consist of not more than 15 members.

Quorum

(6) A majority of the members of a standing or a special committee shall constitute a quorum. In the case of a joint committee, the number of members

constituting a quorum shall be such as the House of Commons acting in consultation with the Senate may determine.

Meetings without quorum

(7) The presence of a quorum shall be required whenever a vote, resolution or other decision is taken by a standing or a special committee, provided that any such committee, by resolution thereof, may authorize the chairman to hold meetings to receive and authorize the printing of evidence when a quorum is not present.

Powers of Standing Committees

(8) Standing committees shall be severally empowered to examine and enquire into all such matters as may be referred to them by the House, and, to report from time to time, and, except when the House otherwise orders, to send for persons, papers and records, to sit while the House is sitting, to sit during periods when the House stands adjourned, to print from day to day such papers and evidence as may be ordered by them, and to delegate to sub-committees all or any of their powers except the power to report direct to the House.

Only members may vote or move motion

(9) Any Member of the House who is not a member of a standing or special committee, may, unless the House or the committee concerned otherwise orders, take part in the public proceedings of the committee, but he may not vote or move any motion, nor shall he be part of any quorum.

Standing Orders apply generally

(10) In a standing or special committee, the Standing Orders of the House shall be observed so far as may be applicable, except the standing orders as to the seconding of motions, limiting the number of times of speaking and the length of speeches.

Decorum in Committee

(11) The Chairman of a standing or special committee shall maintain order in the committees; deciding all questions of order subject to an appeal to the committee; but disorder in a committee can only be censured by the House, on receiving a report thereof.

Reports

(12) Reports from standing and special committees may be made by Members standing in their places, and without proceeding to the bar of the House.

Administration, services and facilities deemed referred

(13) All matters relating to the administration of the House and the provisions of services and facilities to Members shall be deemed to have been referred to the Standing Committee on Management and Members' Services on the first day of each session.

Certificate filed for summons of witnesses

66. (1) No witness shall be summoned to attend before any committee of the House unless a certificate shall first have been filed with the chairman of such committee, by some member thereof, stating that the evidence to be obtained from such witness is, in his opinion, material and important.

Payment

(2) The Clerk of the House is authorized to pay out of the contingent fund to witnesses so summoned a reasonable sum *per diem* during their travel and attendance, to be determined by Mr. Speaker, and a reasonable allowance for travelling expenses.

Claim for payment to be certified by Chairman and Clerk of the Committee

(3) The claim of a witness for payment shall state the number of days during which he has been in attendance, the time of necessary travel and the amount of his travelling expenses, which claim and statement shall, before being paid, be certified by the chairman and clerk of the committee before which such witness has been summoned.

Exception to payment

(4) No witness residing at the seat of government shall be paid for his attendance.

CHAPTER XII

PETITIONS

How and when presented

67. (1) A petition to the House may be presented by a Member at any time during the sitting of the House by filing the same with the Clerk of the House.

Time for presentation

(2) Any Member desiring to present a petition in his place in the House must do so during Routine Proceedings and before Introduction of Bills.

No debate

(3) On the presentation of a petition no debate on or in relation to the same shall be allowed.

Members answerable

(4) Members presenting petitions shall be answerable that they do not contain impertinent or improper matter.

Members endorsation

(5) Every Member presenting a petition shall endorse his name thereon.

Form of petition

(6) Petitions may be either written or printed; provided always that when there are three or more petitioners the signatures of at least three petitioners shall be subscribed on the sheet containing the prayer of the petition.

Reception of petitions

(7) On the next day following the presentation of a petition the Clerk of the House shall lay upon the Table the report of the Clerk of Petitions upon the petitions presented and such report shall be printed in the *Votes and Proceedings* of that day. Every petition so reported upon, not containing matter in breach of the privileges of this House and which, according to the Standing Orders or practice of this House, can be received, shall then be deemed to be read and received.

Immediate discussion when permitted

(8) No debate shall be permitted on the report but a petition referred to therein may be read by the Clerk of the House at the Table, if required; or if it complain of some present personal grievance requiring an immediate remedy, the matter contained therein may be brought into immediate discussion.

CHAPTER XIII

PROCEEDINGS ON PUBLIC BILLS

Introduction of bills upon motion for leave

68. (1) Every bill is introduced upon motion for leave, specifying the title of the bill; or upon motion to appoint a committee to prepare and bring it in.

Brief explanation permitted

(2) A motion for leave to introduce a bill shall be decided without debate

or amendment, provided that any Member moving for such leave may be permitted to give a succinct explanation of the provisions of the said bill.

Imperfect or blank bills

69. No bill may be introduced either in blank or in an imperfect shape.

Motion for first reading and printing

70. (1) When any bill is presented by a Member, in pursuance of an order of the House, the question "That this bill be read a first time and be printed" shall be decided without debate or amendment.

(2) When any bill is brought from the Senate, the question "That this bill be read a first time" shall be decided without debate or amendment.

Printed in English and French before second reading

71. All bills shall be printed before the second reading in the English and French languages.

Three separate readings — Urgent cases

72. Every bill shall receive three several readings, on different days, previously to being passed. On urgent or extraordinary occasions, a bill may be read twice or thrice, or advanced two or more stages in one day.

Clerk certifies readings

73. When a bill is read in the House, the Clerk shall certify upon it the readings and the time thereof. After it has passed, he shall certify the same, with the date, at the foot of the bill.

Reading and referral before amendment

74. (1) Every public bill shall be read twice and referred to a committee before any amendment may be made thereto.

Referral to a committee — No debate

(2) Unless otherwise ordered, in giving a bill a second reading, the same shall be referred to a standing committee, but a bill may be referred to a special or a joint committee. A motion to refer a bill to a standing or a special committee shall be decided without amendment or debate.

Supply and Ways and Means bills

(3) Any bill based on a supply or a ways and means motion, after second reading thereof, shall stand referred to a committee of the whole.

Proceedings on bills in any Committee

75. (1) In proceedings in any committee of the House upon bills, the preamble is first postponed, and if the first clause contains only a short title it is also postponed; then every other clause is considered by the committee in its proper order; the first clause (if it contains only a short title), the preamble and the title are to be last considered.

Proceedings reported

(2) All amendments made in any committee shall be reported to the House. Every bill reported from any committee, whether amended or not, shall be received by the House on report thereof.

Report stage of bill from a standing or special committee

(3) The report stage of any bill reported by any standing or special committee shall not be taken into consideration prior to forty-eight hours following the presentation of the said report, unless otherwise ordered by the House.

Report stage of bill from Committee of the Whole

(4) The consideration of the report stage of a bill from a Committee of the Whole shall be received and forthwith disposed of, without amendment or debate.

Notice to amend at report stage

(5) If, not later than twenty-four hours prior to the consideration of a report stage, written notice is given of any motion to amend, delete, insert or restore any clause in a bill, it shall be printed on a notice paper.

Notice of financial amendments to a bill

(6) When a recommendation of the Governor General is required in relation to any amendment to be proposed at the report stage of a bill, at least twenty-four hours written notice shall be given of the said recommendation and proposed amendment.

Amendment as to form only

(7) An amendment, in relation to form only in a government bill, may be proposed by a Minister of the Crown without notice, but debate thereon may not be extended to the provisions of the clause or clauses to be amended.

Purpose of section (7)

NOTE: The purpose of the section is to facilitate the incorporation into a bill of amendments of a strictly consequential nature flowing from the acceptance of other amendments. No waiver of notice would be permitted in relation to any amendment which would change the intent of the bill, no matter how slightly, beyond the effect of the initial amendment.

Order of the day for report stage

(8) When the Order of the Day for the consideration of a report stage is called, any amendment of which notice has been given in accordance with section (5) of this order shall be open to debate and amendment.

Limits on speeches

(9) When debate is permitted, no member shall speak more than once or longer than twenty minutes during proceedings on any amendment at that stage, except that the Prime Minister, the Leader of the Opposition, a Minister of the Crown or other member sponsoring a bill and the member proposing an amendment, may speak for not more than forty minutes.

Speaker's power on amendments

(10) Mr. Speaker shall have power to select or combine amendments or clauses to be proposed at the report stage and may, if he thinks fit, call upon any member who has given notice of an amendment to give such explanation of the subject of the amendment as may enable Mr. Speaker to form a judgment upon it.

Division deferred

(11) When a recorded division has been demanded on any amendment proposed during the report stage of a bill, Mr. Speaker may defer the calling in of the Members for the purpose of recording the "yeas" and "nays" until any or all subsequent amendments proposed to that bill have been considered. A recorded division or divisions may be so deferred from sitting to sitting.

Motion when report stage concluded

(12) When proceedings at the report stage on any bill have been concluded, a motion "That the bill, as amended, be concurred in" or "That the bill be concurred in" shall be put and forthwith disposed of, without amendment or debate.

Third reading after debate or amendment

(13) When a bill has been amended or debate has taken place thereon at the report stage, the same shall be set down for a third reading and passage at the next sitting of the House.

Third reading when no amendment or after committee of the whole

(14) When a bill has been reported from a standing or special committee,

and no amendment has been proposed thereto at the report stage, and in the case of a bill reported from a Committee of the Whole, with or without amendment, a motion, "That the bill be now read a third time and passed", may be made in the same sitting.

Agreement to allot time

75A. When a Minister of the Crown, from his place in the House, states that there is agreement among the representatives of all parties to allot a specified number of days or hours to the proceedings at one or more stages of any public bill, he may propose a motion, without notice, setting forth the terms of such agreed allocation; and every such motion shall be decided forthwith, without debate or amendment.

Qualified agreement to allot time

75B. When a Minister of the Crown, from his place in the House, states that a majority of the representatives of the several parties have come to an agreement in respect of a proposed allotment of days or hours for the proceedings at any stage of the passing of a public bill, he may propose a motion, without notice, setting forth the terms of the said proposed allocation; provided that for the purposes of this standing order an allocation may be proposed in one motion to cover the proceedings at both the report and the third reading stages of a bill if that motion is consistent with the provisions of Standing Order 75(13). During the consideration of any such motion no Member may speak more than once or longer than ten minutes. Not more than two hours after the commencement of proceedings thereon, Mr. Speaker shall put every question necessary to dispose of the said motion.

Procedure in other cases

75C. A Minister of the Crown who from his place in the House at a previous sitting has stated that an agreement could not be reached under the provisions of Standing Order 75A or 75B in respect of proceedings at the stage at which a public bill was then under consideration either in the House or in any committee and has given notice of his intention so to do may propose a motion for the purpose of allotting a specified number of days or hours for the consideration and disposal of proceedings at that stage; provided that the time allotted for any stage is not to be less than one sitting day and provided that for the purposes of this Standing Order an allocation may be proposed in one motion to cover the proceedings at both the report and the third reading stages on a bill if that motion is consistent with the provisions of Standing Order 75(13). During the consideration of any such motion no Member may speak more than once or longer than ten minutes. Not more than two hours after the commencement of proceedings thereon, Mr. Speaker shall put every question necessary to dispose of the said motion.

CHAPTER XIV

OFFER OF MONEY TO MEMBERS; BRIBERY IN ELECTIONS

A high crime

76. The offer of any money or other advantage to any Member of this House, for the promoting of any matter whatsoever depending or to be transacted in Parliament, is a high crime and misdemeanour, and tends to the subversion of the constitution.

Proceedings in case of bribery

77. If it shall appear that any person has been elected and returned a Member of this House, or has endeavoured so to be, by bribery or any other corrupt practices, this House will proceed with the utmost severity against all such persons as shall have been wilfully concerned in such bribery or other corrupt practices.

CHAPTER XV

INTERNAL ECONOMY

Report within ten days

78. Mr. Speaker shall, within ten days after the opening of each session, lay upon the Table of the House a report of the proceedings for the preceding year of the Commissioners of Internal Economy.

CHAPTER XVI

EFFECT OF PROROGATION ON ORDERS FOR RETURNS

Prorogation not to nullify order or address for returns

79. A prorogation of the House shall not have the effect of nullifying an order or address of the House for returns or papers, but all papers and returns ordered at one session of the House, if not complied with during the session, shall be brought down during the following session, without renewal of the order.

CHAPTER XVII

OFFICERS OF THE HOUSE

Safe-keeping of records — Control of officers and staff

80. The Clerk of the House is responsible for the safe-keeping of all the papers and records of the House, and has the direction and control over all the officers and clerks employed in the offices, subject to such orders as he may, from time to time, receive from Mr. Speaker or the House.

Printing — Order Paper

81. The Clerk of the House shall place on Mr. Speaker's table, every morning, previous to the meeting of the House, the order of the proceedings for the day.

Documents to be tabled

82. (1) It is the duty of the Clerk to make and cause to be printed and delivered to each Member, at the commencement of every session of Parliament, a list of the reports or other periodical statements which it is the duty of any officer or department of the government, or any bank or other corporate body to make to the House, referring to the Act or resolution, and page of the volume of the laws or Journals wherein the same may be ordered; and placing under the name of each officer or corporation a list of reports or returns required of him, or it, to be made, and the time when the report or periodical statement may be expected.

Two copies of every bill introduced sent to Minister of Justice

(2) In order to give effect to the purposes and provisions of section 3 of the Canadian Bill of Rights, it is the duty of the Clerk to cause to be delivered to the Minister of Justice two copies of every bill introduced in or presented to the House of Commons, forthwith after the introduction in or presentation to the House of such bill.

To employ extra writers

83. The Clerk shall employ at the outset of a session, with the approbation of Mr. Speaker, such extra writers as may be necessary, engaging others as the public business may require.

Duties of Law Clerks — Draft legislation — Prepare bills for Senate — Edit annual statutes — Revise bills and insert marginal notes — Revise amendments before third reading — Report on variance in private bills to general Acts

84. It is the duty of the Joint Law Clerks of the House to assist Members of the House and deputy heads in drafting legislation; to prepare bills for the Senate after they have been passed by the House; to supervise the printing and arrangement and extending of the statutes year by year as they are issued at the close of each parliamentary session; to revise, print and put marginal notes upon all bills; to revise before the third reading all amendments made by select committees, or in committees of the whole; and to report to the several chairmen of the various select committees, when requested so to do, any provisions in private bills which are at variance with general Acts on the subjects to which such bills relate or with the usual provisions of private Acts on similar subjects, and any provisions deserving of special attention.

Sergeant-at-Arms responsible for safe-keeping of Mace — Strangers in custody

85.   (1) The Sergeant-at-Arms is responsible for the safe-keeping of the Mace, and of the furniture and fittings of the House.

(2) No stranger who has been committed, by order of the House, to the custody of the Sergeant-at-Arms, shall be released from such custody until he has paid a fee of four dollars to the Sergeant-at-Arms.

Duties

(3) The Sergeant-at-Arms serves all orders of the House upon those whom they may concern and is entrusted with the execution of warrants issued by Mr. Speaker. He issues cards of admission to, and preserves order in, the galleries, corridors, lobbies and other parts. He is responsible for the movable property belonging to the House.

To employ constables and others

(4) The Sergeant-at-Arms shall employ at the outset of a session, with the approbation of Mr. Speaker, such constables, messengers, pages and labourers as may be necessary, engaging others as the service of the House may require.

Supervises constables and others

(5) The Sergeant-at-Arms has the direction and control over all constables, messengers, pages, labourers and other such employees subject to such orders as he may receive from Mr. Speaker or the House.

Completion of work at close of session

86.   It is the duty of the officers of this House to complete and finish the work remaining at the close of the session.

Travelling expenses not allowed

87.   No allowance shall be made to any person in the employ of this House who may not reside at the seat of government, for travelling expenses in coming to attend his duties.

Hours of attendance

88.   The hours of attendance of the respective officers of this House, and the extra clerks employed during the session, shall be fixed from time to time by Mr. Speaker.

Vacancies filled by Mr. Speaker — Salaries to be fixed by Mr. Speaker

89. Before filling any vacancy in the service of the House by Mr. Speaker, inquiry shall be made touching the necessity for the continuance of such office; and the amount of salary to be attached to the same shall be fixed by Mr. Speaker, subject to the approval of the Board of Internal Economy and of the House.

CHAPTER XVIII

PRIVATE BILLS

Time limited for receiving petitions and for presenting bills

90. Petitions for private bills shall only be received by the House if filed within the first six weeks of the session, and every private bill originating in the Commons shall be presented to the House within two weeks after the petition therefor has been favourably reported upon by the Examiner of Petitions or by the Standing Committee on Miscellaneous Private Bills and Standing Orders.

Time limited for depositing bill — Printing and translation cost

91. (1) Any person desiring to obtain any private bill shall deposit with the Clerk of the House not later than the first day of each session, a copy of such bill in the English or French language, with a sum sufficient to pay for translating and printing the same; the translation to be done by the officers of the House, and the printing by the Department of Public Printing.

Fees and charges

(2) After the second reading of a bill, and before its consideration by the committee to which it is referred, the applicant shall in every case pay the cost of printing the Act in the statutes, and a fee of five hundred dollars.

(3) The following charges shall also be levied and paid in addition to the foregoing:

    (a) When any Standing Order of the House is suspended in reference to a bill or the petition therefor, for each such suspension $100

    (b) When a bill is presented in the House after the eighth week of the session and not later than the twelfth week $100

    (c) When a bill is presented in the House after the twelfth week of the session $200

(d) When the proposed capital stock of a company does not exceed
$250,000 .... $100

(e) When the proposed capital stock of a company is over $250,000 and
does not exceed $500,000 .... $200

(f) When the proposed capital stock of a company is over $500,000 and
does not exceed $750,000 .... $300

(g) When the proposed capital stock of a company is over $750,000 and
does not exceed $1,000,000 .... $400

(h) When the proposed capital stock of a company is over $1,000,000
and does not exceed $1,500,000 .... $600

(i) When the proposed capital stock of a company is over $1,500,000
and does not exceed $2,000,000 .... $800

(j) For every additional million dollars or fractional part thereof
.... $200

Capital increased

(4)   When a bill increases the capital stock of an existing company, the
additional charge shall be according to the foregoing tariff, upon the amount
of the increase only.

Borrowing powers increased

(5)   *(a)* When a bill increases or involves an increase in the borrowing
powers of a company without any increase in the capital stock, the additional
charge shall be $300.

Increase of capital and borrowing powers

(b)   When a bill increases both the capital stock and the borrowing
powers of a company, the additional charge shall be made upon both.

Bill stands until charges are paid

(6)   If any increase in the amount of the proposed capital stock or
borrowing powers of a company be made at any stage of a bill, such bill shall
not be advanced to the next stage until the charges consequent upon such
change have been paid.

Interpretation

(7)   In this Standing Order the term "proposed capital stock" includes

any increase thereto provided for in the bill; and where power is taken in a bill to increase at any time the amount of the proposed capital stock, the additional charge shall be levied on the maximum amount of such proposed increase which shall be stated in the bill.

Additional charges apply to Senate bills

(8) The additional charges provided for in this Standing Order shall also apply to private bills originating in the Senate; provided, however, that if a petition for any such bill has been filed with this House within the first six weeks of the session, the additional charges made under paragraphs *(b)* or *(c)* of subsection (3) shall not be levied thereon.

Collection of fees

(9) The Chief Clerk of Private Bills shall prepare and send to the promoter or parliamentary agent in charge of every private bill a statement of fees and charges payable under this Standing Order, and shall collect all such fees and charges and deposit the same with the accountant of the House and shall send a copy of each such deposit slip to the Clerk of the House.

Publication of Standing Orders — Notices in lobbies

92. The Clerk of the House shall publish weekly in the *Canada Gazette* the Standing Orders respecting notices of intended applications for private bills, and shall announce by notice affixed in the lobbies of the House, by the first day of every session, the time limited for receiving petitions for private bills.

Publication of notices

93. (1) All applications to Parliament for private bills, of any nature whatsoever, shall be advertised by a notice published in the *Canada Gazette;* such notice shall clearly and distinctly state the nature and objects of the application, and shall be signed by or on behalf of the applicants, with the address of the party signing the same; and when the application is for an Act of incorporation, the name of the proposed company shall be stated in the notice. If the works of any company (incorporated, or to be incorporated) are to be declared to be for the general advantage of Canada, such intention shall be specifically mentioned in the notice; and the applicants shall cause a copy of such notice to be sent by registered letter to the clerk of each country or municipality which may be specially affected by the construction or operation of such works, and also to the secretary of the province in which such works are, or may be located. Every such notice sent by registered letter shall be mailed in time to reach its destination not later than two weeks before the consideration of the proposed bill by the committee to which it may be referred; and proof of compliance with this requirement by the applicants shall be established by statutory declaration.

Additional notice

(2) In addition to the notice in the *Canada Gazette* aforesaid, a similar notice shall also be published in some leading newspaper as follows:

In case of incorporation

(a) When the application is for an Act to incorporate:

Railway or canal company

    (i) A railway or canal company: in the principal city, town or village in each county or district, through which the proposed railway or canal is to be constructed;

Telegraph or telephone company

    (ii) A telegraph or telephone company: in the principal city or town in each province or territory in which the company proposes to operate;

Construction of works

    (iii) A company for the construction of any works which in their construction or operation might specially affect the particular locality; or obtaining any exclusive rights or privileges; or for doing any matter or thing which in its operation would affect the rights or property of others: in the particular locality or localities in which the business, rights or property of other persons or corporations may be affected by the proposed Act;

Banking, insurance, trust, loan company or industrial company

    (iv) A banking company; an insurance company; a trust company; a loan company; or an industrial company without any exclusive powers: in the *Canada Gazette* only.

In case of amending Act

(b) When the application is for the purpose of amending an existing Act:

Extension of railway

    (i) For an extension of any line of railway, or of any canal; or for the construction of branches thereto: in the place where the head office of the company is situated, and in the principal city, town or village in each county or district through which such extension or branch is to be constructed;

Extension of time

(ii) For an extension of time for the construction or completion of any line of railway or of any branch or extension thereof, or of any canal, or of any telegraph or telephone line, or of any other works already authorized: at the place where the head office of the company is situated and in the principal city or town of the districts affected;

Continuation of charter

(iii) For the continuation of a charter or for an extension of the powers of the company (when not involving the granting of any exclusive rights) or for the increase or reduction of the capital stock of any company; or for increasing or altering its bonding or other borrowing powers; or for any amendment which would in any way affect the rights or interests of the shareholders or bondholders or creditors of the company: in the place where the head office of the company is situated or authorized to be.

Exclusive rights

(c) When the application is for the purpose of obtaining for any person or existing corporation any exclusive rights or privileges or the power to do any matter or thing which in its operation would affect the rights or property of others: in the particular locality or localities in which the business, rights or property of others may be specially affected by the proposed Act.

Duration of notice

(3) All such notices, whether inserted in the *Canada Gazette* or in a newspaper, shall be published at least once a week for a period of four consecutive weeks; and when originating in the Province of Quebec or in the Province of Manitoba shall be published in English in an English newspaper and in French in a French newspaper, and in both languages in the *Canada Gazette,* and if there is no newspaper in a locality where a notice is required to be given, such notice shall be given in the next nearest locality wherein a newspaper is published; and proof of the due publication of notice shall be established in each case by statutory declaration; and all such declarations shall be sent to the Clerk of the House endorsed "Private Bill Notice".

Examiner of private bills

94. (1) The Chief Clerk of Private Bills shall be the Examiner of Private Bills, and, as such, shall examine and revise all private bills before they are printed, for the purpose of insuring uniformity where possible and of seeing that they are drawn in accordance with the Standing orders of the House respecting private bills.

Model bill

(2)   Every bill for an Act of incorporation, where a form of model bill has been adopted, shall be drawn in accordance with a model bill (copies of model bills may be obtained from the Clerk of the House). Any provisions contained in any such bill which are not in accord with the model bill shall be inserted between brackets or underlined, and shall be so printed.

Amending bill

(3)   Where a private bill amends any section, subsection or paragraph of an existing Act, such section, subsection or paragraph shall be repealed in the text of the bill and re-enacted as proposed to be amended, the new matter being indicated by underlining; and the section, subsection or paragraph which is to be so repealed, or so much thereof as is essential, shall be printed in the right-hand page opposite such section, subsection or paragraph.

When a repeal is involved

(4)   When a private bill repeals an existing section, subsection, or other minor division of a section, that section, subsection or division, or so much thereof as is essential, shall be printed opposite the clause.

Explanatory note where necessary

(5)   A brief explanatory note giving the reasons for any clause of an unusual nature or which differs from the model bill clauses or standard clauses shall be printed opposite the clause in the bill.

Map or plan with petition

95.   No petition praying for the incorporation of a railway company, or of a canal company, or for an extension of the line of any existing or authorized railway of canal, or for the construction of branches thereto, shall be considered by the Examiner, or by the Standing Committee on Miscellaneous Private Bills and Standing Orders, until there has been filed with the said Examiner a map or plan, showing the proposed location of the works, and each county, township, municipality or district through which the proposed railway or canal, or any branch or extension thereof, is to be constructed.

Map or plan with bill

96.   No bill for the incorporation of a railway or canal company, or for authorizing the construction of branch lines or extensions of existing lines or of railways or of canals, or for changing the route of the railway or of the canal of any company already incorporated, shall be considered by the Standing Committee on Transport and Communications, until there has been filed with the committee, at least one week before the consideration of the bill, a map or plan drawn upon a scale of not less than half an inch to the mile, showing the location upon which it is intended to construct the proposed work, and showing also the lines of existing or authorized works of a similar character within, or in any way affecting the district, or any part thereof, which the proposed work is intended to serve; and such map or plan shall be signed by the engineer or other person making same.

Examiner of petitions for private bills

97. (1) The Chief Clerk of Private Bills shall be the Examiner of Petitions for Private Bills.

Report to the House

(2) Petitions for private bills, when received by the House, are to be taken into consideration by the Examiner who shall report to the House in each case the extent to which the requirements of the Standing Orders regarding notice have been complied with; and in every case where the notice is reported by the Examiner to have been insufficient or otherwise defective, or if he reports that there is any doubt as to the sufficiency of the notice as published, the petition, together with the report of the Examiner thereon, shall be taken into consideration, without special reference, by the Standing Committee on Miscellaneous Private Bills and Standing Orders, which shall report to the House as to the sufficiency or insufficiency of the notice, and where the notice is deemed insufficient or otherwise defective, shall recommend to the House the course to be taken in consequence of such deficiency or other defect.

Private bills from Senate

(3) All private bills from the Senate (not being based on a petition which has already been so reported on) shall be first taken into consideration and reported on by the Examiner of Petitions, and when necessary by the Standing Committee on Miscellaneous Private Bills and Standing Orders in like manner, after the first reading of such bills, and before their consideration by any other standing committee.

Instruction to committees in certain cases

98. That it be an instruction to all committees on private bills, in the event of promoters not being ready to proceed with their measures when the same have been twice called on two separate occasions for consideration by the committee, that such measures shall be reported back to the House forthwith, together with a statement of the facts and with the recommendation that such bills be withdrawn.

Suspension of rules

99. No motion for the suspension or modification of any provision of the Standing Orders applying to private bills or to petitions for private bills shall be entertained by the House until after reference is made to the Standing Committee on Miscellaneous Private Bills and Standing Orders, or to one of the committees charged with the consideration of private bills, and a report made thereon by one of such committees and, in its report, the said committee shall state the grounds for recommending such suspension or modification.

Private bills introduced on petition

100. (1) All private bills are introduced on petition, and after such petition has been favourably reported upon by the Examiner of Petitions or by the Standing Committee on Miscellaneous Private Bills and Standing Orders, such bills shall be laid upon the Table of the House by the Clerk, and shall be deemed to have been read a first time and ordered to be printed, and to have been ordered for a second reading when so laid upon the Table, and so recorded in the *Votes and Proceedings.*

Senate Bills deemed read a first time

(2) When Mr. Speaker informs the House that any private bill has been brought from the Senate, the bill shall be deemed to have been read a first time and ordered for a second reading and reference to a standing committee at the next sitting of the House and so recorded in the *Votes and Proceedings.*

Bills confirming agreements

101. When any bill for confirming any agreement is presented to the House, a true copy of such agreement must be attached to it.

Bills and petitions referred

102. Every private bill, when read a second time stands referred to one of the standing committees as follows: bills relating to banks, insurance, trade and commerce and to trust and loan companies, to the Standing Committee on Finance, Trade and Economic Affairs; bills relating to railways, canals, telegraphs, canal and railway bridges, to the Standing Committee on Transport and Communications; the bills not coming under these classes, to the Standing Committee on Miscellaneous Private Bills and Standing Orders, and all petitions for or against the bills are considered as referred to such committee.

Notice of sitting of committee

103. (1) No committee on any private bill originating in this House is to consider the same until after one week's notice of the sitting of such committee has been first affixed in the lobby; nor, in the case of any such bill originating in the Senate, until after twenty-four hours' like notice.

Notice to be appended to *Votes and Proceedings*

(2) On the day of the posting of any bill under this standing order, the Clerk of the House shall cause a notice of such posting to be appended to the *Votes and Proceedings* of the day.

Voting in committee — Chairman votes

104. All questions before committees on private bills are decided by a majority of voices including the voice of the chairman; and whenever the voices are equal, the chairman has a second or casting vote.

Provision not covered by notice

105. It is the duty of the committee to which any private bill may be referred by the House, to call the attention of the House specially to any provisions inserted in such bill that does not appear to have been contemplated in the notice or petition for the same, as reported upon by the Examiner of Petitions or by the Standing Committee on Miscellaneous Private Bills and Standing Orders; and any private bill so reported shall not be placed on the Order Paper for consideration until a report has been made by the Examiner as to the sufficiency or otherwise of the notice to cover such provisions.

All bills to be reported

106. The committee to which a private bill may have been referred, shall report the same to the House in every case.

When Preamble not proven

107. When the committee on any private bill reports to the House that they have made any material change in the preamble of a bill, the reasons for making such change shall be stated in their report; and if they report that the preamble of a bill has not been proved to their satisfaction, they must also state the grounds upon which they have arrived at such a decision; and no bill, the preamble of which has been reported as not proven shall be placed upon the Orders of the Day unless by special order of the House.

Chairman to sign bills and to initial amendments

108. The chairman of the committee shall sign with his name at length a printed copy of the bill, and shall also sign with the initials of his name, the preamble and the various sections of the bill and also any amendments which may be made or clauses added in committee; and another copy of the bill with the amendments, if any, written thereon shall be prepared by the clerk of the committee, who shall sign the bill with his name at length and shall also sign with the initials of his name the preamble and the various sections adopted by the committee, and any amendments which may have been made thereto, and shall file the same with the Clerk of the House or attach it to the report of the committee.

Notice of amendments

109. No important amendment may be proposed to any private bill in the House unless one day's notice of the same has been given.

Reprinting of bills when amended

110. Private bills amended by any committee may be reprinted by order of such committee; or after being reported, and before consideration in the House, may be reprinted in whole or in part as the Clerk of the House may direct; and the cost of such reprinting shall, in either case, be added to the cost of the first printing of the bill and be payable by the promoter of the same.

Amendments by the Senate

111. When any private bill is returned from the Senate with amendments, the same not being merely verbal or unimportant, such amendments are, previous to the second reading, referred to the standing committee to which such bill was originally referred.

Record of Private bills

112. A record shall be kept in the private bills office of the name, description, and place of residence of the parties applying for a private bill or of their agent, the amount of fees paid, and all the proceedings thereon, from the time of the deposit of the bill with the Clerk of the House to the passage of the bill; such record to specify briefly each proceeding in the House or in any committee to which the bill or the petition may be referred, and the day on which the committee is appointed to sit; such record shall be open to public inspection during office hours.

List of bills posted in lobbies

113. (1) Lists of all private bills which have been referred to any committee shall be prepared daily by the Chief Clerk of Private Bills, specifying the committee to which each bill has been referred and the date on or after which the bill may be considered by such committee, and shall cause the same to be hung up in the lobby.

Publication of committee meetings

(2) A list of committee meetings shall be prepared from time to time as arranged, by the Chief Clerk of Private Bills, stating the day and hour of each

such meeting, and the room in which it is to be held, which list shall be attached to the *Votes and Proceedings* from day to day; and a list of committee meetings to be held each day shall be hung up in the lobby on the day previous to that on which the meeting is to be held.

Parliamentary agents — Authority conferred by Mr. Speaker

114. (1) No person shall act as parliamentary agent conducting proceedings before the House of Commons or its committees without the express sanction and authority of Mr. Speaker, and all such agents shall be personally responsible to the House and to Mr. Speaker, for the observance of the rules, orders and practice of Parliament and rules prescribed by Mr. Speaker, and also for the payment of all fees and charges.

List of agents

(2) A list of such persons shall be kept by the Chief Clerk of Private Bills and a copy filed with the Clerk of the House.

Fee per session

(3) No person shall be allowed to be registered as a parliamentary agent during any session unless he has paid a fee of twenty-five dollars for such session and is actually employed in promoting or opposing some private bill or petition pending in Parliament during that session.

Liability of agents

115. Any parliamentary agent who wilfully acts in violation of the Standing Orders and practice of Parliament, or of any rules to be prescribed by Mr. Speaker, or who wilfully misconducts himself in prosecuting any proceedings before Parliament, shall be liable to an absolute or temporary prohibition to practice as a parliamentary agent, at the pleasure of Mr. Speaker; provided, that upon the application of such agent, Mr. Speaker shall state in writing the ground for such prohibition.

Standing Orders apply to private bills

116. Except as herein otherwise provided, the Standing Orders relating to public bills shall apply to private bills.

INDEX

N.B. The figures preceded by "§" and "§§" refer to the citation or citations; the figures preceded by "p" and "pp" refer to the page or pages.